The Abrahamic Faiths

Judaism, Christianity, and Islam
Similarities & Contrasts

First Edition
2004 AC / 1425 AH

Reprint
2017AC / 1438 AH

© 2004 AC / 1425 AH
amana publications
10710 Tucker Street
Beltsville, MD 20705-2223 USA
Tel. 301-595-5777, 800-660-1777
Fax 301-595-5888, 240-250-3000

Email: amana@amana-corp.com
Website: www.amanapublications.com

1-59008-031-9 (10-digit ISBN) / 978-1-59008-031-3 (13-digit ISBN)

Library of Congress Cataloging-in-Publication Data

Dirks, Jerald.
  The Abrahamic faiths : Judaism, Christianity, and Islam : similarities &
contrasts / Jerald F. Dirks.-- 1st ed.
      p. cm.
  Includes bibliographical references and index.
  ISBN 1-59008-031-9
  1. Islam--Relations--Christianity. 2. Christianity and other
religions--Islam. 3. Islam--Relations--Judaism. 4.
Judaism--Relations--Islam. 5. Abraham (Biblical patriarch) I. Title.

  BP172.D582 2004
  201'.4--dc22

2004028069

Printed by Mega Printing in Turkey

The Abrahamic Faiths

Judaism, Christianity, and Islam
Similarities & Contrasts

Jerald F. Dirks, M.Div., Psy.D.

amana publications

Table of Contents

Chapter 1

A Muslim in "Atypical Christian" Clothing

ON THE ROAD TO THE MINISTRY

Perhaps I should begin by introducing myself to the reader. I am a former ordained minister who converted to Islam in early 1993.

One of my earliest childhood memories is of hearing the church bell toll for Sunday morning worship in the small, rural town in Kansas in which I was raised. The Methodist Church was an old, wooden structure with a bell tower, two children's Sunday school classrooms cubby holed behind folding, wooden doors to separate it from the sanctuary, and a choir loft that housed the Sunday school classrooms for the older children. It stood less than two blocks from my home. As the bell rang, we would come together as a family and make our weekly pilgrimage to the church.

In that rural setting from the 1950s, the three churches in my hometown of about 500 were the center of community life. The local Methodist Church, to which my family belonged, sponsored ice cream socials with hand-cranked, homemade ice cream, chicken potpie dinners, and corn roasts. My family and I were always involved in all three, but each came only once a year. In addition, there was a two-week community *Bible* school every June, and I was a regular attendee through my eighth grade year in school. However, Sunday morning worship and Sunday school were weekly events, and I strove to keep extending my collection of perfect attendance pins and of awards for memorizing *Bible* verses.

In many ways, small town life in the rural Kansas of the 1950s was very different than American life today. Back then, religion was part and parcel of daily life, a man's word was his bond, a handshake was a more secure foundation for trust than any legally binding contract, divorce was rare, dress was modest, alcohol consumption was minimal, and drugs and pre-marital sex almost never occurred.

By my junior high school days, the local Methodist Church had closed, and we were attending the Methodist Church in the neighboring town, which was only slightly larger than the town in which I lived. It was there that my thoughts first began to focus on the ministry as a personal calling. I became active in the Methodist Youth Fellowship and eventually served as both a district and a conference officer. I also became the regular "preacher" during the annual Youth Sunday service. Eventually my preaching began to draw community-wide attention, and before long I was occasionally filling pulpits at other churches, at a nursing home, and at various church-affiliated youth and ladies' groups, where I typically set attendance records.

By age 17 when I began my freshman year at Harvard College, my decision to enter the ministry had solidified. During my freshman year, I enrolled in a two-semester course in comparative religion, which was taught by Wilfred Cantwell Smith, whose specific area of expertise was Islam. I have to admit that I gave far less attention to Islam during that course than I did to other religions such as Hinduism and Buddhism, as the latter two seemed so much more esoteric and strange to me. In contrast, Islam appeared to be somewhat similar to my own Christianity. As such, I didn't concentrate on it as much as I probably should have, although I can remember writing a term paper for the course on the concept of revelation in the *Qur'an*. Nonetheless, as the course was one of rigorous academic standards and demands, I did acquire a small library of about a half dozen books on Islam, all of which were written by non-Muslims, and all of which were to serve me in good stead 25 years later. I also acquired two different English translations of the meaning of the *Qur'an*, which I read at the time.

That spring, Harvard named me a Hollis Scholar, signifying that I was one of the top pre-theology students in the college. The summer between my freshman and sophomore years at Harvard, I worked as a youth minister at a fairly large United Methodist Church. The following summer, I obtained my License to Preach from the United Methodist Church. Upon graduating from Harvard College in 1971, I enrolled at the Harvard Divinity School, where I also completed a two-year externship program as a hospital chaplain at Peter Bent Brigham Hospital in Boston. In 1972, I was ordained into the Deaconate of the United Methodist Church and received a Stewart Scholarship from the United Methodist Church as a supplement to my Harvard Divinity School scholarships. In 1974, I graduated from Harvard Divinity School with a Master of Divinity degree.

Following graduation from Harvard Divinity School, I spent the summer as the interim minister of two United Methodist churches in rural Kansas, where attendance soared to heights not seen in those churches for several years.

LEAVING THE MINISTRY

In the fall of 1974, I left the parish ministry—never to return. There were several reasons that I did not return to the parish ministry, including the stresses and strains that typically exist on a young minister and his family, my growing interest in psychology, etc. However, the biggest reason had to do with maintaining my own sense of personal integrity.

Seen from the outside, I was a very promising young minister who had received an excellent education, drew large crowds to the Sunday morning worship service, and had been successful at every stop along the ministerial path. However, seen from the inside, I was fighting a constant war to maintain my personal integrity in the face of my ministerial responsibilities. This war was far removed from the ones presumably fought by some later televangelists in unsuccessfully trying to maintain personal sexual morality. Likewise, it was a far different war than those fought by the headline-grabbing pedophilic priests of the current moment. However, my struggle to maintain personal integrity may be the most common one encountered by the better-educated members of the ministry.

A good seminary education is an eye-opening experience for the young minister-to-be. Throughout seminary, I was repeatedly confronted with what the older and more original texts of the various books of the *Bible* had once said. Those texts, supposedly the oldest scriptural foundations of Christianity, raised serious and disturbing questions about such basic Christian doctrines as the trinity of God, the "sonship" of Jesus Christ, the actual historicity of the crucifixion event, and the "atonement in the blood."

My seminary education also provided a systematic review and study of the actual foundations of early Christianity. I was thoroughly exposed to the geo-political machinations and decidedly non-religious considerations that dominated much of the early decision making regarding various doctrines and dogmas of Christianity. I was also educated as to the tremendous breadth of religious and theological opinion that existed within early Christianity and as to how that diversity of thought was methodically reduced by one council and synod after another, often at the expense of systematically attempting to destroy all texts and books at variance with the opinion of the prevailing party. In particular, I was made acutely aware of the conflict that existed between the theology of Paul of Tarsus, a man who had never even met the historical Jesus Christ, and the beliefs and practices of the actual disciples of Jesus as they continued to worship at the Temple in Jerusalem. Ironically, after many centuries of conflict, it was Pauline Christianity that emerged victorious over that of the actual disciples of Jesus.

Given that background, there was no way that I could fill a Sunday morning pulpit, preach a sermon that I knew was at variance with the actual tap root of Christianity, and still maintain my own standards of personal responsibility and integrity. As such, I left the active ministry in the fall of 1974 and pursued my education and professional training in clinical psychology. I was not alone. Approximately half of my graduating class from Harvard Divinity School also opted out of the active ministry and thus demonstrated allegiance to the Harvard motto of *veritas* (truth).

AN "ATYPICAL CHRISTIAN"

For the next 19 years, I was what I referred to as an "atypical Christian." I had a deep and profound belief in God and in the teachings of Jesus Christ, but I could find no satisfactory expression for those beliefs within the confines of contemporary Christianity. A few times a year, I would force myself to attend Sunday morning worship services, primarily because I thought it was an important family function, but typically spent that time gritting my teeth as I heard sermons extolling that which I knew was not the case. Nonetheless, my self-identity was that of being a Christian, however atypical. After all, I was an ordained minister.

The above should not be taken to mean that I abandoned all religious practice or even that I no longer sought spiritual growth. I continued to pray regularly, maintained the worship of God in my own way, and conducted my personal life in conformance with the ethics and morality that I had once been taught in Sunday school and church. I also continued to study and learn. I haunted the bookstore at the local seminary, purchased copies of new books on the archeological discoveries of ancient Christian and Jewish texts, and assiduously read and underlined those texts. I was continuing to grow in my intellectual religious understanding, but I also knew that my spiritual quest was not leading to any deepening of personal religious meaning in my life.

In addition, I was becoming increasingly concerned about the loss of morality, spirituality, and religiousness in the basic fabric of American society. Morality, spirituality, and religiousness are not confined, and cannot be confined, to intellectual exercises and to otherwise empty rites, rituals, and creeds. To really exist within an individual or within a society, they must be living, breathing entities that are manifest and expressed in daily life and in the wide variety of behaviors and actions that comprise daily life. Given this yardstick, American society appeared to have lost its moral and religious compass and to be teetering on the edge of ethical and spiritual bankruptcy.

It was at this juncture that, quite by "accident," I began to come into contact with the local Muslim community in 1991. For some years, my wife and I had been actively involved in doing research on the history of the Arabian horse. Eventually, in order to secure translations of various Arabic documents, this research brought us into contact with Arab Americans who happened to be Muslims. Our first such contact was with Jamal Rabia in the summer of 1991.

After an initial telephone conversation, Jamal visited our home and offered to do some translations for us and to help guide us through the history of the Arabian horse in the Middle East. Before Jamal left that afternoon, he asked if he might: use our bathroom to wash before saying his mandatory scheduled prayers; and borrow a piece of newspaper to use as a prayer rug, so he could say his prayers before leaving our house. We of course obliged but wondered if there was something more appropriate that we could give him to use than a newspaper. Without our ever realizing it at the time, Jamal was practicing a very beautiful form of *Da'wa* (preaching or exhortation). He made no comment about the fact that we were not Muslims, and he didn't preach anything to us about his religious beliefs. He "merely" presented us with his example, an example that spoke volumes if one were willing to be receptive to the lesson.

Over the next 16 months, contact with Jamal slowly increased in frequency until it was occurring on a biweekly to weekly basis. During these visits, Jamal never preached to me about Islam, never questioned me about my own religious beliefs or convictions, and never verbally suggested that I become a Muslim. However, I was beginning to learn a lot. Firstly, there was the constant behavioral example of Jamal observing his scheduled prayers. Secondly, there was the behavioral example of how Jamal conducted his daily life in a highly moral and ethical manner, both in his business world and in his social world. Thirdly, there was the behavioral example of how Jamal interacted with his two children. For my wife, Jamal's wife provided similar examples. Fourthly, always within the framework of helping me to understand Arabian horse history in the Middle East, Jamal began to share with me: (1) stories from Arab and Islamic history, (2) sayings of the Prophet Muhammad, and (3) Qur'anic verses and their contextual meaning. In point of fact, our every visit now included at least a 30-minute conversation centered on some aspect of Islam, but always presented in terms of helping me intellectually understand the Islamic context of Arabian horse history. I was never told "this is the way things are," I was merely told "this is what Muslims typically believe." Since I wasn't being "preached to," and since Jamal never inquired as to my own beliefs, I didn't need to bother attempting to justify my own position. It was all handled as an intellectual exercise, not as proselytizing.

Gradually, Jamal began to introduce us to other Arab families in the local Muslim community. There was Wa'el 'Awad and his family, Khalid Al-Nabhani and his family, and a few others. Consistently I observed individuals and families who were living their lives on a much higher ethical plane than the American society in which we were all embedded. I was beginning to wonder if maybe there was something to the practice of Islam that I had missed during my collegiate and seminary days.

By December, 1992, I was also beginning to ask myself some serious questions about where I was and what I was doing. These questions were prompted by the following considerations. (1) Over the course of the prior 16 months, our social life had become increasingly centered on the Arab component of the local Muslim community. By the end of December, probably 75% of our social life was being spent with Arab Muslims. (2) By virtue of my seminary training and education, I knew how badly the *Bible* had been corrupted (and often knew exactly when, where, and why). I had no belief in any triune Godhead, and I had no belief in anything more than a metaphorical "sonship" of Jesus Christ. In short, while I certainly believed in God, I was as strict a monotheist as my Muslim friends. (3) My personal values and sense of morality were much more in keeping with my Muslim friends than with the "Christian" society around me. After all, I had the non-confrontational examples of Jamal, Khalid, and Wa'el as illustrations.

In short, my nostalgic yearning for the type of community in which I had been raised was finding gratification in the Muslim community. American society might have become morally bankrupt, but that did not appear to be the case for that part of the Muslim community with which I was in contact. Marriages were stable, spouses were committed to each other, and honesty, integrity, self-responsibility, and family values were emphasized. My wife and I had attempted to live our own lives that same way, but for several years I had felt that we were doing so in the context of a moral vacuum. However, my newly found Muslim friends appeared to be different. I admired their religious commitment, their sense of "peace at the core," and their practical application of their religious beliefs into their everyday lives. Their spirituality and commitment to the teachings of their religion were not confined to daily rituals and attendance at some local mosque but were manifest in their family lives, their occupational lives, and their social lives.

It was within the context of the behavioral examples of Jamal, Wa'el, and Khalid that I began to see the type of religious life that I knew was at the heart of what Jesus Christ had taught. I remember expressing that thought once to Jamal: "I don't intend any offense. However, if being a Christian means following the teachings of Jesus Christ, then you are the best Christian that I know." Nonetheless, I maintained my own commitment to being an "atypical Christian."

The different threads were being woven together into a single strand. Arabian horses, my childhood upbringing, my foray into the Christian ministry and my seminary education, my nostalgic yearnings for a moral society, and my contact with the Muslim community were becoming intricately intertwined. My self-questioning came to a head when I finally got around to asking myself exactly what separated me from the beliefs of my Muslim friends. I suppose that I could have raised that question with Jamal, Wa'el, or Khalid, but I wasn't ready to take that step. I had never discussed my own religious beliefs with them, and I didn't think that I wanted to introduce that topic of conversation into our friendship.

As such, I began dusting off my books on Islam and my English translations of the meaning of the *Qur'an* that I had acquired in my collegiate and seminary days. I had not opened them in over 20 years—not since my classes in comparative religion at Harvard. Now, I began to read them again. However, this time I was not reading them from the vantage point of gaining some intellectual mastery in order to pass a class. Now I was reading them to gain insight into the peace, contentment, and religiousness of my Muslim friends. The more I read, the more I found confirmation of what I had been taught so many years before in seminary about the origins of the *Bible* and of Christianity. This was information that could not have been known by an illiterate Arab in seventh century Makkah and Madinah. I rather reluctantly concluded that this was information that could have been known by Muhammad only through some form of divine inspiration, however defined. The implication was obvious, even though I wasn't particularly fond of it: Muhammad was one of the prophets of God. Despite this conclusion, despite the considerable distance separating my own beliefs from the traditional position of the church, and despite how seldom I actually attended church, I still identified myself as being an "atypical Christian."

While I never spoke to my Muslim friends about those books, my wife and I had numerous conversations about what I was reading. By the last week of December of 1992, I was forced to admit to myself that I could find no area of substantial disagreement between my own religious beliefs and the general tenets of Islam. While I was ready to acknowledge that Muhammad was a prophet of (one who spoke for or under the inspiration of) God and while I had absolutely no difficulty affirming that there was no god besides God/Allah, I was still hesitating to make any decision. I could readily admit to myself that I had far more in common with Islamic beliefs, as I then understood them, than I did with the traditional Christianity of the organized church. I knew only too well that I could easily confirm from my seminary training and education most of what the *Qur'an* had to say about Christianity, the *Bible,* and Jesus Christ. Nonetheless, I hesitated. Further, I rationalized my hesitation by maintaining to myself that I really didn't know the nitty-gritty details of Islam and that my areas of agreement were confined to general concepts. As such, I continued to read and then to re-read.

One's sense of identity, of "who one is," is a powerful affirmation of one's own position in the cosmos. In my professional practice, I had occasionally been called upon to treat certain addictive disorders, ranging from smoking, to alcoholism, to drug abuse. As a clinician, I knew that the basic physical addiction had to be overcome to create the initial abstinence. That was the easy part of treatment. As Mark Twain once said, "Quitting smoking is easy; I've done it hundreds of times." However, I also knew that the key to maintaining that abstinence over an extended time period was overcoming the client's psychological addiction, which was heavily grounded in the client's basic sense of identity, i.e., the client identified to himself that he was "a smoker," or that he was "a drinker," etc. The addictive behavior had become part and parcel of the client's basic sense of identity, of the client's basic sense of self. Changing this sense of identity was crucial to the maintenance of the psychotherapeutic "cure." This was the difficult part of treatment. Changing one's basic sense of identity is a most difficult task. One's psyche tends to cling to the old and familiar, which usually seem more psychologically comfortable and secure than the new and unfamiliar.

On a professional basis, I had the above knowledge and used it on a daily basis. However, ironically enough, I was not yet ready to apply it to myself and to the issue of my own hesitation surrounding my religious identity. For 43 years my religious identity had been neatly labeled as "Christian," however many qualifications I might have added to that term over the years. Giving up that label of personal identity was no easy task. It was part and parcel of how I defined my very being. Given the benefit of hindsight, it is clear that my hesitation served the purpose of insuring that I could keep my familiar religious identity of being an "atypical Christian," although an "atypical Christian" who believed like a Muslim believed.

It was now the very end of December 1992, and my wife and I were filling out our application forms for U.S. passports so that a proposed Middle Eastern journey could become a reality. One of the questions had to do with religious affiliation. I didn't even think about it and automatically fell back on the old and familiar as I penned in "Christian." It was easy, it was familiar, and it was comfortable.

However, that comfort was momentarily disrupted when my wife asked me how I had answered the question on religious identity on the application form. I immediately replied, "Christian," and chuckled audibly. Now, one of Freud's contributions to the understanding of the human psyche was his realization that laughter is often a release of psychological tension. However wrong Freud may have been in many aspects of his theory of psychosexual development, his insights into laughter were quite on target. I had laughed! What was this psychological tension that I needed to release through the medium of laughter?

I then hurriedly went on to offer my wife a brief affirmation that I was a Christian, not a Muslim. In response to which, she politely informed me that she was merely asking whether I had filled out the application form with "Christian" or "Protestant" or "Methodist." On a professional basis, I knew that a person does not defend himself against an accusation that hasn't been made. (If, in the course of a session of psychotherapy, my client blurted out, "I'm not angry about that," and I hadn't even broached the topic of anger, it was clear that my client was feeling the need to defend himself against a charge that his own unconscious was making. In short, he really was angry, but he wasn't ready to admit it or to deal with it.) If my wife hadn't made the accusation, i.e., "you are a Muslim," then the accusation had to have come from my own unconscious, as I was the only other person present. I was aware of this, but still I hesitated. The religious label that had been stuck to my sense of identity for 43 years was not going to come off easily.

As the days proceeded to pass by, I continued my reading of the meaning of the *Qur'an* in English translation. Daily, I was pouring over the pages of different English translations of the *Qur'an*—I was not one to trust any single translation. Nonetheless, I continued to identify myself as an "atypical Christian." In January of 1993, I began to experiment with praying the five daily prayers of Islam in secluded privacy. It did not take long before I eagerly looked forward to the five times of prayer each day and found spiritual satisfaction and meaning in their performance. My rationalization was that I was merely an "atypical Christian" who happened to be reading English translations of the *Qur'an* and who happened to be performing the five daily prayers of Islam, because I found those acts enhancing my own sense of spirituality and religiousness.

About a month had gone by since my wife's question to me. It was now late in January of 1993. I had set aside all the books on Islam by the Western scholars, as I had read them all thoroughly. The two English translations of the meaning of the *Qur'an* were back on the bookshelf, and I was busy reading yet a third English translation of the meaning of the *Qur'an*. Maybe in this translation I would find some sudden justification for…

I was taking my lunch hour from my private practice at a local Arab restaurant that I had started to frequent. I entered as usual, seated myself at a small table, and opened my third English translation of the meaning of the *Qur'an* to where I had left off in my reading. I figured I might as well get some reading done over my lunch hour. Moments later, I became aware that Mahmoud, the Syrian owner of the restaurant, was at my shoulder and waiting to take my order. He glanced at what I was reading, but said nothing about it. My order taken, I returned to the solitude of my reading.

A few minutes later, Mahmoud's wife, Iman, an American Muslim who wore the Hijab (scarf) and modest dress that I had come to associate with female Muslims, brought me my order. She commented that I was reading the *Qur'an* and politely asked if I were a Muslim. The word was out of my mouth before it could be modified by any social etiquette or politeness: "No!" That single word was said forcefully and with more than a hint of irritability. With that, Iman politely retired from my table.

What was happening to me? I had behaved rudely and somewhat aggressively. What had this woman done to deserve such behavior from me? This wasn't like me. Given my childhood upbringing, I still used "sir" and "ma'am" when addressing clerks and cashiers who were waiting on me in stores. I could pretend to ignore my own laughter as a release of tension, but I couldn't begin to ignore this sort of unconscionable behavior from myself. My reading was set aside, and I mentally stewed over this turn of events throughout my meal. The more I stewed, the guiltier I felt about my behavior. I knew that when Iman brought me my check at the end of the meal, I was going to need to make some amends. If for no other reason, simple politeness demanded it. Furthermore, I was really quite disturbed about how resistant I had been to her innocuous question. What was going on in me that I responded with that much force to such a simple and straightforward question? Why did that one, simple question lead to such atypical behavior on my part?

Later, when Iman came with my check, I attempted a roundabout apology by saying: "I'm afraid I was a little abrupt in answering your question before. If you were asking me whether I believe that there is only one God, then my answer is yes. If you were asking me whether I believe that Muhammad was one of the prophets of that one God, then my answer is yes." She very nicely and very supportively said: "That's okay; it takes some people a little longer than others."

Perhaps the readers of this will be kind enough to note the psychological games I was playing with myself without chuckling too hard at my mental gymnastics and behavior. I well knew that in my own way, using my own words, I had just said the *Shahadah*, the Islamic testimonial of faith, i.e., "I testify that there is no god but Allah, and I testify that Muhammad is the messenger of Allah." However, having said that and having recognized what I said, I could still cling to my old and familiar label of religious identity. After all, I hadn't said I was a Muslim. I was simply a Christian, albeit an "atypical Christian" who was willing to say that there was One God, not a triune God, and who was willing to say that Muhammad was one of the prophets inspired by that One God. If a Muslim wanted to accept me as being a Muslim, then that was his or her business and his or her label of religious identity. However, it was not mine. I thought I had found my way out of my crisis of religious identity. I was an "atypical Christian" who would carefully explain that I agreed with and was willing to testify to the Islamic testimonial of faith. Having made my tortured explanation and having parsed the English language to within an inch of its life, others could hang whatever label on me they wished. It was their label and not mine.

Ramadan, the Islamic month when Muslims fast from daybreak to sunset, began around March of 1993, and I decided to fast with my Muslim friends. In doing so, I was able, just barely, to convince myself that I was simply being courteous and respectful by not eating and drinking in front of my Muslim friends who were fasting. However, as long as I was going to be fasting in front of Muslims, I might as well do like my Muslim friends and fast from dawn to sunset every day of *Ramadan*. By now, I was merely an "atypical Christian" who regularly read the *Qur'an* in English translation, who assiduously performed the five daily prayers of Islam in private, who was willing to say the *Shahadah* in English translation, and who was fasting during the Islamic month of *Ramadan*. Oh, what an "atypical Christian" I was.

It was now March of 1993, and my wife and I were enjoying a five-week vacation in the Middle East. During this time, I started to perform the five daily prayers of Islam publicly with my newly found Muslim friends in Jordan. After all, I had already been saying them in private for a couple of months. All I had done was transform my private prayers into public, congregational prayers.

I was an "atypical Christian" or so I said. After all, I had been born into a Christian family, had been given a Christian upbringing, had attended church and Sunday school every Sunday as a child, had graduated from a prestigious seminary, and was an ordained minister in a large Protestant denomination. However, I was also a Christian: who didn't believe in a triune God or in the divinity of Jesus Christ; who knew quite well how the *Bible* had been corrupted; who had said the Islamic testimony of faith in my own carefully parsed words; who was fasting during *Ramadan*; who was saying Islamic prayers five times a day; and who was deeply impressed by the behavioral examples I had witnessed in the Muslim community, both in America and in the Middle East. (Time and space do not permit me the luxury of documenting in detail all of the examples of personal morality and ethics I encountered in the Middle East.) If asked if I were a Muslim, I could and did do a five-minute monologue detailing the above and would enter into what had by now become my regular verbal gymnastics, in which I did my round about recitation of the *Shahadah* in my own words, and in which I would end up proclaiming myself to be an "atypical Christian." I thought I had worked things out and that my rationalization was pretty well insulated. I was playing intellectual word games and succeeding at them quite nicely. However, I had not counted on the mercy of Allah.

It was late in March of 1993, and I was coming to the end of my first trip to the Middle East. I was at that moment staying with the extended family of Wa'el, one of my Muslim friends from back in the States. One day, Uncle 'Awad (he will always be my "Uncle" 'Awad), who spoke no English, waved for me to come with him for a drive. The two of us took off, and he drove me to a Palestinian refugee camp. We exited the car and began to stroll down the narrow pathways of the camp.

As we walked down one lane, we were approached by an elderly Muslim who spoke no English. The three of us met—he and Uncle 'Awad spoke only Arabic, and I couldn't even hold a simple conversation in Arabic. We greeted each other with *Al-Salam 'Alaykum* (peace be upon you) and shook hands. The stranger then turned to me and asked a short question in Arabic. Now, my Arabic was limited to a few simple phrases, but even I could translate the question being asked. He was asking if I were a Muslim. All my verbal gymnastics and intellectual rationalizations had just been rendered totally ineffective. I had understood the question, and with my meager Arabic vocabulary I was limited to answering *Nam* (yes) or *La* (no). *Al-Hamdulillah* (all praise be to Allah), I answered, "*Nam*."

The ordained minister who was an "atypical Christian" had become a Muslim despite all of his psychological resistances, intellectual rationalizations, and verbal gymnastics. All of my carefully constructed devices and plans had just been made totally inoperative and useless. As Allah says:

...and Allah too planned, and the best of planners is Allah. (*Qur'an* 3: 54)

...and Allah too plans, but the best of planners is Allah. (*Qur'an* 8: 30)

MORE "ATYPICAL CHRISTIANS"

In the almost ten years since that fateful day, I have become aware that I am not alone. There are many ordained Christian ministers who have converted to Islam. Several Internet web sites proclaim their stories. There are also many ordained Christian ministers who continue their identifications as "atypical Christians." In fact, it is worth sharing a couple of stories about my encounters with those "atypical Christians" who continue to wear the clerical collar.

Only a month or two following my return from the Middle East in 1993, a retired minister who lived not that far from me dropped over unexpectedly one day. In my few, former excursions to the local church, I had previously seen him singing in the church choir. I had also occasionally spoken with him in passing at some local community event. However, he had never before come to my home, and we had never had a conversation that went anywhere besides small talk. Now, he was at my doorstep and was inviting my wife and me over for coffee and snacks for the following evening. In doing so, he stated that he wanted to talk with me about my having become a Muslim. I tried to decline by mentioning the difficulty he and his wife would have in preparing snacks that would conform to Islamic dietary restrictions. Nonetheless, he was most insistent, and there was no way out of his invitation.

The next 24 hours had more than a few moments of trepidation. I did not relish a non-productive confrontation with a senior citizen, and I anticipated that I was about to be involved in one. As such, I began to rehearse mentally what I would say when the subject of my becoming a Muslim was finally raised.

The next evening, my wife and I arrived promptly at the retired minister's home. He greeted us at the door, escorted us in, and helped his wife serve coffee and cookies. Finally, after a round or two of small talk, he came directly to the point. "Why did you, an ordained minister, decide to become a Muslim?" I carefully began my by now well-rehearsed speech. "With your seminary education, you know as well as I the considerations and pressures that led up to the Council of Nicaea..." Before I could get out another word, he cut me off by saying: "So, you finally couldn't stomach the polytheism anymore!" In that single statement, he laid bare the fallacy of the doctrine of the trinity, revealed his complete understanding of and sympathy for my journey from Christianity to Islam, and acknowledged his true beliefs. I was in the presence of another "atypical Christian" who was an ordained minister.

Over nine years had passed since that encounter with the retired minister, and it was now the summer of 2002. I had just finished delivering a lecture on the commonalities and contrasts among Judaism, Christianity, and Islam for an ecumenical meeting sponsored by a Muslim group in Colorado. As I left the auditorium, I was stopped by a young man who took me aside for a private moment and asked to shake my hand. He identified himself as a Christian seminarian who was home over the summer break and was preparing to enter the Christian ministry. He then said: "I just wanted you to know how much I appreciate your courage in being able to maintain your religious integrity. I wish I had that kind of courage." I had found another "atypical Christian" who was about to enter the Christian ministry.

Where Do We Go from Here

As a former Christian minister who is now a Muslim, I am often asked to lecture on various topics pertaining to the interrelationships to be found between Islam and the Judaeo-Christian tradition. In the pages that follow, several of the chapters are drawn from those lectures and from the questions that they generate. Occasionally, I am also asked for my opinion about various points of shared religious history among Islam, Judaism, and Christianity. This often involves sleuthing through the *Bible*, the *Qur'an*, and the narratives (*Ahadith*) about what Prophet Muhammad said and did.

Some of these research endeavors also find expression as individual chapters in the following pages.

In presenting these personal reflections in the following pages and chapters, I must emphasize to my Muslim brothers and sisters that I am not an "official voice" of Christianity. I am merely a former Christian minister. Likewise, I need to stress to my former co-religionists and to other non-Muslims that I am not any "official authority" on Islam. I am merely a Muslim who is struggling to deepen his worship of Allah in Islam (by surrendering to Him).

Two final points need to be mentioned before beginning our journey into the interrelationships that exist between Islam and the Judaeo-Christian tradition. Firstly, it is customary for Muslims to say "peace be upon him" after mentioning the name of any of the prophets recognized by Islam. However, non-Muslim readers often find this religious and literary convention an impediment to ease of reading and comprehension. As such, for the non-Muslim's reading convenience, I am abandoning this convention throughout this book. Secondly, Muslims typically use the Arabic word "Allah" instead of the English word "God." However, as some non-Muslims have negative stereotypes and misconceptions about the word "Allah," the English word "God" will be used throughout the remainder of this book. (A fuller discussion of the Arabic word "Allah," its derivation, its relationship to the Hebrew text of the *Old Testament*, and its relationship to the English word "God" is presented in the following chapter.)

Chapter 2

The Quest for Abraham: Commonalities and Contrasts among Judaism, Christianity, and Islam

Introduction

Prophet Abraham (Ibrahim) is a central and pivotal figure in the shared history and heritage of Judaism, Christianity, and Islam. In the Judaic tradition, he is the recipient of the original covenant between the Hebrew people and God. In the Christian tradition, he is a famed patriarch and the recipient of a formative and original covenant with God, which was later refined as the Mosaic covenant, whereas the second covenant is seen as being ushered in with Jesus Christ. In the Islamic tradition, he is a heralded example of unwavering faith and of steadfast monotheism, a prophet and messenger of God, and the recipient of one of the original books of revelation bestowed upon mankind by God. Across all three religious traditions, Abraham is specifically noted to be the friend of The One God.

Thus, it is that within the Jewish scriptures of the *Nevi'im* and the *Ketuvim,* and within the Christian scriptures of the *Old Testament,* that we find the following words:

> But you, Israel, my servant, Jacob, whom I have chosen, the off-spring of Abraham, my friend… (*Isaiah* 41:8)

> Did you not, O our God, drive out the inhabitants of this land before your people Israel, and give it forever to the descendants of your friend Abraham? (*II Chronicles* 20:7)

Further, within the Christian scriptures of the *New Testament* epistles, it is stated:

> Thus the scripture was fulfilled that says, "Abraham believed God, and it was reckoned to him as righteousness," and he was called the friend of God. (*James* 2:23)

Likewise, within the Islamic scriptures of the *Qur'an*, God says, in the closest English meaning:

> Who can be better in religion than one who submits his whole self to God, does good, and follows the way of Abraham the true in faith? For God did take Abraham for a friend. (*Qur'an* 4:125)

FINDING COMMON GROUND

Against this backdrop of essential commonality, there is little wonder that Islam, Judaism, and Christianity are often classified together as the three Abrahamic faiths. While a classification system based upon a shared and common heritage from Abraham may appear to be overly particularistic to some, no matter what classification system is used, Judaism, Christianity, and Islam consistently group together. For example, the academic discipline of comparative religion offers a variety of ways to classify the various and sundry religions of the world: monotheistic vs. polytheistic, prophetic vs. wisdom tradition, Middle Eastern vs. Eastern. Within the context of the major religions of the contemporary world, the three great monotheistic religions are Judaism, Christianity, and Islam. Within the same context, the three major prophetic religions are Judaism, Christianity, and Islam. Likewise, the three primary Middle Eastern religions are Judaism, Christianity, and Islam.

It is no accident that these three religions consistently group together across a variety of conceptual schemata. While each of the three religions has dogma and doctrine unique to itself, each of them has a core that is essentially similar to the core of the other two. Each of the three religions claims the same historical legacy within the prophetic tradition, although each may interpret specific historical and prophetic events differently. Each of the three religions shares a common core of religious and ethical teaching, although differing in places with regard to specific doctrine and dogma. In fact, using the analogy of a tree, each of the three religions claims to be the one, true, vertical extension of a trunk of primary and divine revelation, with the other two religions being seen as lateral branches that have deviated from the true verticality of the original trunk.

Judaism, Christianity, and Islam share a common trunk of divine revelation and, in their original forms, can be considered to be not just one religious tradition, but one religion. This very point finds repeated and unambiguous expression in the *Qur'an*, where God said that the religion established for Prophet Muhammad and the followers of Islam is the same religion that God established for Prophets Noah, Abraham, Moses, and Jesus.

> The same religion has He established for you as that which He enjoined on Noah—that which We have sent by inspiration to thee—and that which We enjoined on Abraham, Moses, and Jesus: namely, that ye should remain steadfast in religion, and make no divisions therein... (*Qur'an* 42:13a)
>
> Say: "God speaketh the truth: follow the religion of Abraham, the sane in faith; he was not of the pagans." (*Qur'an* 3:95)
>
> And who turns away from the religion of Abraham but such as debase their souls with folly? Him We chose and rendered pure in this world: and he will be in the hereafter in the ranks of the righteous. Behold! his Lord said to him: "Bow (thy will to Me):" he said: "I bow (my will) to the Lord and cherisher of the universe. And this was the legacy that Abraham left to his sons, and so did Jacob; "Oh my sons! God hath chosen the faith for you; then die not except in the state of submission (to God)." Were ye witnesses when death appeared before Jacob? Behold, he said to his sons: "What will ye worship after me?" They said: "We shall worship thy God and the God of thy fathers—of Abraham, Ismail, and Isaac—the One (True) God: to Him we bow (in Islam)." (*Qur'an* 2: 130-133)

And strive in His cause as ye ought to strive, (with sincerity and under discipline). He has chosen you and has imposed no difficulties on you in religion: it is the cult of your father, Abraham. It is He Who has named you Muslims, both before and in this (revelation)… (*Qur'an* 22:78a)

The *Qur'an* further documents that the divine revelation sent to Prophet Muhammad was a continuation of the inspiration sent previously to Prophets Noah, Abraham, Lot, Ismail, Isaac, Jacob, Job, Moses, Aaron, David, Solomon, Elijah (Elias), Elisha, Jonah, Zechariah (Zakariya), John the Baptist, and Jesus. In other words, it was the culmination of the prophetic tradition encoded, however erroneously at times, within the *Bible*.

We have sent thee inspiration, as We sent it to Noah and the messengers after him: We sent inspiration to Abraham, Ismail, Isaac, Jacob and the tribes, to Jesus, Job, Jonah, Aaron, and Solomon, and to David We gave the Psalms. (*Qur'an* 4:163)

Say: "We believe in God, and in what has been revealed to us and what was revealed to Abraham, Ismail, Isaac, Jacob, and the tribes, and in (the books) given to Moses, Jesus, and the prophets, from their Lord: We make no distinction between one and another among them, and to God do we bow our will (in Islam)." (*Qur'an* 3:84)

We gave Moses the book and followed him up with a succession of messengers; We gave Jesus, the son of Mary, clear (signs) and strengthened him with the Holy Spirit. (*Qur'an* 2:87a)

And we gave him (Abraham) Isaac and Jacob: all (three) We guided: and before him We guided Noah, and among his progeny, David, Solomon, Job, Joseph, Moses, and Aaron: thus do We reward those who do good. And Zakariya and John, and Jesus and Elias: all in the ranks of the righteous: and Ismail and Elisha, and Jonah, and Lot: and to all We gave favor above the nations: (to them) and to their fathers and progeny and brethren: We chose them, and We guided them to a straight way. (*Qur'an* 6:84-87)

We did send messengers before thee and appointed for them wives and children: and it was never the part of a messenger to bring a sign except as God permitted (or commanded). For each period is a book (revealed). God doth blot out or confirm what He pleaseth: with Him is the mother of the book. (*Qur'an* 13:38-39)

"For each period is a book (revealed)." Here we begin to encounter the Islamic concept of progressive revelation, of a gradual unfolding of the one, true religion through the medium of successive revelations, a topic that will be addressed more fully in the following chapter. However, for the moment it suffices to note that the three Abrahamic faiths were, in their pristine origins, one religion. Being originally one religion, the three Abrahamic faiths worship the same God, although the three religions may differ in how they conceptualize that one God. God made this very point in the *Qur'an* when He said that the Muslims and the People of the Book (*Ahl Al-Kitab*, i.e., Jews and Christians) have the same deity: "our God and your God is One; and it is to Him we bow (in Islam)."

And dispute ye not with the People of the Book, except with means better (than mere disputation), unless it be with those of them who inflict wrong (and injury); but say, "We believe in the revelation which has come down to us and in that which came down to you; our God and your God is One; and it is to Him we bow (in Islam)." (*Qur'an* 29:46)

God also says in the *Qur'an* that there were many other prophets before Prophet Muhammad. Some of these prophets are directly mentioned in the *Qur'an*, and others of these prophets are not.

We did aforetime send messengers before thee: of them there are some whose story We have related to thee, and some whose story We have not related to thee. (*Qur'an* 40:78a)

Of some messengers We have already told thee the story; of others we have not—and to Moses God spoke directly—messengers who gave good news as well as warning, that mankind, after (the coming) of the messengers, should have no plea against God: for God is exalted in power, wise. (*Qur'an* 4:164)

With regard to those prophets of whom Muslims are aware, i.e., those who are directly mentioned in the *Qur'an*, God directs Muslims not to make hierarchical distinctions among His prophets, but to accept and honor them all.

> Say ye: "We believe in God, and the revelation given to us, and to Abraham, Ismail, Isaac, Jacob, and the tribes, and that given to Moses and Jesus, and that given to (all) prophets from their Lord: we make no difference between one and another of them: and we bow to God (in Islam). (*Qur'an* 2:136)

> The Messenger believeth in what hath been revealed to him from his Lord, as do the men of faith. Each one (of them) believeth in God, His angels, His books, and His messengers. "We make no distinction (they say) between one and another of His messengers." And they say: "We hear, and we obey: (we seek) Thy forgiveness, our Lord, and to Thee is the end of all journeys." (*Qur'an* 2:285)

> Say: "We believe in God, and in what has been revealed to Abraham, Ismail, Isaac, Jacob, and the tribes, and in (the books) given to Moses, Jesus, and the prophets from their Lord: we make no distinction between one and another among them, and to God do we bow our will (in Islam)." (*Qur'an* 3:84)

> To those who believe in God and His messengers and make no distinction between any of the messengers, We shall soon give their (due) rewards: for God is oft-forgiving, most merciful. (*Qur'an* 4:152)

CONFRONTING MISCONCEPTIONS

Introduction

Before continuing our journey into the commonalities and contrasts to be found among Judaism, Christianity, and Islam, it may be helpful to provide a few different conceptual frameworks for understanding the inter-relationships among these three religions. In what follows, three specific issues are addressed: (1) the contrast between the Judaeo-Christian and

Islamic perspectives on the origins of the three Abrahamic faiths; (2) some highly misleading comparisons that are often made when contrasting Judaism, Christianity, and Islam; and (3) the derivation and meaning of the Arabic word "Allah," as well as its relationship to the Hebrew text of the *Old Testament* and to the English word "God."

Origins of the Abrahamic Faiths

Most readers whose religious heritage is from the Judaeo-Christian tradition have probably been taught that Judaism was the first monotheistic religion, that Christianity was a derivation from Judaism, and that Islam was a derivation from both Judaism and Christianity. In fact, these teachings are not facts derived from religious history, but are a Judaeo-Christian interpretation of religious history. The Islamic interpretation of the same historical facts that underlie the Judaeo-Christian interpretation is that Islam began with Prophet Adam, and then it progressively evolved in the unfolding of the prophetic tradition through successive and progressive revelations. As the centuries passed after Prophet Adam, deviations occurred in the true revelation of Islam. Despite additional prophets being sent to call the people back to Islam, some of these religious deviations became codified. Such codifications were the origins of Judaism and Christianity, with Judaism being codified primarily under the influence of Ezra and the Men of the Great Assembly circa 400 BCE, and with Christianity, at least how it has evolved into modern times, being codified primarily under the teachings of Paul (Saul of Tarsus).

Misleading Comparisons

As a second conceptual issue, consider Prophet Jesus and the *Bible* on the one hand and Prophet Muhammad and the *Qur'an* on the other hand. Most non-Muslims immediately assume that Christianity and Islam can be compared by contrasting the role of Prophet Jesus in Christianity with the role of Prophet Muhammad in Islam. In years past, this highly misleading comparison gave rise to the terms "Muhammadans," "Muhammadanism," and "Muhammadism," terms that are deeply offensive to Muslims, as they might imply that Prophet Muhammad is somehow an object of worship for Muslims. An equally inappropriate comparison is to contrast the role of the *Bible* in Christianity with the role of the *Qur'an* in Islam. Much better, although by no means perfect, comparisons have been offered by my former professor of comparative religion, Wilfred Cantwell Smith.

Smith has argued quite cogently that the most frequent error in contrasting Islam and Christianity is to hypothesize a comparison between the roles of Jesus Christ in Christianity and of Prophet Muhammad in Islam. Smith has argued that it is more realistic and more profitable to contrast Prophet Muhammad's role in Islam with the role of Paul (Saul of Tarsus) in Christianity. Both have been referred to as apostles (messengers, envoys, delegates, or ambassadors), who preached a message whose followers believe was of divine origin. Paul's message and the message of Pauline Christianity was the very person of Jesus Christ, whom Christians frequently call the "word of God" and whom Christians typically believe to be the revelation from God—"And the Word became flesh and lived among us..." (*John* 1:14a). In contrast, Muslims believe that Prophet Muhammad preached the message of the *Qur'an*, i.e., the literal words of God. Thus, the role of Prophet Muhammad in Islam can be compared with the role of Paul in Christianity, and the role and status of the *Qur'an* in Islam can be contrasted with the position of Jesus Christ in Pauline Christianity.

Extending Smith's argument further, the *Bible*, i.e., contemporary Christianity's record about the revelation which is Jesus, should not be compared to the *Qur'an*, i.e., Islam's actual and verbatim revelation from God, but perhaps to the *Ahadith*, i.e., the reported narratives regarding what Prophet Muhammad said and did, which contain information regarding the history and context regarding the divine revelation to Prophet Muhammad. As such, Smith argued that within Islam, there is no Qur'anic field of study comparable to Christianity's academic and theological interest in Biblical criticism, including text criticism and literary form criticism. The comparison to Biblical criticism within Christianity would be *Ahadith* criticism within Islam, a field of study that is still somewhat in its early stages compared to the text critical and literary form critical studies that have been undertaken on the *Bible*. Given this presentation, perhaps the Christian reader can understand that asking a Muslim "for historical criticism of the *Qur'an*" is comparable to asking a devout Christian "for a psychoanalysis of Jesus."[1]

Smith's construct has much to commend it but tends to shortchange the type of rational scrutiny by which Muslims have studied and analyzed the *Qur'an*. Such analytical methods have included the study of the circumstances of discrete revelations, the issue of later revelations modifying or abrogating earlier revelations, and the relationship between sound and content. The real contrast is that the *Qur'an* has stood the test of historical and rational analysis in a way that the *Bible* has not.[2]

On the Word "Allah"

The Arabic word "Allah" often sounds quite strange and foreign to non-Muslim ears. Frequently, non-Muslims erroneously conclude that there is some mutually exclusive contrast that is to be made between Allah and God, as though Allah can be understood as some cult deity such as Baal or Osiris. In fact, the English word "God" is merely a translation of the Arabic word "Allah."

The Arabic word "Allah" is a contraction of the Arabic "*Al-Ilah*," which means "the God" and, at least by implication, "the One God." Furthermore, Arabic and Hebrew are sister languages among the Semitic language group, and the Arabic "*Al-Ilah*" is linguistically comparable to the Hebrew "*Elohim*" and "*El-Elohim*," which are the Hebrew words that are typically translated as "God" in most English versions of the *Old Testament*. This can be dramatically illustrated by comparing the Arabic spelling of "*Al-Ilah*" with the Hebrew spelling of "*El-Elohim*."

Neither Arabic nor Hebrew has letters for vowels, with both languages having alphabets consisting only of consonants. Both languages rely on supplemental vowel markings to aid in pronunciation, but such aides are typically found only in highly formal writing. As such, using English letters instead of Arabic and Hebrew letters and omitting the supplemental vowel markings, *Al-Ilah* becomes *Al-Ilh*, and *El-Elohim* becomes *El-Elhm*. If one then removes the plural of respect, which is found only in the Hebrew word, the Arabic remains *Al-Ilh*, while the Hebrew becomes *El-Elh*. Finally, it should be noted that the first and third letters of the Arabic word are transliterations of the Arabic letter "*Alif*" and that the first and third letters of the Hebrew word are transliterations of the Hebrew letter "*Alif*." If each *Alif* in each alphabet is transliterated with the English letter "A," the two words become identical, i.e., "*Al-Alh*" for the Arabic "*Al-Ilah*" and "*Al-Alh*" for the Hebrew "*El-Elohim*."

Given the above understanding, the English word "God" will typically be used throughout this book, rather than the Arabic word "Allah." However, before becoming just too obsessed with whether one uses the Arabic word "Allah" or the English word "God," one does well to heed the words of God as recorded in the *Qur'an*. Perhaps, members of all three Abrahamic faiths can find some insight in these sacred words and thereby find within themselves some measure of greater tolerance for the linguistic practices used by members of the other two Abrahamic faiths when referring to the deity.

> Say: "Call upon Allah (i.e., the One God) or call upon Al-Rahman (i.e., The Most Gracious or The Entirely Merciful): By whatever name ye call upon Him, (it is well): for to Him belong the most beautiful names." (*Qur'an* 17:110a)

On Islam as an Arab Religion

As an additional misconception, consider the oft-stated proposition that Islam is an Arab religion. In point of fact, many Arabs are not Muslims. Iraq houses a Christian population of around one million Arabs, about 05% of the Arabs in Jordan are Christian, and much higher percentages of Christians are to be found among the Arabs of Syria, Lebanon, and Palestine. Furthermore, the vast majority of Muslims are not Arabs. There are over 160 million Muslims in Indonesia, over 100 million in Bangladesh, over 100 million in Nigeria, over 100 million in India, over 90 million in China, over 60 million in Turkey, and several million in Germany, France, and Great Britain.

With regard to Islam in America, it is currently estimated that there are over seven million Muslims in the United States, making it America's second largest religion. Of those over seven million Muslims, it appears that just over 50% are native-born Americans whose parents belong or had once belonged to some other religious tradition. In fact, American conversions to Islam range as high as 25,000 converts each year. During the last decade of the 20th century, the number of mosques in America has more than tripled, climbing from just over 600 to around 2,000. Currently, more Islamic books are being published in English than in Arabic.

Culture vs. Islam

It is sad that many people erroneously assume that some of the worst cultural practices of so-called Muslim countries of the third world are manifestations of Islam. Here, I am referring to such abominations as so-called "honor killings," the subjugation of women, female genital mutilation, the killing of civilian non-combatants, etc. These practices are no more representative of Islam than is the widespread practice in certain areas of so-called Catholic South America of families selling their teenage daughters into white slavery a valid representation of Roman Catholicism. With all religions, it is crucial to distinguish the religion from the cultural milieu in which it may be found.

ONWARD AND UPWARD

Having addressed the foregoing, it is time to turn to some of the specific and detailed commonalities and contrasts that exist among Judaism, Christianity, and Islam. Without in anyway downplaying or minimizing the differences that do exist within these three religious traditions, *Insha'Allah* (the One God willing), the reader will come to appreciate that the commonalities that bind us together are much greater than the differences that keep us apart. In particular, the following chapter highlights some important aspects of religious history and of spiritual and ethical instruction that are shared by the three Abrahamic faiths.

Chapter 3

The *Qur'an, Ahadith,* and Judaeo-Christian Scriptures: Finding Common Ground

INTRODUCTION

This chapter addresses the many and striking similarities that exist between Judaeo-Christian scripture on the one hand and the *Qur'an* and *Ahadith* (singular = *Hadith*) on the other hand. For Muslims, the *Qur'an* represents the divine revelation given to Prophet Muhammad between approximately 610 and 632 CE. Muslims believe that the *Qur'an* contains the actual and verbatim words of God as relayed to Prophet Muhammad by the angel Gabriel. As such, the *Qur'an* is the highest religious authority in Islam. In contrast, the *Ahadith* consist of the narratives of what Prophet Muhammad said and did. Within Islam, the authentic *Ahadith* are second in religious authority only to the *Qur'an*. I emphasize the word "authentic," because it is a matter of historical record that some *Ahadith* were fabricated and others have a weak and questionable provenance. However, there is a corpus of *Ahadith* that is generally accepted as being authentic, and it is this corpus of *Ahadith* that will be used throughout the remainder of this book whenever *Ahadith* are presented.

In an effort to provide some conceptual structure to understanding the commonalities between the Islamic and Judaeo-Christian scriptures, the field of inquiry has been somewhat arbitrarily divided into four areas of concern: (1) religious history and the prophetic tradition, (2) divine revelation in religious history, (3) Jesus Christ and the Virgin Mary, and (4) religious and ethical teachings. The fourth area has been further segmented according to various Biblical passages that find parallel expression in either the *Qur'an* or the *Ahadith*.

RELIGIOUS HISTORY AND THE PROPHETIC TRADITION

The Prophetic Tradition

As a starting point in exploring the similarities between the Judaeo-Christian scriptures and the religious texts of Islam, we can begin by examining the shared prophetic tradition of the three Abrahamic faiths, i.e., Judaism, Christianity, and Islam. However, before beginning this endeavor, it is worthwhile to digress momentarily in order to consider the meaning of the word "prophet."

The English word "prophet" and the related words "prophecy" and "prophesize" are derived from the Greek "*prophetes*." In turn, the Greek "*prophetes*" is a translation of the Hebrew (and Arabic) word "*nabi*," which is derived from the Akkadian language. The Akkadian word "nabi" means "to call," "to announce," or "to speak for." Thus a religious prophet is one who announces or proclaims a divine message or revelation. A prophet is simply someone who speaks for God. As originally intended, prophecy had nothing to do with predicting or seeing into the future.

The prophetic tradition within Judaism and Christianity is firmly encapsulated in what Christianity refers to as the *Old Testament*. Moving from *Genesis* to *Malachi*, Judaism and Christianity trace their prophetic tradition from the creation of Adam, through the pre-Israelite patriarchs (Noah, Enoch, Abraham, and Isaac), and on through the various Israelite prophets and notables (e.g., Jacob, Moses, Joseph, Samuel, David, Solomon, Elijah, Elisha, Jonah, etc.). Within Christianity, the prophetic tradition even encroaches slightly into the *New Testament* gospels, with the inclusion of stories about Zechariah and his son, John the Baptist, who is known as Prophet Yahya within the Islamic tradition.

It may come as a surprise to many non-Muslims to learn that everyone of these aforementioned prophets is mentioned repeatedly in the *Qur'an*. Utilizing a standard English translation of the meaning of the *Qur'an*, one finds Moses being named over 170 times, Abraham over 70 times, Noah over 40 times, Jesus and Joseph (the son of Jacob) over 30 times, Adam, Jacob, and Solomon almost 20 times, Isaac and David over 15 times, and John the Baptist about five times. Within the *Qur'an*, one also finds references to Job (or Prophet Ayyub), Jonah (or Prophet Yunus), Elijah (or Prophet Elias), and Elisha. Clearly, this is a shared prophetic tradition among Judaism, Christianity, and Islam.

When one moves beyond mere names and begins to compare the stories of the prophets mentioned in both the *Bible* and the *Qur'an*, one typically finds that the two sources parallel each other, although occasionally disagreeing about some specific details of the story. This is the case with each of the following stories.

The Creation

Both the *Qur'an* and the *Bible* maintain that God created the cosmos in six days. (*Qur'an* 7:54 vs. *Genesis* 1:1-2:4)

Prophet Adam

Both Islamic and Judaeo-Christian scriptures state that: (1) God created the first human, Adam, from clay or mud; (2) Adam later "fell" by eating from the forbidden tree; and (3) Adam was then expelled from paradise. (*Qur'an* 2:30-39; 7:19-24; 15:28-29; 32:7-9; 38:71-72; and 55:14 vs. *Genesis* 2:4-3:24).

Cain and Abel

Both the *Bible* and the *Qur'an* relate the story of Adam's first two sons, Cain (Qabil) and Abel (Habil). Both accounts state that they quarreled because God accepted Abel's sacrifice and not Cain's. As a result, both sets of scripture maintain that Cain killed Abel. (*Qur'an* 5: 27-31 vs. *Genesis* 4:1-16).

Prophet Noah and the flood

Both the *Qur'an* and the *Bible* relate the following data regarding Prophet Noah. (1) God directed Prophet Noah and his followers to build an ark. (2) Once completed, the ark was boarded by Prophet Noah and his followers, as well as by representatives from the animal kingdom. (3) Thereafter, a flood destroyed mankind, but the inhabitants of the ark were saved. (4) Noah lived 950 years. (*Qur'an* 11:25-34, 36-48; 23:23-30; 26:105-122; 29:14-15; 37:75-82; 54:9-15; and 71:1-28 vs. *Genesis* 6: 9-9:29).

The Sacrifice of Prophet Abraham

Both the *Qur'an* and the *Bible* relate that Prophet Abraham was tried by God by being asked to sacrifice his son. As Prophet Abraham was complying with this test, God ransomed Abraham's son with a ram, which was sacrificed in place of Abraham's son. (*Qur'an* 37:99-112 vs. *Genesis* 22:1-19).

Prophet Lot and the Destruction of Sodom

Both the *Qur'an* and the *Bible* state the following details regarding Prophet Lot. (1) Prophet Lot eventually left Prophet Abraham and moved to a city (Sodom). (2) Angels of God came to Sodom and stayed in Prophet Lot's home, where they were threatened by the inhabitants of Sodom. (3) Prophet Lot tried to appease these men of Sodom by offering his daughters as brides if these men would leave his guests alone. (4) Prophet Lot's offer was rejected. (5) The angels then blinded the inhabitants of Sodom and destroyed Sodom and all its inhabitants, with the exception of Prophet Lot and his followers. (6) Even Prophet Lot's wife was killed. (*Qur'an* 7:80-84; 11:77-83; 15:57-77; 21:74-75; 26:160-175; 27:54-58; 29:28-35; 37:133-138; 51:31-37; and 54:33-39 vs. *Genesis* 19:4-28).

Prophet Joseph

Both the *Qur'an* and the *Bible* relate the following narrative events concerning Prophet Joseph. (1) Prophet Joseph, the son of Prophet Jacob, had a dream or vision in which 11 stars (his brothers), the sun (his father), and the moon (his mother) prostrated to him. (2) This dream or vision earned Prophet Joseph the enmity of his brothers. (3) His brothers subsequently faked Prophet Joseph's death. (4) Instead of dying, Prophet Joseph was first placed into a well or pit and then was later sold into slavery in Egypt. (5) In Egypt, he was sexually confronted by his owner's wife. (6) Prophet Joseph was then placed in prison, where he interpreted the dreams of two former servants of the Egyptian monarch. (7) Later, Prophet Joseph correctly interpreted the monarch's dream of seven years of plenty to be followed by seven years of famine and was made the vizier of ancient Egypt. (8) Subsequently, Prophet Joseph's brothers came to Egypt to buy grain during the time of famine, and the family was eventually reunited in Egypt. (*Qur'an* 12:4-101 vs. *Genesis* 37:3-37:36; 39:1-47:12).

Prophets Moses and Aaron

Both the *Qur'an* and the *Bible* detail the following events concerning Prophet Moses and his brother, Prophet Aaron. (1) Moses was cast out on the water as an infant by his mother, but he was then rescued and taken in by a member of the Egyptian royal family. (2) As an adult, Moses killed an Egyptian who was oppressing an Israelite. (3) Moses then escaped to Midian (Madyan), where he helped the Sheykh of Midian's daughters water their flock at a well. (4) Having been summoned to be a prophet of God on a mountain in Midian, Prophet Moses later returned to Egypt, where he and Prophet Aaron confronted the pharaoh with mighty signs (e.g., a staff being turned into a serpent and Prophet Moses's hand turning a leprous white in color) and demanded that the Israelites be set free. (5) Pharaoh initially refused this request but finally granted it after Egypt was afflicted with a series of plagues, including death, locusts, lice, frogs, and blood (*Qur'an*) or water turned to blood, frogs, gnats, flies, diseased livestock, boils, thunder and hail, locusts, darkness, and death (*Bible*). (6) Pharaoh released the Israelites into the custody of Prophets Moses and Aaron before changing his mind and pursuing them to the sea. (7) The sea parted, allowing the Israelites to pass by, but then closed on the pursuing Egyptians and drowned them. (8) The Israelites subsequently wandered in the wilderness, where God provided for their sustenance with manna and quail. Nonetheless, the Israelites complained about not having a variety of vegetables and fruits to eat. (9) Early in the Israelite sojourn in the wilderness, the Israelites sent spies into Palestine to survey their potential opposition. Upon returning, all of the spies, excepting only two (identified as Joshua and Caleb in *Numbers* 13:1-14:10), maintained that the opposition was too strong for the Israelites to proceed into Palestine. As punishment for their lack of faith, God made the Israelites wander in the wilderness for 40 years. (10) In the wilderness, Prophet Moses relieved the thirst of the Israelites by striking a rock with his staff, causing water to come gushing forth by God's leave. (11) Also in the wilderness, Prophet Moses was called up to a mountain where God gave him the tablets of the law. (12) In the meantime, the Israelites abandoned the worship of God and forced (*Qur'an*) or seduced (*Bible*) Prophet Aaron into helping to construct a golden calf as an idol. (*Qur'an* 2:51-61; 5:20-26;

7:104-156; 10:75-92; 11:96-97; 17:101-103; 19:51-53; 20:9-73, 77-98; 23:45-48; 26:10-66; 28:7-39; 43:46-56; 51:38-40; and 79:15-24 vs. *Exodus* 2:1-4:17; 5:1-14:31; 16:4-35; 17:1-7; 31:18-32:35; *Numbers* 11:1-9,   31-32; 13:1-14:10, 26-34; 20:1-11; and *Deuteronomy* 9:8-29).

Prophet Samuel and King Saul

Both the *Bible* and the *Qur'an* relate the following details concerning Prophet Samuel and King Saul (Talut). (1) The Israelites demanded that one of their prophets (identified as Samuel in the *Bible*) appoint for them a king. (2) The prophet anointed Saul as King of Israel, but the Israelites then questioned the prophet's choice of Saul as their king. (3) Saul subsequently led the Israelites out into battle against Goliath (Jalut) and his army (the Philistines according to the *Bible*). (*Qur'an* 2:246-250 vs. *I Samuel* 8:4-10:8; 17:1-11).

Prophet David

Both the *Qur'an* and the *Bible* state that when King Saul's army was confronted by Goliath and the Philistines, Prophet David marched forth and killed Goliath. (*Qur'an* 2:251 vs. *I Samuel* 17:1-54).

Prophet Jonah

Both the *Qur'an* and the *Bible* relate the following events concerning the life of Prophet Jonah. (1) Prophet Jonah tried to escape and flee on a ship. (2) While he was onboard lots were cast, and he was thrown overboard. (3) Once in the sea, he was swallowed by a big fish. (4) Inside the big fish, Prophet Jonah prayed to God for forgiveness. (5) His prayer was answered, and he was cast forth on a shore. (6) Thereafter, a plant grew over Prophet Jonah, and he preached the message of God, converting over 100,000 with his preaching. (*Qur'an* 37:123-132 vs. *Jonah* 1:1-4:6)

Prophets Zechariah and John The Baptist

Both the *Qur'an* and the *Bible* provide the same, following details regarding the miraculous birth of Prophet John the Baptist. (1) Prophet Zechariah was a care-giver to the Virgin Mary. (2) Prophet Zechariah, as an aged and childless man who was married to a barren woman, prayed that he might yet father a child. (3) His prayer was answered, and his wife conceived Prophet John the Baptist. (4) As a sign, Prophet Zechariah was made mute for three nights (*Qur'an*) or throughout the conception, gestation, and first eight days of life of Prophet John the Baptist (*Bible*). (*Qur'an* 3:37-41; 19:2-15; 21:89-90 vs. *Luke* 1:5-80).

Differences in the Prophetic Tradition

Having summarized some of the commonalities to be found in the shared prophetic tradition of Judaism, Christianity, and Islam, it must also be acknowledged that one often finds that the respective stories of the prophets from the *Bible* and the *Qur'an* tend to complement each other without overlapping. Thus, the *Qur'an* gives considerable detail about Abraham's early life, presumably in Ur. While such information is not to be found in the *Bible*, it does not contradict Biblical accounts. In contrast, the *Bible* gives information about Abraham's life in Palestine that is not to be found in the *Qur'an* but that does not contradict the *Qur'an*. Further, the *Qur'an* presents a much fuller story regarding the visit of the Queen of Sheba (Bilqis) to Prophet Solomon than is to be found in the *Bible*. In contrast, the *Bible* gives much more information than the *Qur'an* when it comes to the stories regarding Prophet Solomon's building programs and judicial wisdom. However, once again, these specific differences in emphasis are not contradictions.

Furthermore, it should be noted that many of the Qur'anic stories of the prophets that are not found in the *Bible* are found in parallel or variant versions in the Jewish *Talmud* or in various Jewish Targum and Midrashim. Such is the case with all of the following Qur'anic stories. (1) Prophet Adam, having previously been taught the names of all things by God, named the various entities of creation after the angels were unable to do so (*Qur'an* 2:30-33 vs. Midrash Rabbah on *Leviticus* and *Genesis*; and Sanhedrin 28). (2) God commanded the angels to bow down to Prophet Adam (*Qur'an* 2:34; 7:11; 15:28-29; 17:61; 18:50; 20:116; 38:71-74 vs. Midrash of Rabbi Moses). (3) A raven's scratching on the ground served as the inspiration for Cain's (*Qur'an* 5:31) or Prophet Adam's (Pirke Rabbi Elieser 21) idea of burying Prophet Abel's body after he was murdered by Cain. (4) As a youth, Prophet Abraham destroyed numerous idols, earning him the enmity of the idol worshippers who then unsuccessfully attempted to burn him to death (*Qur'an* 21:51-70; 29:24; 37:83-98 vs. Midrash Rabbah on *Genesis*). (5) Prophet Joseph is found to be innocent of attempting to rape his Egyptian owner's wife when it is found that she tore Prophet Joseph's garment from the back (indicating that she had chased him) and not from the front (*Qur'an* 12:21-29 vs. Midrash Jalkut). (6) The wife of Prophet Joseph's Egyptian owner invited other Egyptian women to a meal, where-upon they all cut their hands with knives in amazement when they were confronted by the magnificence of Prophet Joseph (*Qur'an* 12:30-31vs. Midrash Jalkut). (7) Prophet Jacob urged his sons to enter the Egyptian city by different gates when they went to Egypt to get food during a time of famine (*Qur'an* 12: 67-68 vs. Midrash Rabbah on *Genesis*). (8) The golden calf made by the Israelites in the wilderness, while Prophet Moses was on the mountain, actually seemed to low (*Qur'an* 7:148; 20:83-89 vs. Pirke Rabbi Elieser).[3]

True, there are places where the Judaeo-Christian and Islamic traditions contradict each other, or at least differ rather more dramatically than previously illustrated. For example, while both traditions maintain that God created the universe in six days, the *Qur'an* offers no parallel to the Biblical account of God resting from his work on the seventh day. While both traditions maintain that Prophet Adam "fell" from grace by eating of the forbidden fruit in the garden, Islam, unlike traditional Western Christianity, does not interpret this event as creating a state of Original Sin, in which all of humanity inherits Adam's initial sin through being conceived through sexual intercourse. Further, Islam does not necessarily see Adam's earthly sojourn as being a divine punishment for his original mistake.[4] While both traditions maintain that Prophet Abraham was called upon to offer his son in sacrifice, the Judaeo-Christian tradition maintains that the sacrificial vic-tim was Prophet Isaac and that the site of sacrifice was Jerusalem, while the Islamic tradition usually holds that it was Prophet Ismail and that the site of sacrifice was just outside Makkah at Mina.[5] While both the Islamic and Christian traditions maintain the virgin birth of Jesus Christ, Islam sees this as a miraculous act of divine creation, while traditional Christianity interprets this as a divine begetting.

DIVINE REVELATION IN HISTORY

At this point, it might be helpful to digress for a moment and consider the Islamic view of the concept of revelation, a topic that was briefly introduced in the preceding chapter. Islam views the prophetic tradition as being a series of progressive revelations, with each prophet being given a divine covenant. Therefore, unlike the Christian notion of a first covenant with Prophet Abraham (later ratified and expanded in the so-called Mosaic covenant) and a second covenant with Jesus Christ, Islam sees a multiplicity of covenants, in which each prophet and his followers were given a covenant by God. Furthermore, Islam does not limit the prophetic tradition to the Israelites and their precursors, with the *Qur'an* specifically mentioning such non-Israelite prophets as Ismail (the eldest son of Abraham), Hud of the 'Ad people, Salih of the Thamud people, Shu'ayb of the Midianites (Madyan), and Muhammad (the last of the prophets of God). In addition, the *Qur'an* specifically states that God sent a messenger or prophet to every people, although many of their names and identities may no longer be known to us.

> Before thee We sent (messengers) to many nations, and We afflicted the nations with suffering and adversity that they might learn humility. (*Qur'an* 6:42)
>
> Verily, We have sent thee in truth, as a bearer of glad tidings and as a warner: and there never was a people without a warner having lived among them (in the past). (*Qur'an* 35:24)
>
> To every people (was sent) a messenger: when their messenger comes (before them), the matter will be judged between them with justice, and they will not be wronged. (*Qur'an* 10:47)

As the sequence of prophets unfolded over time and across different ethnic groups, successive revelations would sometimes add to or abrogate prior revelations. Thus, the totality of the revelation given to Prophet Moses might be somewhat different than that previously given to Prophet Abraham, the revelation given to Prophet Jesus might be different than that received by Prophet Moses, and the revelation presented to Prophet

Muhammad different than that taught by Prophet Jesus. From an Islamic perspective, this evolution in the revelatory message indicates a gradual unfolding of God's divine plan and message, with specific changes paced to the spiritual development of humanity or to that of a specific group of people.[6]

> O People of the Book! There hath come to you Our messenger, revealing to you much that ye used to hide in the book and passing over much (that is now unnecessary): there hath come to you from God a (new) light and a perspicuous book—wherewith God guideth all who seek His good pleasure to ways of peace and safety and leadeth them out of darkness, by His will, unto the light—guideth them to a path that is straight. (*Qur'an* 5:15-16)
>
> None of Our revelations do We abrogate or cause to be forgotten, but We substitute something better or similar: knowest thou not that God hath power over all things. (*Qur'an* 2:106)
>
> This *Qur'an* is not such as can be produced by other than God; on the contrary it is a confirmation of (revelations) that went before it and a fuller explanation of the book—wherein there is no doubt— from the Lord of the worlds. (*Qur'an* 10:37)
>
> We did send messengers before thee, and appointed for them wives and children: and it was never the part of a messenger to bring a sign except as God permitted (or commanded). For each period is a book (revealed). God doth blot out or confirm what He pleaseth: with Him is the mother of the book. (*Qur'an* 13:38-39)

However, throughout all of the progressive revelations given to successive prophets, Islamic thought maintains that two core elements of the revelations remained constant. Firstly, there is no god but God Who alone is to be worshiped in His Oneness. Secondly, avoid evil and wickedness, for there will be a general resurrection and a Day of Judgment.

> For we assuredly sent amongst every people a messenger (with the command), "Serve God and eschew evil:" of the people were some whom God guided and some on whom error became inevitably

(established). So travel through the earth and see what was the end of those who denied (the truth). (*Qur'an* 16:36)

With those two constants, one again meets the essential commonality that is to be found among Islam, Christianity, and Judaism, for these same two constants may be seen as being fundamental within both Judaism and Christianity.

THE ISLAMIC VIEW OF MARY AND JESUS

As noted earlier, Jesus is mentioned by name over 30 times across multiple passages in the *Qur'an*. However, much of the information on Jesus in the *Qur'an* is confined to two lengthy passages (chapter 3, verses 35-60; and chapter 19, verses 1-40), both of which, like *Luke*, preface the account of the birth of Jesus with the story of the miraculous birth of John the Baptist, and the former of which prefaces the story of the birth of John the Baptist with the story of the birth of Mary. In what follows, the Islamic portrayal of Jesus and Mary is drawn from the *Qur'an* and from the sayings of Prophet Muhammad.

Qur'an 3:35-37 begins the story of Mary (Maryam) with a brief statement about her birth. The reader is first introduced to an otherwise unidentified "woman of 'Imran," i.e., descendant of 'Imran[7], presumably a reference to the Biblical Amran, who was the father of Prophets Moses and Aaron (*Exodus* 6:16-20), and who was the founding ancestor of one of the clans of the Israelite tribe of Levi (*Numbers* 3:14-27). This "woman of 'Imran" supplicated to God and dedicated her unborn daughter to "Thy special service." The girl was born, was named Mary, and was accepted by God, Who "made her grow in purity and beauty." She then entered the care of Prophet Zechariah, the father of Prophet John the Baptist, at which time she was "supplied with sustenance" from God. Additionally, *Qur'an* 3:44 states that several individuals "cast lots with arrows" to see who would have final care of Mary.

> Behold! A woman of 'Imran said: "O my Lord! I do dedicate unto Thee what is in my womb for Thy special service: so accept this of me: for Thou hearest and knowest all things." When she was

delivered, She said: "O my Lord!   Behold!   I am delivered of a female child!"—and God knew best what she brought forth—"and no wise is the male like the female.[8] I have named her Mary, and I commend her and her offspring to Thy protection from the evil one, the rejected." Right graciously did her Lord accept her: He made her grow in purity and beauty; to the care of Zakariya was she assigned. Every time that he entered (her) chamber to see her, he found her supplied with sustenance. He said: "O Mary! Whence (comes) this to you?" She said: "From God: for God provides sustenance to whom He pleases without measure."...they cast lots with arrows, as to which of them should be charged with the care of Mary... (*Qur'an* 3:35-37, 44)

While much of the above may be unfamiliar to many Christians, each of the above statements has important parallels in early Christian scripture and apocryphal writing. For example, *The Gospel of the Birth of Mary* 1:6 states that Mary's parents devoted her "to the service of the Lord" even before she was conceived, and 5:6 of the same apocryphal gospel further states that her parents rededicated her to that service after she reached puberty. A variant fragment of *The Gospel of the Birth of Mary*, preserved in a statement by Faustus, the bishop of Riez in Provence, states that Mary was a Levite. *The Protoevangelion of James* 8:2 notes that an angel fed Mary during her stay at the Temple in Jerusalem and that Zechariah petitioned the High Priest about Mary. *The Protoevangelion of James* 8:6-16 and *The Gospel of the Birth of Mary* 5:4-6:7 both state that various males cast lots by way of their rods for the care of Mary and that Joseph, to whom Mary was later betrothed, was the winner. Finally, *Luke* 1:39-45, 56 reports that Mary stayed with Zechariah and his wife, Elizabeth, for three months.

The above noted fragment of *The Gospel of the Birth of Mary* is not the only Christian reference suggesting that the family of Mary was of the Israelite tribe of Levi. In addition, there are at least two Biblical references that may provide circumstantial evidence of a link between the tribe of Levi and the family of Mary and Jesus. Firstly, *Luke* 1:36 reports that Elizabeth, the mother of John the Baptist, was a relative of Mary, while *Luke* 1:5 clearly states that Elizabeth was a descendant of Aaron, who was of the tribe of Levi (*Exodus* 4:14). If Elizabeth was a Levite and if Mary was Elizabeth's relative, is it not probable that Mary was also a Levite? Secondly, *Luke* 3:23 notes that Jesus was "about thirty years old" when he began his mission and ministry. This reference becomes important when one realizes that the Levites began their religious duties at the tabernacle (later the temple) at 30 years of age.

> The following were the sons of Levi, by their names: Gershon, Kohath, and Merari...The Lord spoke to Moses and Aaron, saying: Take a census of the Kohathites separate from the other Levites, by their clans and their ancestral houses, from thirty years old up to fifty years old, all who qualify to do work relating to the tent of meeting...Take a census of the Gershonites also, by their ancestral houses and by their clans; from thirty years old up to fifty years old you shall enroll them, all who qualify to do work in the tent of meeting...As for the Merarites, you shall enroll them by their clans and their ancestral houses; from thirty years old up to fifty years old you shall enroll them, everyone who qualifies to do the work of the tent of meeting. (*Numbers* 3:17; 4:1-3, 22-23, 29-30)

Resuming the Islamic portrayal of Mary, *Qur'an* 66:12 states that Mary was a virtuous woman who guarded her chastity, who testified to the truth of the words of God and of His revelations, and who was a devout servant of God. In addition, *Qur'an* 3:42 declares that God purified Mary and chose her above the women of all nations, while *Qur'an* 3:45 notes that an angelic visitor announced to Mary the coming virgin birth of one who would be called Christ Jesus and who would be "held in honor in this world and the Hereafter and of (the company of) those nearest to God." These last two verses from the *Qur'an* are remarkably similar to the themes enunciated in *Luke* 1:26-33 and further illustrate the inherent similarity between the Islamic and early Christian portrayals of Mary.

> Behold! The angels said: "O Mary!   God hath chosen thee and purified thee—chosen thee above the women of all nations..."...Behold! the angels said: "O Mary! God giveth thee glad tidings of a word from Him: his name will be Christ Jesus.

The son of Mary, held in honor in this world and the hereafter and
of (the company of) those nearest to God..." (*Qur'an* 3:43, 45)

...The virgin's name was Mary. And he came to her and said,
"Greetings, favored one! The Lord is with you."...The angel said
to her, "Do not be afraid, Mary, for you have found favor with God.
And now, you will conceive in your womb and bear a son, and you
will name him Jesus. He will be great, and will be called the Son of
the Most High, and the Lord God will give to him the throne of
his ancestor David. (*Luke* 1:27b-28, 30-32)

Both Islam and Christianity proclaim the virgin birth of Jesus.
However, there is a fundamental difference between the two religions in
terms of how the virgin birth is typically conceptualized. Contemporary
Christianity portrays the virgin birth of Jesus in terms of Jesus being the
"begotten" son of God. For example, *Matthew* 1:18 states that Mary was
"with child from the Holy Spirit," and *Luke* 1:35 has an angel telling Mary
that the "Holy Spirit will come upon you." While these Biblical verses may
be seen as rather ambiguous by some, the Nicene Creed [9] of Christianity
allows for no such ambiguity when it states: "We believe in one Lord,
Jesus Christ, the only Son of God, eternally begotten of the Father, God
from God, Light from Light, true God from true God, begotten, not made,
one in Being with the Father." Further, the so-called Apostles' Creed holds
that: "I believe in God the Father Almighty; maker of heaven and earth; and
in Jesus Christ his only Son, our Lord; who was conceived by the Holy
Ghost..." [10] In contrast, Islam's portrayal of the virgin birth is that of a
miraculous creation, not that of divine begetting. With regard to that point,
two verses from the *Qur'an* are especially relevant:

She said: "O my Lord! How shall I have a son when no man
hath touched me?" He said: "Even so: God createth what He
willeth: when He hath decreed a plan, He but saith to it 'Be', and
it is!"...The similitude of Jesus before God is as that of Adam;
He created him from dust, then said to him: "Be:" and he was.
(*Qur'an* 3:47, 59)

While many passages in the *Qur'an* deal with the mission, ministry, and miracles of Jesus, *Qur'an* 3:49 provides the most succinct encapsulation. This single verse informs the reader that Jesus was appointed by God as a messenger to the "children of Israel," that he performed many miracles "by God's leave" (e.g., turning a clay figure of a bird into a living bird, healing the blind and the lepers, and quickening the dead), and that he declared "what ye eat, and what ye store." In addition, *Qur'an* 19:27-34 states that Jesus spoke during infancy, and *Qur'an* 5:46 reports that God gave Jesus a gospel containing "guidance and light, and confirmation of the law that had come before him."

The story of the clay birds and of Jesus speaking in infancy may be new to most Christians, but both stories appear in early Christian literature. *The First Gospel of the Infancy of Jesus Christ* 1:2 details Jesus speaking in infancy, while 15:6 of the same apocryphal gospel and 1:2-10 of *Thomas's Gospel of the Infancy of Jesus Christ* narrate the story of the clay birds coming to life. Further, the list of miracles given in *Qur'an* 3:49 appears to overlap quite comfortably with similar lists given in the *New Testament* gospels. For example, the *Qur'an* has Jesus saying:

...I heal those born blind and the lepers, and I quicken the dead, by God's leave; and I declare to you what ye eat and what ye store in your houses. Surely therein is a sign for you if ye did believe. (*Qur'an* 3:49b)

Similarly, the *New Testament* gospels have Jesus saying:

..."Go and tell John what you have seen and heard: the blind receive their sight, the lame walk, the lepers are cleansed, the deaf hear, the dead are raised, the poor have good news brought to them..." (*Luke* 7:22)

..."Go and tell John what you hear and see: the blind receive their sight, the lame walk, the lepers are cleansed, the deaf hear, the dead are raised, and the poor have good news brought to them..." (*Matthew* 11:4b-5)

Additionally, there are certain affinities between the statement in *Qur'an*

5:46 regarding Jesus being "confirmation of the law that had come before him" and *Matthew* 5:17-19, where Jesus is reported to have said that he did not come to abolish the law, but to fulfill it.

> Do not think that I have come to abolish the law or the prophets; I have come not to abolish but to fulfill. For truly I tell you, until heaven and earth pass away, not one letter, not one stroke of a letter, will pass from the law until all is accomplished. Therefore, whoever breaks one of the least of these commandments, and teaches others to do the same, will be called least in the kingdom of heaven; but whoever does them and teaches them will be called great in the kingdom of heaven.(*Matthew* 5:17-19)

Finally, Islam, like Christianity, maintains that there is yet a future role for Jesus in the end times prior to the Day of Judgment. In a remarkable similarity to Christian thought, numerous sayings of Prophet Muhammad (*Muslim, Ahadith* #293, 6924, 6931-6934, 7015, and 7023; *Abu Dawud, Hadith* #4310; and *Al-Bukhari, Ahadith* #3:425, 656; and 4:657-658) contribute to the Islamic perspective that Jesus will descend back to earth, will slay Dajjal (the Antichrist), and will establish an earthly rule before dying.

> An-Nawwas b. Sam'an reported that God's Messenger (said)...God will send Christ, son of Mary, and he will descend at the white minaret in the eastern side of Damascus wearing two garments lightly dyed with saffron and placing his hands on the wings of two angels. When he would lower his head, there would fall beads of perspiration from his head, and when he would raise it up, beads like pearls would scatter from it. Every non-believer who would smell the odor of his self would die for him (Dajjal or the Antichrist) until he (Jesus) would catch hold of him (the Antichrist) at the gate of Ludd and would kill him. Then a people whom God had protected would come to Jesus, son of Mary, and he would wipe their faces and would inform them of their ranks in paradise...then God would send Gog and Magog and they would swarm down from every slope. The first of them would pass the lake of Tiberias

(the Sea of Galilee) and drink out of it. And when the last of them would pass, he would say: "There was once water there." Jesus and his companions would then be besieged here (at Tur, and they would be so much hard pressed) that the head of the ox would be dearer to them than one hundred dinars and God's Apostle, Jesus, and his companions would supplicate to God, Who would send to them insects (which would attack their besiegers' necks) and in the morning they (the besiegers) would perish like one single person…God's Apostle, Jesus, and his companions would then again beseech God…Then God would send rain which no house of clay or (the tent of) camels hairs would keep out, and it would wash away the earth until it could appear to be a mirror. Then the earth would be told to bring forth its fruit and restore its blessing and, as a result thereof, there would grow (such a big) pomegranate that a group of persons would be able to eat that and seek shelter under its skin, and the milk cow would give so much milk that a whole party would be able to drink it. And the milk camel would give such milk that the whole tribe would be able to drink out of that, and the milk sheep would give so much milk that the whole family would be able to drink out of that. At that time, God would send a pleasant wind that would soothe (people) even under their armpits and would take the life of every Muslim. Only the wicked would survive who would commit adultery like asses, and the Last Hour would come to them. (*Muslim, Hadith* #7015)

There is a particularly dramatic *Old Testament* passage that many Christians interpret as referring to this coming Messianic reign. It is striking for its contrasts and juxtapositions.

The wolf shall live with the lamb, the leopard shall lie down with the kid, the calf and the lion and the fatling together, and a little child shall lead them. The cow and the bear shall graze, their young shall lie down together; and the lion shall eat straw like the ox. The nursing child shall play over the hole of the asp, and the weaned child shall put its hand on the adder's den. They will not hurt or destroy on all my holy mountain; for the earth will be full of the knowledge of the Lord as the waters cover the sea. On that day the root of Jesse shall stand as a signal to the peoples; the nations shall inquire of him, and his dwelling shall be glorious. (*Isaiah* 11:6-10)

The Messianic reign is described in remarkably similar terms in the following *Hadith*.

During Jesus's reign, such security will exist that a camel will graze with the lion and the beast of prey with cows and sheep. Children will play with snakes, and none harm the other. (*Musnad* 406:2[11])

Insha'Allah (the One God willing), this brief treatment illustrates that there are several and major similarities in the understanding of Jesus and Mary by Islam and early Christianity. Although differing in their assessment of the nature of Jesus, a topic to be addressed in the following chapter, both contemporary Christianity and Islam view Jesus as being an instrument of God. In contrast, no such perspective is to be found in traditional Judaism. In fact, quite the opposite perspective is demonstrated in some of the ancient Jewish texts. For example, consider the following statements, the first of which appears in the Baraitha, and the second of which appears in the Tosefta, both being supplements to the *Mishnah*, the older of the two main parts of the *Talmud*.

It has been taught: on the eve of Passover they hanged Yeshu (Jesus)...because he practiced sorcery and enticed and led Israel astray... (Baraitha, *Babylonian Talmud*, Sanhedrin 43a)

It happened with Rabbi Elazar ben Damah, whom a serpent bit, that Jacob, a man of Kefar Soma, came to heal him in the name of Yeshu(a) (Jesus) ben Pantera; but Rabbi Ishmael did not let him. (Tosefta, Hullin (Profane Things) 11, 22, 23)

The first of the above quoted statements clearly identifies Jesus Christ as having been a sorcerer who led the children of Israel astray from true worship and religious practice. In the second statement, the reference to "Yeshu(a) ben Pantera," i.e., Jesus the son of Pantera, reflects the once prevalent view within Judaism that Jesus Christ was the bastard son of an illegitimate union between Mary and a Roman soldier named Pantera.[12] Fortunately, this is a view that has seldom been propagated publicly for many years.

Nonetheless, this ancient Jewish belief that Jesus was the illegitimate son of Pantera may be echoed in the following *New Testament* verses, in which the Jews of Jesus's day appear to contrast themselves with Jesus by: (1) announcing that they are the legitimate children of both Abraham and of God; and (2) stating that they, at least, are not illegitimate children, implying perhaps that Jesus was illegitimate in his lineage.

> They (the Jews) answered him (Jesus), "Abraham is our father." Jesus said to them, "If you were Abraham's children, you would be doing what Abraham did, but now you are trying to kill me, a man who has told you the truth that I heard from God. This is not what Abraham did. You are indeed doing what your father does." They said to him, "We are not illegitimate children; we have one father, God himself." (*John* 8:39-41)

The ancient Jewish propaganda that Jesus Christ was the illegitimate son of Pantera and Mary also appears to find an echo in two passages from the *Qur'an*. In the first, it is stated that the Jews slandered Mary with a "grave false charge." In the second, Jesus speaks in infancy to define his prophethood and thus defend his mother's honor and chastity against the innuendo of onlookers.

> ...they (the Jews) uttered against Mary a grave false charge. (*Qur'an* 4:156b)

> At length she brought the (babe) to her people, carrying him (in her arms). They said, "O Mary! Truly an amazing thing hast thou brought! O sister of Aaron! Thy father was not a man of evil, nor thy mother a woman unchaste!" But she pointed to the babe. They said, "How can we talk to one who is a child in the cradle?" He said: "I am indeed a servant of God: He hath given me revelation and made me a prophet; and He hath made me blessed wheresoever I be

and hath enjoined on me prayer and charity as long as I live: (He) hath made me kind to my mother and not overbearing or miserable; so peace is on me the day I was born, the day that I die, and the day that I shall be raised up to life (again)." Such (was) Jesus the son of Mary: (it is) a statement of truth, about which they (vainly) dispute. (*Qur'an* 19:34)

Before ending our discussion of the Islamic perspective on Jesus Christ, it should be noted that the Qur'anic statement that "the day that I die, and the day that I shall be raised up to life (again)" does not in anyway support the alleged crucifixion and resurrection of Jesus, as the *Qur'an* explicitly denies that Jesus was crucified, an issue that will be more fully discussed in the next chapter. Rather, the statement refers to a future death, following the return of Jesus Christ to earth in the end times, which will be followed by his resurrection during the general resurrection.

Abu Huraira narrated that the Prophet said: "...Jesus...will descend (to the earth)...He will destroy the Antichrist, will live on the earth for forty years, and then he will die. The Muslims will pray over him." (*Abu Dawud, Hadith* #4310)

'Abdullah ibn Salam narrated that the description of Muhammad is written in the Torah, and also that Jesus, son of Mary, will be buried along with him. Abu Mawdud said that a place for a grave had remained in the house (where Prophet Muhammad was buried). (*Al-Tirmidhi, Hadith* # 5772)

RELIGIOUS AND ETHICAL TEACHINGS

Introduction

So far, we have been confining our exploration of the three Abrahamic faiths to the domain of religious history. However, it is equally profitable to consider the realm of religious and ethical instruction. All three Abrahamic faiths stress that proper adherence to the divine revelation involves establishing a proper relationship with God and with one's fellow man. In what follows, various examples of such religious and ethical instruction will be identified from the *Bible*, and then the Islamic parallels to those Biblical passages will be presented from the *Qur'an* and *Ahadith*.

The Unity of God

A central tenet of Judaism is the concept of the Unity of God. This is succinctly expressed in the following verse, which is known as the *Shema*.

Hear O Israel, the Lord our God, the Lord is One. (*Deuteronomy* 6:4)

According to the *New Testament* and in what appears to be a clear refutation of the doctrine of the trinity, Jesus quoted these very words of the *Shema* when he was asked about the greatest of all commandments.

One of the scribes came near and heard them disputing with one another, and seeing that he answered them well, he asked him, "Which commandment is the first of all?" Jesus answered, "The first is, 'Hear, O Israel: the Lord our God, the Lord is one...'" (*Mark* 12:28-29)

Further, the anonymous author of *James* also stressed the Unity of God, noting that even the demons (jinn in Islam) believe in God's Oneness.

You believe that God is one; you do well. Even the demons believe—and shudder. (*James* 2:19)

The Unity of God is also repeatedly emphasized in the *Qur'an*. The following represent just a couple of those verses.

And your God is One God: there is no god but He: most gracious, most merciful. (*Qur'an* 2: 163)

Say: He is God, the One and Only... (*Qur'an* 112:1)

God, The Beginning and The End

The *New Testament* uses many illustrations and metaphors to refer to the majesty and greatness of God. One of the more dramatic examples states that God is the "first and the last, the beginning and the end."

I am the Alpha and the Omega, the first and the last, the beginning and the end. (*Revelation* 22:13)

The same concept regarding the nature of God is succinctly stated in the *Qur'an*, where God refers to Himself as "the first and the last, the evident and the hidden."

> He is the first and the last, the evident and the hidden… (*Qur'an* 57:3a)

God's Omnipotence

The three Abrahamic faiths all stress that God is all-powerful and that there is nothing beyond His competence and ability. Numerous *Old Testament* verses praise and glorify the unlimited power of God, and the following verses are just a few representations of that fact.

> The Lord said to Moses, "Is the Lord's power limited? Now you shall see whether my word will come true for you or not." (*Numbers* 11:23)

> Yours, O Lord, are the greatness, the power, the glory, the victory and the majesty; for all that is in the heavens and on the earth is yours; yours is the kingdom, O Lord, and you are exalted as head above all. (*I Chronicles* 29:11)

> Great is our Lord, and abundant in power… (*Psalms* 147:5a)

> Daniel said: "Blessed be the name of God from age to age, for wisdom and power are his." (*Daniel* 2:20)

All three of the Synoptic Gospels of the *New Testament* report that Jesus even more directly spoke of the omnipotence of God by noting that "for God all things are possible."

> Jesus looked at them and said, "For mortals it is impossible, but not for God; for God all things are possible." (*Mark* 10:27; see also *Matthew* 19:26 and *Luke* 18:27)

Similarly, the concept of the omnipotence of God is recognized and taught by Islam.

> …knowest thou not that God hath power over all things. (*Qur'an* 2:106b)

The Omniscience of God

The omniscience of God is also a central concept within all three of the Abrahamic faiths. There is nothing that happens under heaven and earth that is not visible and known to God. More specifically, God knows our innermost thoughts, hopes, wishes, and fantasies. In the following *New Testament* passage, Jesus reportedly makes this point by way of a metaphor.

…but God knows your hearts… (*Luke* 16:15)

The same point is made with an almost identical metaphor in the *Qur'an*, when it is said that God knows the secrets hidden in our hearts. An even stronger statement regarding the omniscience of God is made in a second Qur'anic passage that stresses that God knows all "that is in the heavens and on earth."

For God knoweth well the secrets of your hearts. (*Qur'an* 3:154)

Seest thou not that God doth know (all) that is in the heavens and on earth? There is not a secret consultation between three, but He makes the fourth among them—nor between five but He makes the sixth—nor between fewer nor more, but He is with them, wheresoever they be: in the end will He tell them the truth of their conduct, on the Day of Judgment. For God has full knowledge of all things. (*Qur'an* 58:7)

The Ten Commandments

One of the earliest classical expressions of an ethical system is presented in the Decalogue or Biblical Ten Commandments, as found in *Exodus* 20: 1-17 and *Deuteronomy* 5:1-21. In summary form, these commandments may be summarized as: (1) you shall have no other gods before God; (2) you shall not make any graven images or idols; (3) you shall not take the name of the Lord, your God, in vain; (4) remember the Sabbath day, and keep it holy; (5) honor your father and your mother; (6) you shall not murder; (7) you shall not commit adultery; (8) you shall not steal; (9) you shall not bear false witness; and (10) you shall not covet. These Ten Commandments serve as a basic underpinning of the Judaeo-Christian system of ethics and are reflected quite dramatically in the ethical teachings of the *Qur'an*.

> Thy Lord hath decreed that ye worship none but Him and that
> ye be kind to parents. Whether one or both of them attain old age
> in thy life, say not to them a word of contempt, nor repel them,
> but address them in terms of honor...Nor come nigh to adultery;
> for it is a shameful (deed) and an evil, opening the road (to other
> evils). Nor take life—which God has made sacred—except for just
> cause...Give full measure when ye measure, and weigh with a
> balance that is straight: that is the most fitting and the most advan-
> tageous in the final determination...And in nowise covet those
> things in which God hath bestowed His gifts more freely on some
> of you than on others...(*Qur'an* 17:23, 32-33a, 35; 4:32a)

Let's pause for a moment to consider these Qur'anic injunctions. (1)
"Thy Lord hath decreed that ye worship none but Him" is a direct restate-
ment of you shall have no other gods before God. (2) "...be kind to parents.
Whether one or both of them attain old age in thy life, say not to them a
word of contempt, nor repel them, but address them in terms of honor..."
Honor your father and your mother. (3) "Nor come nigh to adultery; for it
is a shameful (deed) and an evil, opening the road (to other evils)." You shall
not commit adultery. (4) "Nor take life—which God has made sacred—
except for just cause..." You shall not murder. (5) "Give full measure when
ye measure, and weigh with a balance that is straight: that is the most
fitting and the most advantageous in the final determination..." You shall
not steal, and, perhaps also, you shall not bear false witness. (6) "And in
nowise covet those things in which God hath bestowed His gifts more freely
on some of you than on others..." You shall not covet.

As to the remaining three or four moral injunctions of the Ten
Commandments, one can easily find Qur'anic parallels to most of
them. The command not to make any graven images or idols is consistent
with Islam's traditional avoidance of creating artistic likenesses of any living
creature, and with the following Qur'anic injunction.

> ...shun the abomination of idols... (*Qur'an* 22:30)

You shall not take the name of the Lord, your God, in vain is paralleled by the following Qur'anic passage.

> They swear their strongest oaths by God that, if only thou wouldst command them, they would leave (their homes). Say: "Swear ye not; obedience is (more) reasonable; verily God is well acquainted with all that ye do." (*Qur'an* 24:53)

You shall not bear false witness finds expression in many passages of the *Qur'an* (e.g., 2:42; 4:112; 25:72-75; 40:28; 45:27; 51:10; 56:92; and 58: 14-15), but is perhaps expressed best in the following verses.

> And cover not truth with falsehood, nor conceal the truth when ye know (what it is)…Woe to the falsehood mongers— (*Qur'an* 2:42; 51:10)

Thus, only the Decalogue's injunction to remember the Sabbath day is not to be found in Islam.

The *Lex Talionis*

A second fundamental ethical precept of the *Old Testament* is the *Lex Talionis* (law of retaliation in kind), which is found in the so-called Mosaic Law of *Exodus*. Briefly stated, the *Lex Talionis* authorized the victim of a wrongdoing to seek equivalent retaliation or retribution against the perpetrator of the wrongdoing.

> If any harm follows, then you shall give life for life, eye for eye, tooth for tooth, hand for hand, foot for foot, burn for burn, wound for wound, stripe for stripe. (*Exodus* 21:23-25)

Of note, the *New Testament* reports that Jesus Christ urged his followers not to insist on their rights under this Lex Talionis when he reportedly said:

> You have heard that it was said, "An eye for an eye and a tooth for a tooth." But I say to you, do not resist an evildoer. But if anyone strikes you on the right cheek, turn the other also; and if anyone wants to sue you and take your coat, give your cloak as well; and if anyone forces you to go one mile, go also the second mile.

(*Matthew* 5:38-41; see also *Luke* 6:29)

In the above verses, Jesus reportedly suggests that the *Lex Talionis* should be softened with charity, mercy, and forgiveness. This call for a compassionate modification of the *Lex Talionis* is also found in two separate passages in the *Qur'an*. In neither case is the *Lex Talionis* forbidden per se, but in both cases the alternative of forgiveness, patience, and charity is recommended   to the victim. In the first example presented below, remission of retaliation   is said to result in "an act of atonement for" the victim. In the second example, the replacing of retribution by patience and forgiveness is stated to be "an exercise of courageous will and resolution in the conduct of affairs."

> We ordained therein for them: "Life for life, eye for eye, nose for nose, ear for ear, tooth for tooth, and wounds equal for equal." But if anyone remits the retaliation by way of charity, it is an act of atonement for himself... (*Qur'an* 5:45)

> The recompense for an injury is an injury equal thereto (in degree): but if a person forgives and makes reconciliation, his reward is due from God: for (God) loveth not those who do wrong. But indeed if any do help and defend themselves after a wrong (done) to them, against such there is no cause of blame. The blame is only against those who oppress men with wrongdoing and insolently transgress beyond bounds through the land, defying right and justice: for such there will be a penalty grievous. But indeed if any show patience and forgive, that would truly be an exercise of courageous will and resolution in the conduct of affairs. (*Qur'an* 42:40-43)

Similar sentiments can be found in two other passages from the *Qur'an*, both of which are quoted immediately below.

> Repel evil with that which is best: We are well-acquainted with the things they say. (*Qur'an* 23:96)

> Nor can goodness and evil be equal. Repel (evil) with what is better: then will he between whom and thee was hatred become as it

were thy friend and intimate! (*Qur'an* 41:34)

God's Burden Upon Us

In a passage of great tenderness and compassion, the *New Testament* reports that Jesus addressed the issue of being "burdened" by following God's message and commandments.

> "Come to me, all you that are weary and are carrying heavy burdens, and I will give you rest. Take my yoke upon you, and learn from me; for I am gentle and humble in heart, and you will find rest for your souls. For my yoke is easy, and my burden is light." (*Matthew* 11:28-30)

God's "burden" upon us is light, and His yoke is easy. In fact, accepting the yoke of God allows one to lay down our worldly burdens and to find rest from the weariness of the demands of this early life. In two different Qur'anic passages, God's words strike a similar theme. In the first verse, we are reassured that God recognizes our weaknesses and wishes to lighten our burdens. In the second, God comforts us by noting that none of us will actually be called upon to carry a burden greater than he or she can bear.

> God doth wish to lighten your (difficulties): for man was created weak (in flesh). (*Qur'an* 4:28)

> No soul shall have a burden laid on it greater than it can bear. (*Qur'an* 2:233)

God's Caring for Us

Not only does God wish to lighten our burdens, He actively cares for us and sustains us. As such, we are free to concentrate less on our material lives, and focus more on our spiritual being. This point is made quite beautifully in the Sermon on the Mount.

> Look at the birds of the air; they neither sow nor reap nor gather into barns, and yet your heavenly Father feeds them. Are you not of more value than they? (*Matthew* 6:26)

Remarkably similar sentiments are stated in the *Qur'an*, even to the point of illustrating that God makes sustenance available for the animals of the earth.

> How many are the creatures that carry not their own sustenance? It is God Who feeds (both) them and you, for He hears and knows (all things). (*Qur'an* 29:60)

God vs. Caesar

How does one balance one's duties to God vs. one's duties to secular and governmental authority? All three of the Synoptic Gospels relate that the Pharisees attempted to trap Jesus into giving an incriminating answer to this question by asking him if they were obliged to pay taxes to Rome. In response, Jesus reportedly asked to see a coin from them, and asked them whose image appeared on the throne. They responded that it was the Roman emperor's. At that, Jesus reportedly said:

> "Give therefore to the emperor the things that are the emperor's, and to God the things that are God's." (*Matthew* 22:21; see also *Mark* 12:13-17 and *Luke* 20:20-25)

This pithy answer demonstrates that in the normal course of human events there is typically no conflict between fulfilling one's secular and national duties and fulfilling one's religious duties to God. The following *Hadith* of Prophet Muhammad conveys the same message, but adds an additional caveat pertaining to those exceptions where a conflict exists between secular and religious responsibilities. It is hard to imagine that any devout Christians would object to the fundamental truth of this addition.

> Ibn 'Umar narrated that the Prophet said: "It is obligatory for one to listen to and obey (the ruler's orders) unless these orders involve one's disobedience (to God); but if an act of disobedience (to God) is imposed, he should not listen to or obey it." (*Al-Bukhari, Hadith* #4:203; see also *Hadith* #9:258)

Social Duty and Responsibility

Let us consider another of the great ethical teachings attributed to Jesus in the *New Testament*, one that dramatically illustrates our social duty and responsibility to our fellow man.

> Then he will say to those at his left hand, "You that are accursed, depart from me into the eternal fire prepared for the devil and his angels; for I was hungry and you gave me no food, I was thirsty and you gave me nothing to drink, I was a stranger and you did not welcome me, naked and you did not give me clothing, sick and in prison and you did not visit me." Then they also will answer, "Lord, when was it that we saw you hungry or thirsty or a stranger or naked or sick or in prison, and did not take care of you?" Then he will answer them, "Truly I tell you, just as you did not do it to one of the least of these, you did not do it to me." And these will go away into eternal punishment, but the righteous into eternal life. (*Matthew* 25:41-46)

Islam offers an almost identical ethical instruction, which is found in the sayings of Prophet Muhammad.

> Abu Huraira narrated that God's Apostle said:"Verily, God, the exalted and glorious, will say on the Day of Resurrection: 'O son of Adam, I was sick but you did not visit Me.' He will say: 'O my Lord, how could I visit Thee when Thou art the Lord of the worlds?' Thereupon He will say: 'Didn't you know that a certain servant of Mine was sick, but you did not visit him, and were you not aware that if you had visited him, you would have found Me by him? O son of Adam, I asked you for food but you did not feed Me.' He will say: 'My Lord, how could I feed Thee when Thou art the Lord of the worlds?' He will say: 'Didn't you know that a certain servant of Mine asked you for food but you did not feed him, and were you not aware that if you had fed him you would have found him by My side?' (The Lord will again say:) 'O son of Adam, I asked you for something to drink, but you did not provide Me with any.' He will say: 'My Lord, how could I provide Thee with something to drink when Thou art the Lord of the worlds?' Thereupon, He will

say: 'A certain servant of Mine asked you for a drink but you did not provide him with one, and had you provided him with a drink you would have found him near Me.'" (*Muslim, Hadith* #6232)

Abu Musa Al-Ash'ari narrated that the Prophet said: "Feed the hungry, visit the sick, and ransom the prisoner." (*Fiqh Al-Sunnah,* 3:93c)

False Piety and Charity

In another passage, the *New Testament* reports that Jesus warned his followers against false piety and stressed that one's heavenly reward is based upon one's intentions as much as one's behavior. In conveying this message, Jesus reportedly focused initially on the issue of charity and suggested that one's acts of charity should not be made public simply to be seen by men.

> Beware of practicing your piety before others in order to be seen by them; for then you have no reward from your Father in heaven. So whenever you give alms, do not sound a trumpet before you, as the hypocrites do in the synagogues and in the streets, so that they may be praised by others. Truly I tell you, they have received their reward. But when you give alms, do not let your left hand know what your right hand is doing, so that your alms may be done in secret; and your Father who sees in secret will reward you. (*Matthew* 6:1-4)

Remarkably similar sentiments are recorded in the *Qur'an*, where God informs that the rewards associated with behavioral acts of charity are actually canceled out by "reminders of your generosity."

> O ye who believe! Cancel not your charity by reminders of your generosity or by injury—like those who spend their substance to be seen of men, but believe neither in God nor in the Last Day...If ye disclose (acts of) charity, even so it is well, but if ye conceal them, and make them reach those (really) in need, that is best for you: it will remove from you some of your (stains of) evil. And God is well-acquainted with what ye do. (*Qur'an* 2:264a, 271)

However, the Islamic parallels to *Matthew* 6:1-4 are not just confined to the *Qur'an*. Even more dramatic convergence is to be found in the following *Hadith* of Prophet Muhammad.

> Anas ibn Malik narrated that God's Messenger said: "When God created the earth…the angels…asked if anything in His creation was stronger than wind, and He replied, 'Yes, the son of Adam who gives charity with his right hand while concealing it from his left.'" (*Al-Tirmidhi*, *Hadith* #192; see also *Al-Bukhari*, *Ahadith* #1:629, 2:504, & 8:798)

False Piety and Prayer

According to *Matthew*, Jesus did not confine his teachings against false piety to the issue of charity. Immediately following his reported discourse in *Matthew* 6:1-4, Christ reportedly preached against false piety creeping into someone's prayer.

> And whenever you pray, do not be like the hypocrites; for they love to stand and pray in the synagogues and at the street corners, so that they may be seen by others. Truly I tell you, they have received their reward. But whenever you pray, go into your room and shut the door and pray to your Father who is in secret; and your father who sees in secret will reward you. When you are praying, do not heap up empty phrases as the Gentiles do; for they think that they will be heard because of their many words. (*Matthew* 6:5-7)

The following passages from the *Qur'an* appears to be a direct parallel to the ethical sentiments expressed in the above *New Testament* verses about false piety while praying.

> Call on your Lord with humility and in private: for God loveth not those who trespass beyond bounds. (*Qur'an* 7:53)

> The hypocrites—they think they are over-reaching God but He will over-reach them: when they stand up to prayer, they stand without earnestness to be seen of men, but little do they hold God in remembrance. (*Qur'an* 4:142)

So woe to the worshippers who are neglectful of their prayers, those who (want but) to be seen (of men) but refuse (to supply even) neighborly needs. (*Qur'an* 107:4-7)

The ethical considerations stated in *Matthew* 6:5-7 also find clear and unambiguous expression in several sayings of Prophet Muhammad. Perhaps, the most dramatic such example can be seen when Muhammad implied that the Antichrist was less of a threat to a believer, than was the believer doing an otherwise virtuous act for reasons of false piety.

God's Messenger came out to them when they were discussing the Antichrist and asked if they would like him to tell what caused him more fear for them than the Antichrist. They replied that they certainly would, so he said, "Latent polytheism, meaning that a man will stand up and pray and lengthen his prayer because he sees someone looking at him." (*Al-Tirmidhi, Hadith* #5333)

Within Islam, worshipful prayer to God is one of the most virtuous acts a person can undertake. However, if he lengthens that prayer for show or for praise because someone is watching him, he is, in essence, performing that prayer for the sake of show or praise and not for the sake of God. Further, there is a subtle implication that he has compromised his belief in the Oneness of God by assigning a weight to the onlooker's praise or commendation, which is equal to or superior to the weight that he is assigning to God. (Within the framework of Islamic law (*Shariah*), this type of action is known as *Riyaa*, i.e., to perform acts that are pleasing to God with the intention of pleasing others than God.[13])

Running throughout reported teachings of Prophet Jesus against false piety in both charity and prayer in *Matthew* 6:1-7, one can identify the clear theme that one must not only do the proper action and behavior, but that one should also have the correct intention. Given this consideration, it may be helpful to quote another example from the sayings of Prophet Muhammad, one which parallels the reported teaching of Prophet Jesus that one's intentions are crucial in evaluating the moral, ethical, and spiritual worth of any action.

God's Apostle said, "The reward of deeds depends upon the intention, and every person will get the reward according to what he has intended. (*Al-Bukhari*, *Hadith* #1:51; see also *Al-Bukhari*, *Hadith* #7:8, *Muslim*, *Ahadith* #4692-4693, and *Abu Dawud*, *Hadith* #2195)

Avoid false piety, one's actions are judged on one's intentions, and do not make a public display of acts of charity and prayer. These are the three mainstays of *Matthew* 6:1-7, and all three points are amply illustrated and confirmed in the *Qur'an* and in the sayings of Prophet Muhammad.

Adultery and Intentions

The *New Testament* alleges that Jesus also addressed the issue of one's intention with regard to the specific issue of adultery.

You have heard that it was said, "You shall not commit adultery." But I say to you that everyone who looks at a woman with lust has already committed adultery with her in his heart. (*Matthew* 5:27-28)

Once again, these reported words of Jesus find a direct parallel in the sayings of Prophet Muhammad.

Ibn 'Abbas narrated that he did not see anything so resembling minor sins as what Abu Huraira said from the Prophet, who said: "God has written for the son of Adam his inevitable adultery whether he is aware of it or not. The adultery of the eye is looking (at something that is sinful to look at), and the adultery of the tongue is to utter (what it is unlawful to utter), and the inner self wishes and longs for (adultery), and the private parts turn that into reality or refrain from submitting to the temptation." (*Al-Bukhari*, *Hadith* #8:609; see also *Al-Bukhari*, *Hadith* #8:260)

The Golden Rule

For many Christians, the pinnacle of the reported ethical instruction of Jesus Christ can be found in the so-called Golden Rule.

In everything do to others as you would have them do to you; for this is the law and the prophets. (*Matthew* 7:12; see also *Luke* 6:31)

Variations on the Golden Rule can also be found in prior Jewish writings. For example, a "negative" version of the Golden Rule is attributed to Rabbi Hillel, in which he instructed that one should not do to others what one would not want done to oneself.[14] An additional "negative" version of the Golden Rule can be identified in the *Old Testament* apocryphal writings.

And what you hate, do to no man. (*Tobit* 4:14)

The Islamic parallel to the Golden Rule can be found in the teachings of Prophet Muhammad.

Anas narrated that the Prophet said: "None of you will have faith till he wishes for his brother what he likes for himself." (*Al-Bukhari, Hadith* #1:12)

Man's Search for God

The *New Testament* author of the epistle of *James* offers a concise guide and instruction regarding man's search for God. In so doing, the unknown author states two basic principles. Firstly, "submit" to God. (It should immediately be noted that in the single word "submit," one finds the English translation of a variant form of the Arabic word "Islam.") Secondly, whatever action man takes in reaching out to God, God will reciprocate in turn.

Submit yourselves therefore to God. Resist the devil, and he will flee from you. Draw near to God, and he will draw near to you. (*James* 4:7-8a)

"Draw near to God, and he will draw near to you" are words of great spiritual comfort and assurance. However, the Islamic teaching goes even further in offering spiritual comfort and assurance than does the author of *James*. Prophet Muhammad instructed not only that God will reciprocate any attempt man makes to reach out to Him, but that, in reaching back to man, God will multiply whatever effort man has made.

Abu Huraira narrated that the Prophet said, "God says: ... I am with him (man) if he remembers Me. If he remembers Me in himself, I too, remember him in Myself; and if he remembers Me in a group of people, I remember him in a group that is better than they; and if he comes one span (about eight to nine inches) nearer to Me, I go one cubit (about 18-20 inches) nearer to him; and if he comes one cubit nearer to Me, I go a distance of two out-stretched arms nearer to him; and if he comes to Me walking, I go to him running.'" (*Al-Bukhari, Hadith* #9:502)

Anas narrated that the Prophet said: "My Lord says, 'If My slave comes nearer to me for a span, I go nearer to him for a cubit; and if he comes nearer to Me for a cubit, I go nearer to him for the span of outstretched arms; and if he comes to Me walking, I go to him running.'" (*Al-Bukhari, Hadith* #9:627)

God and Supplication in Prayer

In a moving passage that uses the metaphor of a father and his child, the *New Testament* reports that Jesus preached the efficacy of supplicating to God in prayer.

Ask, and it will be given you; search, and you will find; knock, and the door will be opened for you. For everyone who asks receives and everyone who searches finds, and for everyone who knocks, the door will be opened. Is there anyone among you who, if your child asks for bread, will give a stone? Or if the child asks for a fish, will give a snake? If you then, who are evil, know how to give good gifts to your children, how much more will your father in heaven give good things to those who ask him! (*Matthew* 7:7-11; see also *Luke* 11:9-13)

Likewise, the *Qur'an* offers direct reassurance that God will not turn away from those who call on Him.

And your Lord says: "Call on Me; I will answer your (prayer)..."

(*Qur'an* 40:60a)

Backbiting

The author of *James* does not just address the issue of man's relationship to God but also confronts man's relationship to his fellow man. Thus, the reader of this epistle is told to refrain from any backbiting regarding one's fellow congregants. One is not to "speak evil against one another," for others are one's "brothers and sisters."

> Do not speak evil against one another, brothers and sisters. Whoever speaks evil against another or judges another, speaks evil against the law and judges the law; but if you judge the law, you are not a doer of the law but a judge. There is one lawgiver and judge who is able to save and to destroy. So who, then, are you to judge your neighbor? (*James* 4:11-12)

The *Qur'an* also instructs believers to avoid backbiting and speaking "ill of each other behind their backs." However, the words of God go well beyond those of the writer of *James*. God instructs Muslims to avoid all mockery, sarcasm, and ridicule of others, and to refrain from all needless and inappropriate suspicion of others.

> O ye who believe! Let not some men among you laugh at others: it may be that the (latter) are better than the (former): nor let some women laugh at others: it may be that the (latter) are better than the (former): nor defame nor be sarcastic to each other, nor call each other by (offensive) nicknames: ill-seeming is a name connoting wickedness, (to be used of one) after he has believed: and those who do not desist are (indeed) doing wrong. O ye who believe! Avoid suspicion as much (as possible): for suspicion in some cases is a sin: and spy not on each other, nor speak ill of each other behind their backs... (*Qur'an* 49:11-12a)

> Those who love (to see) scandal...broadcast among the believers, will have a grievous penalty in this life and in the hereafter: God

knows, and ye know not. (*Qur'an* 24:19)

Insha'Allah or God Willing

The author of *James* warns man against taking himself too seriously, and of becoming so arrogant that he believes that he can actually say what he will be doing later in the day or during the following day. Rather than saying, "I will do such and such," one is instructed to say, "I will do such and such, God willing or if God wishes."

> Come now, you who say, "Today or tomorrow we will go to such and such a town and spend a year there, doing business and making money." Yet you do not even know what tomorrow will bring. What is your life? For you are a mist that appears for a little while and then vanishes. Instead you ought to say, "If the Lord wishes, we will live and do this or that." As it is, you boast in your arrogance; all such boasting is evil. (*James* 4:13-16)

Likewise, in the *Qur'an*, God warns against this specific type of arrogance and instructs His believers to temper their statements about their future actions by saying "*Insha'Allah*" (God willing or so please God).

> Nor say of anything, "I shall be sure to do so and so tomorrow"— without adding, "So please God!" And call thy Lord to mind when thou forgetest, and say, "I hope that my Lord will guide me ever closer (even) than this to the right road."(*Qur'an* 18:23-24)

Priorities during War

The so-called Mosaic Law of the *Old Testament* specifies that a man is excused from bearing arms and from all modes of warfare during the first year of his married life.

> When a man is newly married, he shall not go out with the army or be charged with any related duty. He shall be free at home one year, to be happy with the wife whom he has married. (*Deuteronomy* 24:5)

This sentiment, i.e., that marital responsibilities early on in a marriage take precedence over serving in the army, also finds direct expression in at least two sayings of Prophet Muhammad on this subject.

> Jabir ibn 'Abdullah narrated: "I participated in a military expedition along with God's Apostle…Then I said, 'O God's Apostle! I am a bridegroom,' and requested him to allow me to go home. He allowed me…(*Al-Bukhari, Hadith* #4:211; see also *Al-Bukhari, Hadith* #3:589)

Furthermore, Prophet Muhammad taught that certain marital responsibilities may override a man's duty to serve in the military even later in married life.

> Ibn 'Abbas narrated that a man came to the Prophet and said, "O God's Apostle! I have enlisted in the army for such and such military expedition, and my wife is leaving for Hajj (the Muslim's pilgrimage to Makkah)." God's Apostle said, "Go back and perform Hajj with your wife." (*Al-Bukhari, Hadith* #4:295; see also *Al-Bukhari, Hadith* #4:250;)

> Ibn 'Umar narrated that 'Uthman did not join the Battle of Badr, because he was married…and (his wife) was ill. So, the Prophet said to him, "(Take care of your wife and) you will get a reward and a share (from the war booty) similar to the reward and the share of one who has taken part in the Battle of Badr." (*Al-Bukhari, Hadith* #4:359)

The Final Day

In response to questions concerning the Final Day or Day of Judgment, the *New Testament* informs the reader that Jesus reportedly said that no one knew the time except "the Father." Of note, these reported words of Jesus Christ clearly state that Jesus was not privy to certain information known only to God and suggest the subordination of Jesus to God.

> But about that day and hour no one knows, neither the angels of heaven, nor the Son, but only the Father. (*Matthew* 24:36; see also the parallel in *Mark* 13:32-37)

As repeatedly stated in the *Qur'an*, the timing of the Final Day is knowledge that rests solely with God, glorified and exalted is He. No man, no jinn, no angel, and no prophet or messenger has that knowledge. During his ministry, Prophet Muhammad was asked repeatedly about the timing of the Day of Judgment. In response to such questioning, God provided the following revelations to Prophet Muhammad through the angel Gabriel.

> They ask thee about the (final) Hour—when will be its appointed time? Say: "The knowledge thereof is with my Lord (alone): none but He can reveal as to when it will occur. Heavy were its burden through the heavens and the earth. Only, all of a sudden will it come to you." They ask thee as if thou wert eager in search thereof: say: "The knowledge thereof is with God (alone), but most men know not." (*Qur'an* 7:187)

> They ask thee about the Hour—"When will be its appointed time?" Wherein art thou (concerned) with the declaration thereof? With thy Lord is the limit fixed therefor. Thou art but a warner for such as fear it. (*Qur'an* 79:42-45)

> Men ask thee concerning the Hour: say, "The knowledge thereof is with God (alone):" and what will make thee understand?—perchance the hour is nigh! (*Qur'an* 33:63)

> Say: "As to the knowledge of the time, it is with God alone: I am (sent) only to warn plainly in public." (*Qur'an* 67:26)

> Verily the knowledge of the Hour is with God (alone). (*Qur'an* 31:34a)

Dietary Restrictions

The *Old Testament* lists numerous dietary restrictions that were reportedly placed upon the Israelites by God. Of these, two of the best known are the prohibition against eating pork and the prohibition against eating carrion.

> But among those that chew the cud or have divided hoofs, you shall not eat the following...The pig, for even though it has divided hoofs and is cleft-footed, it does not chew the cud; it is unclean

for you. Of their flesh you shall not eat, and their carcasses you shall not touch; they are unclean for you. (*Leviticus* 11:4a, 7-8)

You shall not eat any abhorrent thing. These are the animals you may not eat...And the pig, because it divides the hoof but does not chew the cud, is unclean for you. You shall not eat their meat, and you shall not touch their carcasses...You shall not eat anything that dies of itself... (*Deuteronomy* 14:3-4a, 8, 21a)

These same dietary restrictions are found in three separate passages of the *Qur'an*. In all three cases, Muslims are prohibited from eating pork and carrion. However, the Qur'anic prescriptions do allow for the issue of necessity. If a person were starving or if there were some medical necessity, the prohibition does not apply to that person, so long as the person is not engaged in "willful disobedience" and in "transgressing due limits." Other dietary restrictions mentioned in these Qur'anic verses prohibit eating: (1) the meat of animals slaughtered under an invocation to some deity other than God, (2) the meat of animals that have been sacrificed on stone altars (implying a pagan sacrifice), and (3) meat that has been raffled off (gambling is prohibited in Islam).

He hath only forbidden you dead meat (carrion) and blood and the flesh of swine, and that on which any other name hath been invoked besides that of God. But if one is forced by necessity, without willful disobedience, nor transgressing due limits—then is he guiltless, for God is oft-forgiving, most merciful. (*Qur'an* 2:173)

Forbidden to you (for food) are dead meat, blood, the flesh of swine, and that on which hath been invoked the name of other than God; that which hath been killed by strangling, or by a violent blow, or by a headlong fall, or by being gored to death; that which hath been (partly) eaten by a wild animal; unless ye are able to slaughter it (in due form), that which is sacrificed on stone (altars); (forbidden) also is the division (of meat) by raffling with arrows: that is impiety...But if any is forced by hunger, with no inclination to transgression, God is indeed oft-forgiving, most merciful.

(*Qur'an* 5:3a,c)

Say: "I find not in the message received by me by inspiration any (meat) forbidden to be eaten by one who wishes to eat it, unless it be dead meat, or blood poured forth, or the flesh of swine—for it is an abomination—or what is impious, (meat) on which a name has been invoked other than God's." But (even so), if a person is forced by necessity, without willful disobedience, nor transgressing due limits—thy Lord is oft-forgiving, most merciful. (*Qur'an* 6:145)

The *Qur'an* also speaks directly to the issue of where Islamic dietary restrictions differ from those practiced by the Jews. For example, Muslims may eat camel meat and shellfish, while Jews may not. In short, such differences are said to have resulted from the Jews having been prohibited certain foods as a direct punishment "for their willful disobedience."

For those who followed the Jewish law, We forbade every (animal) with undivided hoof, and We forbade them the fat of the ox and the sheep, except what adheres to their backs or their entrails, or is mixed up with a bone: this in recompense for their willful disobedience: for We are true (in our ordinances). (*Qur'an* 6:146)

Gaining Entrance to Heaven

All three of the Synoptic Gospels report that Jesus referred to the difficulties of a rich man in gaining entrance to heaven. Presumably, such a rich man's gains were ill-gotten or were amassed through miserly disregard of the requirements of brotherly love and charity.

Again I tell you, it is easier for a camel to go through the eye of a needle than for someone who is rich to enter the kingdom of God. (*Matthew* 19:24; see also *Mark* 10:25 and *Luke* 18:25)

The identical metaphor, i.e., that of a camel passing through the eye of a needle, is used in the *Qur'an* in referring to the likelihood of someone entering heaven who has rejected the signs of God.

To those who reject Our signs and treat them with arrogance, no opening will there be of the gates of heaven, nor will they enter the garden, until the camel can pass through the eye of the needle: such is Our reward for those in sin.(*Qur'an* 7:40)

Do Not Aggrandize God's Messengers

In what appears to be a direct repudiation of any claim to divinity, three different *New Testament* gospels imply that Jesus Christ denied that he was good and insisted that only God was good.

As he was setting out on a journey, a man ran up and knelt before him, and asked him, "Good Teacher, what must I do to inherit eternal life?" Jesus said to him, "Why do you call me good? No one is good but God alone." (*Mark* 10:17-18; see parallel versions in *Luke* 18:18-19 and *Matthew* 19:16-17)

"Why do you call me good? No one is good but God alone." In other words, Jesus is saying do not aggrandize me and do not attribute to me that which should only be attributed to God. Remarkably similar sentiments were expressed by Prophet Muhammad in several *Ahadith*, six of which are quoted below.

At the time of the Prophet there was a hypocrite who rendered so much harm to the believers that some of them summoned the others to ask the help of the Prophet against him. When the Prophet heard of it, he said: "No man may seek my help. Only the help of God is worthy of being sought." (*Kitab Al-Tawhid*, page 43)

Narrated 'Umar: "I heard the Prophet saying, 'Do not exaggerate in praising me as the Christians praised the son of Mary, for I am only a slave. So, call me the slave of God, and His apostle.'" (*Al-Bukhari*, *Hadith* #4:654)

Mutarrif said, quoting his father ('Abd Allah ibn Al-Shikhkhir): "I went with a deputation of Banu 'Amir to the Apostle of God, and we said: 'You are our lord (Sayyid).' To this he replied: 'The Lord is

God, the blessed and exalted.' Then we said: 'And the one of us most endowed with excellence and superiority.' To this, he replied: 'Say what you have to say, or part of what you have to say, and do not let the devil make you his agents.'" (*Abu Dawud, Hadith* # 4788)

When some people addressed the Prophet with the words, "O Prophet of God," "O the best of us," "O son of the best," "our master," or "son of our master," he interrupted them and said: "O men, say what you came here to tell and lend not your feelings to Satan. I am but Muhammad, the servant of God and His prophet. I do not approve of your raising me above my station assigned to me by God—may He be praised and glorified." (*Kitab Al-Tawhid*, page 163)

Al-Nasa'i also reported from Ibn 'Abbas: "Once, a man said to the Prophet, 'How wonderful that God and you have willed it!' The Prophet objected: 'Have you made me an equal associate to God? Rather, say, 'How wonderful that God alone has willed it!'"" (*Kitab Al-Tawhid*, page 121)

Ibn Majah reported from Tufayl, 'Aisha's half-brother on her mother's side, that Tufayl said: "I came upon a group of Jews. I said to them: 'You are indeed the people of God, if only you didn't claim that 'Uzayr (Ezra) is His son.' They answered: 'You are indeed the people of God, if only you didn't say, 'How wonderful that God and Muhammad have willed it!'" Then, I came upon a group of Christians, and said to them: 'You are indeed the people of God, except that you claim that Christ is the son of God.' They said: 'You too are indeed the people of God, except that you say, 'How wonderful that God and Muhammad have willed it!'" I related what happened to some of my fellows and then went to the Prophet. He asked: 'Did you tell anyone else?' I answered, 'Yes.' He praised God and thanked Him and then said: 'Tufayl has already communicated to some of you his judgment or vision. You have been repeating words, which I would rather have forbidden you to use much earlier, but did not for such and such reasons. Henceforth, do not say, 'How wonderful that God and Muhammad have willed it,' but 'How wonderful that God alone has willed it.'"…(*Kitab Al-Tawhid*, pages 121-122)

The Message of the Prophets

As an additional consideration regarding the inappropriate aggrandizement of the prophets of God, the *New Testament* reports that Jesus clearly stated that the message he conveyed was not of his own making, but was the message conveyed to him from God.

> Then Jesus answered them, "My teaching is not mine but his who sent me. Anyone who resolves to do the will of God will know whether the teaching is from God or whether I am speaking on my own. Those who speak on their own seek their own glory; but the one who seeks the glory of him who sent him is true, and there is nothing false in him." (*John* 7:16-18)

Likewise, the *Qur'an* states that Prophet Muhammad was explicitly instructed to say that the message he preached was merely his recitation of the revelation that he had received from God. Additionally, he was told to point out that he was without treasures and that he had no secret knowledge beyond that conveyed to him through revelation.

> Say: "I tell you not that with me are the treasures of God, nor do I know what is hidden, nor do I tell you I am an angel. I but follow what is revealed to me." (*Qur'an* 6:50)

Family Ties vs. Loving One's Prophet

In a striking *New Testament* passage, Jesus reportedly warned that one was not worthy of him unless one loved Jesus more than one loved his father, mother, son, daughter, etc.

> Whoever loves father or mother more than me is not worthy of me; and whoever loves son or daughter more than me is not worthy

of me... (*Matthew* 10:27; see also *Luke* 14:26)

In two different narrations, Prophet Muhammad voiced similar sentiments regarding how individuals were to relate to their prophet. Prophet Muhammad's contemporaries were to love him above their own families, just as Jesus had instructed his contemporaries to love him above their own families.

> Anas narrated that the Prophet said, "None of you will have faith till he loves me more than his father, his children, and all mankind." (*Al-Bukhari, Hadith* #1:14)

> 'Abd Allah ibn Hisham narrated that...the Prophet said..."(you will not have complete faith) till I am dearer to you than your own self." (*Al-Bukhari, Hadith* #8:628)

False Prophets

Both Jesus and Prophet Muhammad warned against the dangers of false prophets, people who attempted to use religion for their own nefarious ends. Furthermore, in giving these warnings, these two prophets used striking similar words.

> Beware of false prophets, who come to you in sheep's clothing but inwardly are ravenous wolves. (*Matthew* 7:15)

> Abu Huraira narrated that God's Messenger said, "In the last times, men will come forth who will fraudulently use religion for worldly ends and wear sheepskins in public to display meekness. Their tongues will be sweeter than sugar, but their hearts will be the hearts of wolves..." (*Al-Tirmidhi, Hadith* #5323)

Serving Multiple Masters

In the so-called Sermon on the Mount, Jesus reportedly instructed his followers that it is impossible to serve more than one master and to do justice to both. Thus, one must chose between serving God and the worldly life.

No one can serve two masters; for a slave will either hate the one and love the other, or be devoted to the one and despise the other. You cannot serve God and wealth. (*Matthew* 6:24)

In a similar vein but with a slightly different twist, the *Qur'an* speaks about the person who vainly tries to serve multiple masters and raises the rhetorical question as to whether he is really as well off as the person who serves only a single, unitary master, i.e., God.

God puts forth a parable—a man belonging to many partners at variance with each other, and a man belonging entirely to one master: are those two equal in comparison? Praise be to God! But most of them have no knowledge. (*Qur'an* 39:29)

Love vs. Hate

The *New Testament* gospels say that Jesus preached a message of love to one's fellow man and insisted that one should even love one's enemies. By so doing, one would be a brother to one's fellow man, as we all are children of God.

You have heard that it was said, "You shall love your neighbor and hate your enemy." But I say to you, love your enemies and pray for those who persecute you, so that you may be children of your Father in heaven... (*Matthew* 5:43-45; see also *Luke* 6:27)

Likewise, Prophet Muhammad disavowed hatred and taught that we all are brothers.

Anas ibn Malik narrated that God's Apostle said, "Do not hate one another, nor be jealous of one another, and do not desert one another. But O God's worshippers, be brothers!" (*Al-Bukhari, Hadith* #8:99; see also *Ahadith* 8:90-92 & 717)

Meekness and Humility

For many Christians, the Sermon on the Mount represents the finest in the reported ethical instruction of Jesus Christ. In particular, many Christians are drawn to the simplicity and beauty of the Beatitudes as reported in *Matthew*. In a concise and pithy manner, these Beatitudes   highlight the characteristics of the truly virtuous and religious individual. For example, the Beatitudes stress that meekness and humility are to be prized.

Blessed are the meek, for they will inherit the earth. (*Matthew* 5:5)

Meekness and humility are also characteristics that are valued in Islam. As illustrated in the following verse from the *Qur'an*, the true servants of God are said to be those who live their lives in humility and graciousness.

And the servants of (God) most gracious are those who walk on the earth in humility, and when the ignorant address them, they say, "Peace!" (*Qur'an* 25:63)

Righteousness

The *New Testament* Beatitudes continue with a statement of reassurance for those who "hunger and thirst for righteousness." Likewise, the *Qur'an* emphasizes that "(every) blessedness" awaits those who "work righteousness."

Blessed are those who hunger and thirst for righteousness, for they shall be filled. (*Matthew* 5:6)

For those who believe and work righteousness is (every) blessedness and a beautiful place of (final) return. (*Qur'an* 13:29)

The Peacemakers

In yet a third Beatitude, Jesus reportedly taught that being a peacemaker was a virtue and a blessing. Once again, the basic meaning of a Beatitude finds expression in the *Qur'an*, where Muslims are instructed to make peace between and reconcile contending parties.

Blessed are the peacemakers, for they will be called the children of God. (*Matthew* 5:9)

So make peace and reconciliation between your two (contending) brothers; and fear God that ye may receive mercy. (*Qur'an* 49:10)

Mercy and Forgiveness

The *New Testament* instructs us that we are to be merciful and to follow the example of God's mercy to us when dealing with our fellow man. In fact, in one particularly telling passage, we are instructed that God's forgiveness of our own sins is contingent upon our having forgiven those who have wronged us.

> Be merciful, just as your Father is merciful. (*Luke* 6:36)

> For if you forgive others their trespasses, your heavenly Father will also forgive you, but if you do not forgive others, neither will your Father forgive your trespasses. (*Matthew* 6:14-15)

The *Qur'an* also teaches that God is most merciful. Further, the *Qur'an* suggests that if we forgive others, then God will be "oft-forgiving" and "most merciful" to us.

> But God is the best to take care (of him), and He is the most merciful of those who show mercy. (*Qur'an* 12:64)

> But if ye forgive and overlook, and cover up (their faults), verily God is oft-forgiving, most merciful. (*Qur'an* 64:14b)

The Greeting of Peace

In an interesting *New Testament* passage, Jesus reportedly taught proper etiquette upon entering a house. Such etiquette includes addressing the worthy occupants of the house with the greeting of "peace." However, if the occupants are unworthy, one is instructed to "let your peace return to you."

> As you enter the house, greet it. If the house is worthy, let your peace come upon it; but if it is not worthy, let your peace return to you. (*Matthew* 10:12-13)

The *Qur'an* teaches a similar etiquette regarding the entering of houses. Upon entering a house, a Muslim is to salute the occupants with "a greeting or blessing and purity as from God." As to the nature of this greeting, a previously quoted passage from the *Qur'an* instructs Muslims to address others with the greeting of "peace." However, there is no instruction to "let your peace return to you" if one judges the occupants to be unworthy. As noted previously, one is to greet even the ignorant with the greeting of "peace."

> But if ye enter houses, salute each other—a greeting or blessing and purity as from God... (*Qur'an* 24:61)

> And the servants of (God) most gracious are those who walk on the earth in humility, and when the ignorant address them, they say, "Peace!" (*Qur'an* 25:63)

An Offending Hand

Many non-Muslims are deeply troubled by that aspect of Islamic law that prescribes the amputation of a hand in certain situations of thievery. Typically, they fail to understand that the punishment is only carried out in certain situations and not in every case. Nonetheless, they still find the punishment cruel and barbaric. Ironically, the same reaction is not engendered by an almost identical prescription reportedly given by Jesus in the *New Testament*, an instruction that most Christians prefer to treat as a metaphor, even though the reported words of Jesus are quite straightforward and unambiguous.

> If your hand or your foot causes you to stumble, cut it off and throw it away; it is better for you to enter life maimed or lame than to have two hands or two feet and to be thrown into the eternal fire. (*Matthew* 18:8; see also *Mark* 9:43-45)

The corresponding concept from the *Qur'an* is presented below. Again, it is emphasized that Islamic law prescribes the amputation of a thief's hand only in certain situations.

> As to the thief, male or female, cut off his or her hands: a punishment by way of example from God for their crime: and God is exalted in power, full of wisdom. (*Qur'an* 5:38)

Treasures on Earth and in Heaven

In the Sermon on the Mount, Jesus reportedly warned against storing up treasures on earth, and noted that such treasures are transitory at best. Rather than seeking treasures on earth, the *New Testament* has Jesus suggesting that one should strive for eternal treasures in heaven and that one's heart will typically be with one's treasure.

> Do not store up for yourselves treasures on earth, where moth and rust consume and where thieves break in and steal; but store up for yourselves treasures in heaven, where neither moth nor rust consumes and where thieves do not break in and steal. For where your treasure is, there your heart will be also. (*Matthew* 6:19-21; see also *Luke* 12:33-34)

The *Qur'an* conveys a similar message, noting that those who desire the "tilth of the hereafter" will find that tilth increasing for them. In contrast, those who desire the "tilth of this world" will be granted a portion thereof but will be denied an eternal reward in the hereafter. Further, the *Qur'an* notes that "what is with you must vanish," while "what is with God will endure."

> To any that desires the tilth of the hereafter, We give increase in his tilth; and to any that desires the tilth of this world, We grant somewhat thereof, but he has no share or lot in the hereafter. (*Qur'an* 42:20)

> What is with you must vanish: what is with God will endure. And We will certainly bestow on those who patiently persevere their reward according to the best of their actions. (*Qur'an* 16:96)

Being Tested with Gifts

The *New Testament* says that Jesus taught that God's expectation of each of us is based in part on the amount of blessings we have been given in this earthly life. More will be expected from those of us who have been given much.

> From everyone to whom much has been given, much will be required; and from the one to whom much has been entrusted, even more will be demanded. (*Luke* 12:48b)

The *Qur'an* states a parallel message and speaks of the gifts that we have been given in this life as actually being a trial for us.

It is He Who hath made you (His) agents, inheritors of the earth: He hath raised you in ranks, some above others: that He may try you in the gifts He hath given you: for thy Lord is quick in punishment: yet He is indeed oft-forgiving, most merciful.(*Qur'an* 6:165)

One's Light on Judgment Day

All three Abrahamic faiths stress that there will be a final Day of Judgment at the end of time. Within the *New Testament*, Jesus reportedly taught that one must constantly be vigilant and prepared for this Day of Judgment, for it may come "as a thief in the night." To illustrate this point, the *New Testament* attributes the following parable to Jesus.

Then the kingdom of heaven will be like this. Ten bridesmaids took their lamps and went to meet the bridegroom. Five of them were foolish, and five were wise. When the foolish took their lamps, they took no oil with them; but the wise took flasks of oil with their lamps. As the bridegroom was delayed, all of them became drowsy and slept. But at midnight there was a shout, "Look! Here is the bridegroom! Come out to meet him." Then all those bridesmaids got up and trimmed their lamps. The foolish said to the wise, "Give us some of your oil, for our lamps are going out." But the wise replied, "No! There will not be enough for you and for us; you had better go to the dealers and buy some for yourselves."

And while they went to buy it, the bridegroom came, and those who were ready went with him into the wedding banquet; and the door was shut. Later the other bridesmaids came also, saying, "Lord, lord, open to us." But he replied, "Truly I tell you, I do not know you." Keep awake therefore, for you know neither the day nor the hour. (*Matthew* 25:1-13)

According to the above passage from *Matthew*, there will be some who will not enter heaven because their lamps are incapable of giving light. They have foolishly left their oil behind and have to beg vainly for oil from those who are prepared. Because they have no light, they are unable to enter heaven. A similar metaphor is found in the *Qur'an*. Once again, there are those who have no light and are not able to enter heaven. Once again, these unfortunate ones beg their more fortunate and prepared others for the ability to generate light. Once again, they ask in vain.

> One day shalt thou see the believing men and the believing women—how their light runs forward before them and by their right hands: (their greeting will be): "Good news for you this day! Gardens beneath which flow rivers! To dwell therein for aye! This is indeed the highest achievement!" One day will the hypocrites—men and women—say to the believers: "Wait for us! Let us borrow (a light) from your light!" It will be said: "Turn ye back to your rear! Then seek a light (where ye can)!" So a wall will be put up betwixt them, with a gate therein. Within it will be mercy throughout, and without it, all alongside, will be (wrath and) punishment! (*Qur'an* 57:12-13)

The Saved and the Condemned

In illustrating the relative positions of the saved and the condemned following the Day of Judgment, the *New Testament* says that Jesus provided a parable about a rich man and a poor man. The rich man was later condemned to hell, and the poor man (Lazarus) was rewarded with heaven. According to the parable, the suffering rich man later gazed from hell upwards to heaven, and begged that Lazarus might come down and ease his thirst just a bit. His request was denied, as there was an impenetrable chasm between heaven and hell.

> There was a rich man who was dressed in purple and fine linen and who feasted sumptuously every day. And at his gate lay a poor man named Lazarus, covered with sores, who longed to satisfy his hunger with what fell from the rich man's table; even the dogs would come and lick his sores. The poor man died and was carried away by the

angels to be with Abraham. The rich man also died and was buried. In Hades, where he was being tormented, he looked up and saw Abraham far away with Lazarus by his side. He called out, "Father Abraham, have mercy on me, and send Lazarus to dip the tip of his finger in water and cool my tongue; for I am in agony in these flames." But Abraham said, "Child, remember that during your lifetime you received your good things, and Lazarus in like manner evil things; but now he is comforted here, and you are in agony. Besides all this, between you and us a great chasm has been fixed, so that those who might want to pass from here to you cannot do so, and no one can cross from there to us." (*Luke* 16:19-26)

The same exact message is provided in the *Qur'an*, even extending to the issue of the condemned begging water from the saved. Once again, the request of the condemned is denied.

The companions of the fire will call to the companions of the garden: "Pour down to us water or anything that God doth provide for your sustenance." They will say: "Both these things hath God forbidden to those who rejected Him—such as took their religion to be mere amusement and play, and were deceived by the life of the world." That day shall We forget them as they forgot the meeting of this day of theirs, and as they were wont to reject Our signs. (*Qur'an* 7:50-51)

Summary and Conclusions

In closing this chapter, it may be helpful to note just one more example of the commonalities between the *Bible* and the *Qur'an*. The gospels of *Matthew* and *Luke* detail an alleged saying of Jesus that is probably immortalized by song in the mental recesses of each reader who ever spent much childhood time in Sunday school or in vacation *Bible* school.

Everyone then who hears these words of mine and acts on them will be like a wise man who built his house on rock. The rain fell, the floods came, and the winds blew and beat on that house, but it did not fall, because it had been founded on rock. And everyone who hears these words of mine and does not act on them will be like a foolish man who built his house on sand. The rain fell, and the floods came, and the winds blew and beat against that house, and it fell—and great was its fall! (*Matthew* 7:24-27; see also *Luke* 6: 47-49)

The above sentiments also find expression in the *Qur'an*, where God warns mankind to build the foundation of his religious and spiritual edifice on the bedrock of "piety to God." Mankind is to avoid building his foundation on the weakness of "an undermined sand-cliff," which will "crumble to pieces" and which "is never free from suspicion and shakiness."

Which then is best? He that layeth his foundation on piety to God and His good pleasure, or he that layeth his foundation on an undermined sand-cliff, ready to crumble to pieces? And it doth crumble to pieces with him into the fire of hell. And God guideth not people that do wrong. The foundation of those who so build is never free from suspicion and shakiness in their hearts, until their hearts are cut to pieces. And God is all-knowing, wise. (*Qur'an* 9:109-110)

As one can see, there is substantial overlap between the Judaeo-Christian scriptures and the Islamic religious texts. These areas of commonality include both religious history and ethical teachings. These similarities are, indeed, quite impressive and obviously go beyond the realms of chance and happenstance. For Muslims, such similarities attest to the divine revelation that lies behind all three of the Abrahamic faiths, however much the non-Islamic Abrahamic faiths may have deviated from that divine revelation.

Chapter 4

From Jesus to Muhammad: Early Christianity and Islam

INTRODUCTION

The immediately previous chapter explored some of the essential similarities among the three Abrahamic faiths—Judaism, Christianity, and Islam. Those similarities included a shared religious history, although occasionally marked by differences in interpretation and details, and a common set of religious and ethical instructions derived from divine revelation. The present chapter focuses on the centuries that separate Prophet Jesus from Prophet Muhammad. Specifically, we will look at five primary issues, the interpretation of which divides contemporary Christianity from Islam. These issues are: (1) the mission and ministry of Jesus Christ, (2) the alleged crucifixion of Jesus Christ, (3) the nature of Jesus, (4) the nature of God, and (5) the prophethood of Muhammad. In reviewing these five issues, each will be examined in turn and, where appropriate, will be traced along chronological trajectories.

However, before beginning this endeavor, it should be noted that, contrary to the popular belief of the modern Christian laity, early Christianity was not a single, monolithic structure. There were many branches to early Christianity, and each local church, e.g., the church at Corinth, Damascus, Alexandria, Jerusalem, etc., was independent of every other church. Each church had its own ecclesiastical hierarchy and its own set of recognized scripture. Thus, the *Epistle of Barnabas* was recognized as scripture by the church at Alexandria, but not in other local churches. Some churches recognized the *Gospel of Thomas* and the *Shepherd of Hermas*, and others did not. With regard to that issue, it should be noted that most of the apocryphal books of the *New Testament* that were referenced in the prior chapter and that will be referenced later in this chapter were recognized as authoritative by one or another local church, and it was not until the sixth century that the books of the *New Testament* became completely standard- ized, although attempts at standardization had begun about two centuries before that.

Not only did the local churches of early Christianity differ as to what was and was not recognized scripture, they also differed in their religious doctrine and dogma. Such differences are especially apparent when one considers the first four issues under consideration in this chapter. As will be shown, there were branches of early Christianity that approached each of these four issues in a manner quite consistent with Islamic interpretation and in a manner at variance with that of contemporary Christianity.

A DISCLAIMER

It is quite outside of the current time parameters to cover all of the different positions advanced by one or another early Christian church with regard to each one of the five issues to be discussed. As such, it is noted at the outset that the following review is highly selective and is not repre- sentative of the breath of differing opinion that existed within the early Christian churches. Quite simply, it is not my intent to present the full range of opinion that existed within early Christianity. Rather, I intend to highlight those early branches of Christianity that were more or less consistent with Islam's position on the five issues under consideration.

The reason for this arbitrary selectivity is simple and straightforward. The Islamic proposition that Jesus was a prophet of Islam and that the religion that he taught was an earlier form of Islam more or less demands that one should be able to find residual traces consistent with Islamic teaching within the historical record of early Christianity. It is the purpose of this chapter to begin to illuminate this Islamic residual within early Christianity with regard to the mission and ministry of Jesus, the alleged crucifixion of Jesus, the nature of Jesus, the nature of God, and the prophethood of Muhammad.

THE MISSION AND MINISTRY OF JESUS

Introduction

Qur'an 3:49 informs the reader that Jesus was appointed by God as a messenger to the "children of Israel." In contrast, contemporary Christianity typically maintains that Jesus's ministry and mission were to the world at large. Nonetheless, there are several *New Testament* passages that appear to agree with the Islamic position that he was sent only to the "children of Israel." For example, consider the following Biblical verses.

> These twelve Jesus sent out with the following instructions: "Go nowhere among the Gentiles, and enter no town of the Samaritans, but go rather to the lost sheep of the house of Israel." (*Matthew* 10:5-6).

> Jesus left that place and went away to the district of Tyre and Sidon. Just then a Canaanite woman from that region came out and started shouting, "Have mercy on me, Lord, Son of David, my daughter is tormented by a demon." But he did not answer her at all. And his disciples came and urged him, saying, "Send her away, for she keeps shouting after us." He answered, "I was sent only to the lost sheep of the house of Israel." But she came and knelt before him, saying, "Lord, help me." He answered, "It is not fair to take the children's food and throw it to the dogs." She said, "Yes, Lord, yet even the dogs eat the crumbs that fall from their masters' table." Then Jesus answered her, "Woman, great is your faith! Let it be done for you as you wish." And her daughter was healed instantly. (*Matthew* 15:21-28)

Jesus reportedly answered, "I was sent only to the lost sheep of the house of Israel." As reported in *Matthew*, Jesus gave a clear, precise, and unambiguous answer as to the field of his mission. It was limited to "the lost sheep of the house of Israel," and it was to this community that he sent his disciples in their missionary efforts.[15]

The Role of Paul

We might also consider how the actual disciples of Jesus, as well as the immediate followers of those disciples, continued Jesus's ministry after the end of his earthly sojourn. However, at this point we must interject a very important proviso that is often overlooked, even though known, by most contemporary Christians, namely that Paul (a former Jewish Pharisee who was once known as Saul of Tarsus) was never a disciple of Jesus and apparently never even met Jesus during the latter's earthly ministry. In short, Paul, who was the foremost proponent of the concept of a universal ministry for Jesus, does not represent the tradition of the disciples of Jesus and in fact was frequently in marked conflict with the Jerusalem church, which was the headquarters of the actual disciples of Jesus. This can be readily substantiated by turning to the *New Testament.*

> When he (Paul) had come to Jerusalem, he attempted to join the disciples; and they were all afraid of him, for they did not believe that he was a disciple. (*Acts* 9:26)

Other *New Testament* passages, e.g., *Acts* 15:1-5, *Acts* 21:17-26, and *Galatians* 2:1-9, dramatically illustrate that Paul, with his insistence on preaching to the gentiles, was in frequent conflict with the Jerusalem church. With regard to these three passages, it is instructive to note that both *Acts* and *Galatians* are Pauline documents and do not reflect the teachings of the Jerusalem church and of the actual disciples of Jesus. As an illustration of this Pauline bias, one can profitably examine *Acts* 21:17-26, where the Pauline writer of this text attempts to show that the Jerusalem church supported Paul in the final analysis. However, the fact of the matter was, as recorded in that very passage, the elders of the Jerusalem church made Paul undergo the temporary rites of being a Nazarite, indicating that he was made to purify himself and to pay penance for what he had been doing.

Despite this Pauline bias, *Acts* does preserve a statement indicating what the actual disciples of Jesus and their immediate followers did when it came to preaching the message of Jesus.

> Now those who were scattered because of the persecution that took place over Stephen traveled as far as Phoenicia, Cyprus, and Antioch, and they spoke the word to no one except Jews. (*Acts* 11:19)

Jewish Christianity

In short, any serious student of early Christianity must recognize a fundamental divergence of thought between the Pauline church with its message to the gentiles, and the Jerusalem church of Jesus's actual disciples. The latter restricted its message to the "children of Israel," continued to worship in the temple in Jerusalem, and did not even call themselves Christians, a term that first arose in the gentile church in Antioch, as witnessed by *Acts* 11:20-26. In fact, the early Christian church of Jerusalem, led by the disciples and immediate followers of Jesus, was proclaimed at the time to be authentically Jewish by no less a Jewish authority than Rabbi Gamaliel, the grandson of Rabbi Hillel, both of whom are recognized as being the preeminent Jewish scholars surrounding the time of Christ.[16] (Of note, Rabbi Gamaliel was the reported Pharisaic instructor of Paul (*Acts* 21:39-22:3), a fact that Paul apparently used whenever he needed to stress his Jewish credentials.)

Many scholars of the history of early Christianity, recognizing that the actual disciples of Jesus did not preach to other than the "children of Israel," refer to the Jerusalem church as being "Jewish-Christian." Of marked importance to the current discussion, this Jewish-Christian tradition continued well after the destruction of the temple of Jerusalem in 70 CE. Such early Christian movements as the Ebionites, the Nazarenes (not to be confused with the modern Christian denomination), and the Elkasites appear to have represented this Jewish-Christian tradition. With regard to the longevity of this Jewish-Christian movement within early Christianity, one can point particularly to the Ebionites, who were apparently established shortly before the destruction of the temple in 70, whereupon they fled from the vicinity of Jerusalem, and spread to what is today Jordan, Syria, Turkey, and Egypt. Of note, the Ebionites continued as a viable movement within greater Christianity through the second, third, and fourth centuries. Likewise, the Nazarenes were known to have existed in greater Syria at least as late as the fourth century, while the Elkasites thrived from the second through fourth centuries.[17]

Summary

Reviewing the preceding historical record, one finds evidence of a trajectory within early Christianity that can be traced back to *Matthew*, *Acts*, and the Jerusalem church, that continued to exist well into at least the fourth century, and that continued to restrict active preaching to the "children of Israel." Of note, the groups represented by this longitudinal trajectory also firmly rejected the Pauline abrogation of the so-called Mosaic laws governing dietary restrictions, circumcision, etc. In this way, these groups were also more or less consistent with Islam.

THE CRUCIFIXION

Introduction

As noted in the previous chapter, there are major similarities in the understanding of Jesus and Mary by Islam and early Christianity. However, when we consider the alleged crucifixion of Jesus Christ, we come to a fundamental discrepancy between Islam and contemporary Christianity. The *Qur'an* declares that Jesus was not crucified, even though his persecutors thought that they had crucified him.

> That they said (in boast), "We killed Christ Jesus the son of Mary, the messenger of God"—but they killed him not, nor crucified him, but so it was made to appear to them, and those who differ therein are full of doubts, with no (certain knowledge), but only conjecture to follow, for of a surety they killed him not—nay, God raised him up unto Himself, and God is exalted in power, wise— (*Qur'an* 4:157-158)

The *Qur'an* says that Jesus was not crucified, a position in marked conflict with contemporary Christianity, which has built its entire theological edifice upon the alleged crucifixion and resurrection of Jesus. In contrast, the *Qur'an* maintains that God saved Jesus and "raised him up unto Himself," a statement having parallels with the ascension of Jesus as portrayed in *Mark* 16:19 and *Luke* 24:50-51.

For most modern day Christians, indeed, for most inhabitants of the Western world, it is almost unthinkable that anyone could seriously maintain that Jesus was not crucified. Such Christian critics of Islam might even maintain that the alleged resurrection of Jesus is a matter of religious belief but that the crucifixion of Jesus is a matter of an unblemished historical record. However, as will soon be see, the actual historical record is otherwise than one might expect.

The Historical Record

Outside of the *New Testament* and other early Jewish and Christian scriptural writings, there are only two references to Jesus being crucified in the entire historical record of the first century. The first was made by Josephus bin Matthias, a first century Jewish historian, and the second by Tacitus, a first and second century Roman. Neither writer was a witness to the crucifixion event. For that matter, most Biblical scholars maintain that none of the *New Testament* authors who wrote about the crucifixion event were actual witnesses of that event. Nonetheless, the skeptic of the Islamic position that Jesus was not crucified will rightly insist that any serious attempt to question the crucifixion of Jesus must marshal an impressive array of documentation that there was serious controversy about whether or not Jesus was actually crucified. "Where is that documentation?" they may well ask. The answer is that it is to be found within the writings of early Christianity itself. In short, the discrepancy between Islam and contemporary Christianity about the crucifixion event obscures the fact that many branches of early Christianity maintained quite adamantly that it was not Jesus Christ who was crucified. This can be verified by examining the writings of the so-called Apostolic Fathers of the early Christian churches, the so-called *New Testament* apocrypha, and even the *New Testament* itself.

The Apostolic Fathers

The writings of the Apostolic Fathers frequently noted that there were Christian sects that rejected the proposition that Jesus had been crucified. Such references can be found in the writings of Ignatius, Polycarp, Justin, Irenaeus, Tertullian, and Hippolytus. Together, these Apostolic Fathers represent a veritable *Who's Who* of early Christianity. As a specific example, we can turn to *Trallians*, a book authored by Ignatius, the bishop of Antioch, who died circa 110. In referring to the crucifixion event, Ignatius wrote that there were Christians of his day who denied that Jesus was crucified in   reality and maintained that Jesus was crucified only in appearance or in   illusion.

> But if, as some say...his suffering was only an appearance, then why am I a prisoner, and why do I long to fight with the wild beasts? In that case, I am dying in vain.

"(S)ome say...(Jesus's) suffering was only an appearance." In considering this quotation from Ignatius, one must acknowledge that Ignatius could not be attacking a belief among early Christians that did not in fact already exist. His attack against those early Christians who believed that Jesus's crucifixion was only illusory demonstrates the existence of that belief among early Christians as early as 110, i.e., by the time of Ignatius's death. Further, the fact that Ignatius even bothered to attack this doctrine suggests that the belief in the illusory nature of the crucifixion was quite widespread by 110.

Christianity's Apocryphal Writings

The fact that many branches of early Christianity maintained that it was not Jesus Christ who was crucified can also be readily verified by considering the so-called apocryphal gospels. For example, the *Gospel of Barnabas* maintained that it was Judas Iscariot, not Jesus Christ, who was crucified. In addition, the *Apocalypse of Peter* 81:4-82:33 maintained that Jesus was crucified only in appearance, not in reality, with the one who was crucified being a substitute or simulacrum of Jesus. Likewise, the *Second Treatise of the Great Seth* 55:10-56:25 stated that it was not Jesus who was crucified, but Simon (presumably Simon of Cyrene, who is identified in *Matthew* 27:32, *Mark* 15:21, and *Luke* 23:26 as being the person who carried Christ's cross for him), and that Simon appeared as though he were Jesus. This position, i.e., that it was Simon of Cyrene who was crucified in place of Jesus, was a cardinal tenet of the early Christian group known as Basilideans, which flourished in Egypt during the second century, and which claimed to be based directly on the teachings of Glaucias, the alleged interpreter of Peter, the disciple of Jesus Christ. Additionally, the *Acts of John* 97-101 reported that the crucifixion of Jesus was an illusion.[18]

The Canonical Gospels

However, it is not just within the so-called apocryphal writings that one finds evidence that it was not Jesus who was crucified. The canonical gospel of *Matthew* 27:11-26 states that Pilate gave the crowd a choice between releasing "Jesus who is called the Messiah" or "Jesus Barabbas." (Any Christians who might wonder about the name "Jesus Barabbas" are urged to consult the New Revised Standard Version of *Matthew* 27:17 for this identification, which is based on some of the oldest surviving texts of this verse.) Matthew then goes on to state that the crowd chose Jesus Barabbas and that Pilate released Jesus Barabbas. Of note, Barabbas, i.e., "*bar Abbas,*" is not a given name but is a patronymic, i.e., a statement that one is the son of so-and-so. Translating from the Aramaic language, the language spoken by Jesus, "bar Abbas" may be translated as "son of the father." In short, *Matthew* tells the discerning reader that Pilate released "Jesus, the son of the Father," and condemned a different Jesus, who was claiming to be the Messiah, i.e., the anointed one.[19] So, who was who? Does this help explain why Pontius Pilate was canonized as a saint by the Coptic Christian Church? Does one justify sainthood for the man who condemned Jesus or for the man who released him? Certainly, *Matthew* raises the very real question of who was actually released and who was actually crucified.

However, if Jesus was not crucified, what does this say about the Christian doctrine of the atonement in the blood? After all, was not the crucifixion of Jesus the crowning pinnacle of his divine mission? Was it not an absolutely indispensable part of his divine work? In addressing these questions, one has only to turn to the *New Testament* to discover what Jesus reportedly had to say about these very questions. His answer appears to be reported in a prayer attributed to Jesus in the gospel of *John*. Of note, *John* places this prayer prior to the crucifixion event.

> And this is eternal life, that they may know You, the only true God, and Jesus Christ whom You have sent. I glorified You on earth by finishing the work that You gave me to do. (*John* 17:3-4)

"I...finish(ed) the work that You gave me to do" and did so prior to the crucifixion event. As reported by *John*, Jesus specifically excluded the later crucifixion event and alleged resurrection as being part of his "work that You gave me to do." This would also negate any possibility that the "atonement in the blood" was in any manner part of the mission or work of Jesus Christ.

Of some interest with regard to this last point, Origen, perhaps the greatest Christian theologian of the third century, specifically rejected the concept that salvation came through the alleged crucifixion of Jesus, and stressed that salvation was solely contingent upon man's proper exercise of his own free will, i.e., by proper belief and action.[20]

Summary

In summary, while there is no glossing over the fact that Islam and contemporary Christianity disagree as to whether or not Jesus was crucified, it is equally clear that there were branches of early Christianity that, like Islam, maintained that Jesus was not crucified. Whether or not contemporary Christians begin to rethink their own belief in the crucifixion of Jesus, it is hoped that they will have a more tolerant understanding of how it is that Islam can maintain that Jesus was not crucified.

THE NATURE OF JESUS CHRIST
Introduction

Islam holds that Jesus was a man, but one who was selected by God to be a prophet and messenger. He was not one of three persons sharing a common substance in some tripartite God, nor was he the literal "son of God," but he was God's prophet and messenger to the Israelite people.

O People of the Book! Commit no excesses in your religion: nor say of God aught but the truth. Christ Jesus, the son of Mary, was (no more than) a messenger of God and His word, which He bestowed on Mary, and a spirit proceeding from Him: so believe in God and His messengers. Say not "trinity:" desist: it will be better for you: for God is One God: glory be to Him: (far exalted is He) above having a son. To Him belong all things in the heavens and on earth. And enough is God as a disposer of affairs. (*Qur'an* 4:171)

Christ, the son of Mary, was no more than a messenger; many were the messengers that passed away before him. His mother was a woman of truth. They had both to eat their (daily) food. (*Qur'an* 5:75a)

...(Jesus) the son of Mary... was no more than a servant: We granted Our favor to him, and We made him an example to the children of Israel. (*Qur'an* 43:57-59)

Despite Islam's adherence to the virgin birth of Jesus, Islam maintains that Jesus was created by God, not begotten by him. As such, the phrase "son of God" is nothing more than a misleading metaphor.

Say, He is God, the One and Only; God, the Eternal, Absolute. He begetteth not, nor is He begotten, and there is none like unto Him. (*Qur'an* 112:1-4)

She (Mary) said: "O my Lord! How shall I have a son when no man hath touched me?" He said: "Even so: God createth what He willeth: when He hath decreed a plan, He but saith to it 'Be', and it is!"...The similitude of Jesus before God is as that of Adam; He created him from dust, then said to him, "Be," and he was. (*Qur'an* 3:47, 59)

Each of these Islamic positions regarding Jesus Christ, i.e., that he was a prophet and messenger of God and that he was miraculously created by God, not begotten by Him, finds significant support within early Christianity. In what follows, each issue is addressed in turn, with the latter issue leading naturally into a review of Christian Adoptionism.

Biblical Support for Jesus-as-Prophet

The Biblical evidence that Jesus was a prophet of God is primarily confined to two types of *New Testament* information. The first consists of those verses in which the contemporaries of Jesus reportedly refer to him as a prophet, while the latter consists of verses in which Jesus is alleged to have referred to himself as a prophet of God. Each type of information will be presented in turn.

There are several places in which the contemporaries of Jesus refer to him as being a prophet of God. Of most importance, in none of these examples does Jesus refute this claim, nor does the author of the *New Testament* book in which the claim is reported.

> When he entered Jerusalem, the whole city was in turmoil, asking, "Who is this?" The crowds were saying, "This is the prophet Jesus from Nazareth in Galilee." (*Matthew* 21:10-11)

> When the chief priests and the Pharisees heard his parables, they realized that he was speaking about them. They wanted to arrest him, but they feared the crowds, because they regarded him as a prophet. (*Matthew* 21:45-46)

> King Herod heard of it, for Jesus' name had become known. Some were saying, "John the baptizer has been raised from the dead; and for this reason these powers are at work in him." But others said, "It is Elijah." And others said, "It is a prophet, like one of the prophets of old." (*Mark* 6:14-15; see parallel version in *Luke* 9:7-8)

> Jesus went on with his disciples to the villages of Caesarea Philippi; and on the way he asked his disciples, "Who do people say that I am?" And they answered him, "John the Baptist; and others, Elijah; and still others, one of the prophets." He asked them, "But who do you say that I am?" Peter answered him, "You are the Messiah." (*Mark* 8:27-29; parallel versions may be found in *Luke* 9:18-20 and *Matthew* 16:13-16a, with the latter being followed by a later interpolation into the text, which consists of verses 16b-19)

Then he came forward and touched the bier, and the bearers stood still. And he said, "Young man, I say to you, rise!" The dead man sat up and began to speak, and Jesus gave him to his mother. Fear seized all of them; and they glorified God, saying, "A great prophet has risen among us!" and "God has looked favorably on his people!" (*Luke* 7:14-16)

He asked them, "What things?" They replied, "The things about Jesus of Nazareth, who was a prophet mighty in deed and word before God and all the people." (*Luke* 24:19)

Jesus said to her, "Go call your husband, and come back." The woman answered him, "I have no husband." Jesus said to her, "You are right in saying, 'I have no husband'; for you have had five husbands, and the one you have now is not your husband. What you have said is true!" The woman said to him, "Sir, I see that you are a prophet..." (*John* 4:16-19)

When the people saw the sign that he had done, they began to say, "This is indeed the prophet who is to come into the world." (*John* 6:14)

When they heard these words, some in the crowd said, "This is really the prophet." Others said, "This is the Messiah." (*John* 7: 40-41a)

So they said again to the blind man, "What do you say about him? It was your eyes he opened." He said, "He is a prophet." (*John* 9:17)

As the above verses demonstrate, the contemporaries of Jesus Christ repeatedly considered him to be a prophet. It mattered not whether those contemporaries were the crowds of Jerusalem, the Israelite people in general, those who had witnessed the reported miracles of Jesus, those who had talked with Jesus and been confronted by him, or those who were healed by him. Across all these groups, the above verses of the *New Testament* indicate that there was a consensus that Jesus was a prophet of one kind or another.

Having presented the above, it must be acknowledged that the Christian reader will probably be quick to claim that these contemporaries of Jesus were wrong and that they misperceived him and did not know him well enough to understand him and his "divine" nature. However, what about the actual disciples of Jesus? Surely, they would know whether Jesus was man or God. Surely, they would be able to differentiate whether Jesus was a prophet or God.

> But Peter, standing with the eleven, raised his voice and addressed them..."You that are Israelites, listen to what I have to say: Jesus of Nazareth, a man attested to you by God with deeds of power, wonders, and signs that God did through him among you, as you yourselves know..." (*Acts* 2:14a, 22)

Peter, arguably the disciple closest to Jesus Christ, reportedly said quite simply and quite plainly that Jesus was merely "a man," albeit "a man attested to you by God." He was "a man" who came with miraculous "deeds of power, wonders, and signs." However, these miraculous "deeds of power, wonders, and signs" were not his doing but were only things "that God did through him." All in all, the above quoted words, attributed by the author of *Acts* to Peter, are remarkably similar to the Islamic position regarding Jesus Christ.

However, one does not have to stop with Peter's reported appraisal of the nature of Jesus. One can also consider the words that the *New Testament* attributes to Jesus Christ himself, in which Jesus appears to be referring to his own nature.

> Whoever welcomes you welcomes me, and whoever welcomes me welcomes the one who sent me. Whoever welcomes a prophet in the name of a prophet will receive a prophet's reward; and whoever welcomes a righteous person in the name of a righteous person will receive the reward of the righteous... (*Matthew* 10:40-41)

There are several points that need to be made with regard to the above quoted verses. (1) The statement that "whoever welcomes me welcomes the one who sent me" cannot be used to equate the nature of Jesus with that of

God, unless one is willing to use the statement that "whoever welcomes you welcomes me" equates the nature of others with that of Jesus and then by extension with that of God. (2) The first sentence also has Jesus referring to "the one who sent me," clearly implying that Jesus was subordinate to the One who sent him. (3) If the statement that "whoever welcomes a prophet" is not a self-reference to his own prophethood, then to what prophet is Jesus referring? This becomes a crucial question, because the alleged statement of Jesus is not made in the past tense.

In a second statement attributed to Jesus, he refers to himself and to his having just been rejected by the people of Nazareth after attempting to preach there.

> But Jesus said to them, "Prophets are not without honor except in their own country and in their own houses." (*Matthew* 13:57; see parallel versions of this saying in *Mark* 6:1-4, *Luke* 4:16-24, and *John* 4:43-44)

In a third statement attributed to Jesus, albeit one that is sometimes interpreted by Christians as referring to the alleged crucifixion of Jesus, Jesus again refers to himself as being a prophet.

> Yet today, tomorrow, and the next day I must be on my way, because it is impossible for a prophet to be killed outside of Jerusalem. Jerusalem, Jerusalem, the city that kills the prophets and stones those who are sent to it! (*Luke* 13:33-34)

Obviously, each Christian must decide for him or herself whether the totality of the verses quoted above are sufficient, given other Biblical verses that may point in a different direction, to justify a personal belief that Jesus Christ was no more than a prophet, messenger, and servant of God. Nonetheless, any fair-minded Christian should recognize that the totality of the above quoted verses does demonstrate some Biblical support for such a proposition. However, there is much more to say about how early Christianity regarded the nature of Jesus.

Early Christianity on the Nature of Jesus

When considering the issue of the nature of Jesus within early Christianity, one is immediately confronted with the major differences that existed among the various early Christian churches. As seen above, Jesus and his disciples appeared to stress the humanity of Jesus. In contrast, the alleged divinity of Jesus appears to be a Pauline creation, as illustrated by the following verses.

> Let the same mind be in you that was in Christ Jesus, who, though he was in the form of God, did not regard equality with God as something to be exploited, but emptied himself, taking the form of a slave, being born in human likeness. (*Philippians* 2:5-7)

Once again, Pauline Christianity was early on at odds with the Christianity practiced by the followers and disciples of Jesus, and this division of Christological thought was to continue down throughout the first centuries of Christianity. At the risk of oversimplifying, the ways in which early Christianity answered the question of the nature of Jesus can be grouped into three broad categories: Jesus was God; Jesus was man and God simultaneously; and Jesus was a man, although one who was an instrument of God.

The first position, i.e., that Jesus was God, denies the humanity of Jesus. This position was represented in early Christianity by many forms of Christian Gnosticism, especially by Docetism. The Docetist position was that Jesus did not have a real or material body, but only a phantom or apparent body. As such, the Docetists maintained that Jesus could not have suffered and died on the cross, because he did not have a physical body. Likewise, because he had no physical body, there could have been no resurrection.

The second position, i.e., that Jesus was both God and man simultaneously, is the one that evolved into the typical and orthodox doctrines of contemporary Christianity. That Jesus is neither simply God, nor simply man, but is both God and man simultaneously is directly stated in the so-called Nicene Creed issued by the Council of Constantinople in 381: "...We believe in one Lord, Jesus Christ, the only Son of God, eternally begotten of the Father, God from God, Light from Light, true God from true God, begotten, not made, one in being with the Father...he came down from heaven by the power of the Holy Spirit, he was born of the Virgin Mary, and became man."[21] Likewise, in the creedal formulation issued by the Council of Ephesus in 431, one finds the following statement. "We, therefore, acknowledge our Lord Jesus Christ, the Son of God, the Only-begotten, complete God and complete man...begotten of the Father before the ages according to (his) divinity...of Mary the Virgin according to (his) humanity; that he is of the same nature with the Father according to (his) divinity, and of the same nature with us according to (his) humanity. For a union of the two natures has taken place..."[22] However, the simultaneous god-man dichotomy finds its fullest expression in the statement issued by the Council of Chalcedon in 451: "...our Lord Jesus Christ, perfect in deity and perfect in humanity...in two natures, without being mixed, transmuted, divided, or separated. The distinction between the natures is by no means done away with through the union, but rather the identity of each nature is preserved and concurs into one person and being."[23] There are two natures that are neither "mixed" nor "separated." Clearly, this is a doctrine that can be promulgated only through recourse to the phrase "divine mystery," because the doctrine defies all human reason, logic, and intellect.

The third position, i.e., that Jesus was man, although one standing in a special relationship with God, is represented in early Christianity by the various subordinationist and Adoptionist theologies, including Dynamic Monarchianism, Arianism, Nestorianism, the Paulicians of Armenia, etc. These early Christian movements basically maintained that Jesus's relationship to God was like that of an adopted son to his adoptive father, not like a begotten son to his begetting father. This position is consistent with Islamic thought, which views Jesus as being a man, albeit as a man who was a prophet and messenger of God, and who thus stood in a special relationship with God.

Biblical Support for the Non-Divinity of Jesus

Was Jesus divine? There are numerous Biblical passages that suggest that he was not and that maintain that Jesus was subordinate and inferior to God. The following are a representative sampling of such verses, all of which are attributed to sayings of Jesus by the *New Testament*.

But about that day and hour no one knows, neither the angels of heaven, nor the Son, but only the Father. (*Matthew* 24:36; see also *Mark* 13:32)

Jesus said to him, "Why do you call me good? No one is good but God alone." (*Mark* 10:18; see also *Matthew* 19:17 and *Luke* 18:19)

Jesus said to them, "Very truly, I tell you, the Son can do nothing on his own, but only what he sees the Father doing; for whatever the Father does, the Son does likewise." (*John* 5:19)

I can do nothing on my own. As I hear, I judge; and my judgment is just, because I seek to do not my own will but the will of him who sent me. (*John* 5:30)

You heard me say to you, "I am going away and am coming to you." If you loved me, you would rejoice that I am going to the Father, because the Father is greater than I. (*John* 14:28)

Jesus said to her, "Do not hold on to me, because I have not yet ascended to the Father. But go to my brothers and say to them, 'I am ascending to my Father and your Father, to my God and your God.'" (*John* 20:17)

Of these verses, the last is particularly striking, for Jesus reportedly said that he was going "to my God and your God," which appears to be an explicit denial of his being God. However, there is one more verse that needs to be presented, one which says that after his ascension Jesus "sat down at the right hand of God," obviously implying that Jesus and God are separate and distinct entities.

So then the Lord Jesus, after he had spoken to them, was taken up into heaven and sat down at the right hand of God. (*Mark* 16:19)

Of most importance in considering this last verse, one should note that the verse does not say that Jesus sat down at the right hand of "the Father" but that he "sat down at the right hand of God." Thus, attempts to salvage a Jesus-as-God concept from this verse cannot resort to contrasting "the Son" with "the Father" but are forced to contrast Jesus with God.

The Scriptural Basis for Adoptionism

If Jesus is not divine, then how does one account for the title of "Son of God?" The answer is to be found in the Adoptionist movement within early Christianity. The Adoptionist trajectory in early Christianity begins with the baptism of Jesus by John the Baptist. According to the usual Adoptionist formulations, it was at his moment of baptism that Jesus moved into his special relationship with God—not at his conception or birth. With regard to the baptism of Jesus, the account of *Luke* is especially relevant. As noted in appropriate footnotes to the *Revised Standard Version* and the *New Revised Standard Version* of the *Bible*, the oldest Greek manuscripts of and quotations from *Luke* render the key verse in question as follows.

> Now when all the people were baptized, and when Jesus also had been baptized and was praying, the heaven was opened, and the Holy Spirit descended upon him in bodily form like a dove. And a voice came from heaven, "You are my son; today I have begotten you." (*Luke* 3:21-22)

"Today I have begotten you," i.e., at the time of baptism, not at the time of conception. Given that Jesus was clearly an adult at the time of his baptism, under this ancient reading of *Luke*, "begotten" must be understood metaphorically, not physically or literally. In other words, the "sonship" of Jesus was a created relationship, not a begotten relationship. Furthermore, before the contemporary Christian rejects this probably original wording of *Luke* 3:22, he or she should consider that this exact wording is also to be found in *Hebrews* 1:5a, *Hebrews* 5:5, and *Acts* 13:33 in what are obvious references to the baptism of Jesus. This same wording is also to be found in *Psalms* 2:7 and in the *Gospel of the Ebionites*, the latter of which reads as follows.

> When the people were baptized, Jesus also came and was baptized by John. And as he came up from the water, the heavens were opened and he saw the Holy Spirit in the form of a dove that descended and entered into him. And a voice (sounded) from heaven that said:"Thou art my beloved son, in thee I am well

pleased." And again: "I have this day begotten thee." (*Gospel of the Ebionites*, as quoted by Epiphanius in *Panarian* 30.13.7-8)

This Adoptionist legacy finds additional support in the *New Testament* in words attributed to Jesus Christ himself. In the following verses, Jesus quotes from *Psalms* 82:6, in which "those to whom the word of God came," i.e., all of the prophets, are referred to as "gods" and as "children of the Most High." If taken at face value, these verses suggest that Jesus did not distinguish between his own role as "God's son" and the role held by all of the previous prophets as "gods" and as "children of the Most High."

Jesus answered, "Is it not written in your law, 'I said, you are gods'? If those to whom the word of God came were called 'gods'—and the scripture cannot be annulled—can you say that the one whom the Father has sanctified and sent into the world is blaspheming because I said, 'I am God's Son'?" (*John* 10:34-36)

For the sake of completeness, the verses to which Jesus is allegedly referring are quoted immediately below.

I say, "You are gods, children of the Most High, all of you; nevertheless, you shall die like mortals, and fall like any prince." (*Psalms* 82:6-7)

"You are gods, children of the Most High, all of you..." If "all of you" refers to the prophets, as implied in *John* 10:34-36, then all of the prophets are the "children of the Most High," and no special significance should be accorded to Jesus as the "son of God." Furthermore, unless one wants to maintain that all of the prophets were the begotten children of God, then the Adoptionist position regarding a created sonship appears to be affirmed by Jesus's own words. If "all of you" refers to all people, then we are all children of God, and the sonship of Jesus must be seen and interpreted solely within that light.

The Subordinationist/Adoptionist Trajectory

Given this scriptural legacy, it is not surprising that subordinationism and Adoptionism were potent forces within early Christianity from the first through the seventh centuries. In fact, their influence was so clearly felt throughout Christendom that one can trace the chronological trajectory of the subordinationist/Adoptionist position with some precision.

As early as the first century, the Adoptionist position was a key doctrine of the Ebionites, who maintained that Jesus became the Messiah and adopted son of God at his baptism and that this was secondary to Jesus having obeyed the Mosaic Law. As noted previously, the Ebionite movement began in the vicinity of Jerusalem by around 70 and continued as a force within Christianity into the fourth century, having spread to Jordan, Syria, Turkey, and Egypt. Over and beyond its Adoptionist theology, the Ebionites continued to adhere to the so-called Mosaic Law of Judaism, rejected the sacrificial cult aspects of traditional Judaism, appear to have denied the virgin birth of Jesus Christ, and practiced vegetarianism.[24]

Circa 100, Elkesai, the founder of the Elkesaites, began to preach an early Christian doctrine in Parthia. Elkesai stressed the need to be circumcised, the necessity of keeping the so-called Mosaic Law of Judaism, the practice of baptism, the rejection of sacrifices, and the turning to face Jerusalem during prayer. Central to the preaching of Elkesai was the concept that Jesus Christ was simply a prophet of God.[25]

Early in the second century, Cerinthus preached a Gnostic version of the Adoptionist position. Cerinthus denied the virgin birth of Jesus, kept the so-called Mosaic Law, and taught that Jesus was an exemplary man upon whom descended the Christ (who was to be differentiated from Jesus) at the time of the baptism. In short, Cerinthus taught that Jesus was a great prophet upon whom divine power descended.[26]

Circa 160-170, Theodotus the Gnostic also taught a Gnostic brand of Adoptionist theory, which he promulgated throughout Turkey. Influenced by Valentinus, Theodotus taught that Jesus was a man who was created by God, and who was united with God in a special relationship at the baptism, in order to bring sacred knowledge (gnosis) to man.[27]

Circa 189, Theodotus the Tanner traveled from Byzantium to Rome, where he propounded an Adoptionist position that maintained that Jesus was a mere man, although miraculously conceived. According to this Theodotus, Jesus was the metaphorical son of God only to the extent that God granted him divine wisdom and power at his baptism. In short, Theodotus was adamant about rejecting the concept that Jesus was the Son of God and was to be worshiped, in order to preserve the Unity of God and the distinction between Jesus and God. Despite being excommunicated by Pope Victor I, Theodotus acquired numerous followers, who continued his Adoptionist preaching. The movement grew in numbers and vitality and began to be known as Theodotianism or Dynamic Monarchianism. This movement lasted well into the third century, being supported by Artemon of Rome (who was excommunicated by Pope Zephyrinus) among others.[28]

Origen (Oregenes Adamantius) was born circa 185 and died circa 254 in Tyre (now Sur, Lebanon). He became the head of the catechetical school at Alexandria under Bishop Demetrius and was ordained into the priesthood circa 229 at Caesarea. Origen was a celebrated writer and theologian, who contributed numerous volumes to early Christian literature. Among the notable aspects of Origen's theology was his insistence that "the Son (was) inferior to the Father." Clearly a subordinationist when it came to the nature of Jesus, Origen's teachings were later to influence Dionysius of Alexandria, Eusebius of Nicomedia, Arius, and the rise of Arianism.[29]

Dionysius of Alexandria became head of the catechetical school at Alexandria circa 231 and bishop of Alexandria in 248, a position that he held until 264. Following in the footsteps of Origen, Dionysius stressed the subordination of Jesus Christ to God, arguing that Jesus did not exist before being engendered, that therefore there was a time in which Jesus did not exist and that therefore Jesus was not eternal. Not being eternal, Jesus had to be a creation (*poiema*) and a product (*geneton*) that was foreign to the being and substance of God, just as the vine is foreign to the gardener and the ship is foreign to the ship builder. It needs to be emphasized that here was a bishop, a peer of the early Christian church, who actively proclaimed the subordination of Jesus Christ to God and who stressed that Jesus was a creation of God. As will be seen, he was hardly the last bishop to take this position.[30]

Circa 260, Paul of Samosata, the bishop of Antioch, advanced the Adoptionist position of Dynamic Monarchianism once again. Paul held that Jesus was a man who was born of Mary, that he was the one through whom God spoke his word, and that Jesus was divine only to the extent that he was the human vehicle through whom God spoke. In addition, he condemned hymns in honor of Jesus as being a late innovation within Christianity. As a result of Paul's preaching this Adoptionist doctrine, at least three different church councils were held at Antioch to debate Paul's orthodoxy. Rather amazingly, it was only after the third council in 268 that Paul was pronounced deposed from his episcopacy. In short, the combined ecclesiastical structure of the first two church councils was unwilling to remove Paul from his episcopacy merely because he espoused an Adoptionist position. Furthermore, even after being deposed by proclamation in 268, it took an additional four years before Paul was deposed in fact, thanks to the support that he received from Zenobia, the Queen of Palmyra. Despite having been finally deposed from his episcopacy, Paul's Adoptionist message was picked up by his followers, who later evolved into the Paulicians of Armenia, a Christian movement active as late as the seventh century.[31]

Lucian of Antioch was born circa 240 in Samosata (now Samsat, Turkey) and died on January 7, 312, in Nicomedia (now Izmit, Turkey). Lucian became a celebrated Christian teacher and theologian, whose theological formulations regarding the nature of Jesus appeared to have been influenced by the Dynamic Monarchianism of Paul of Samosata. In turn, Lucian's teachings were to be influential in the later thinking of Eusebius of Nicomedia and of Arius, the founder of Arianism. Despite his Adoptionist teachings regarding the nature of Jesus, Lucian was canonized a saint of the church, in part secondary to his being tortured and starved to death for his refusal to eat meat that had been ritually offered to the pagan gods of Rome during the persecution of Christians by Emperor Maximinus.[32]

The Adoptionist position in early Christianity reached its zenith under the teachings of Arius. Arius had been born about 250 in Libya, was ordained into the priesthood, and became a presbyter in charge of the church at Baucalis in Alexandria, Egypt. His Adoptionist teachings were often uncannily in line with later Islamic teachings on the nature of Jesus and on the nature of God. For example, Arius taught that God is absolutely unique and incomparable, is alone self-existent, unchangeable, and infinite, and must be understood in terms of his absolute Oneness. Given this all-important first premise, Arius concluded that: (1) the life of Jesus as portrayed in the canonical gospels demonstrates that Jesus was not self-existent, that he changed and grew over time, if in no other way than in passing through the stages of birth, childhood, adolescence, and adulthood, and that he was finite, having a definite time of conception and birth; therefore (2) Jesus was God's created being, who was called into existence out of nothingness, who could not have shared in the absolute uniqueness, immutability, and infinity of God without compromising them, who could not have been of the same substance as God without compromising the Oneness of God, and who could have had no direct knowledge of God, other than that which God chose to reveal to him. As subsequently pointed out by Athanasius, an implacable foe of Arius, an important corollary to these fundamental conclusions was that only God could redeem mankind to God, which undermined the concept of "atonement in the blood of Christ."[33]

Arian Christianity was publicized about 323 in Arius's poetic work, *Thalia* (Banquet), and quickly grew in popularity, spreading throughout the Middle East with amazing rapidity, in part due to the many songs that popularized Arianism among the laity and that proclaimed that Jesus was created and was not co-eternal with the Father. As a result, bathers at the public baths might be regaled by a bath attendant who was preaching that Jesus was created by God from nothingness. Before being given the local currency exchange rate, customers of a money changer were likely to have to listen to a sermon on the distinction between the creation, which included Jesus, and the Creator. Those seeking to buy a loaf of bread were first subjected to the baker's oration on how Jesus was subordinate to God.[34]

It was due to the rapid rise of Arianism that the Synod at Alexandria met in September of 323 and formally excommunicated Arius. This excommunication was promptly reversed one month later at the Synod of Bithynia in October of 323. Finally, Emperor Constantine was forced to convene the Council of Nicaea in May of 325, which, under the force of Constantine's army, formalized the doctrine that Jesus was of one substance (*homoousion*) with the Father. Arius refused to sign this creed and was thence branded as a heretic. However, the Arian position within Christianity was so strong that Constantine was forced to reinstate Arius at the Synod of Jerusalem in 335! Later that same year, Arius died at Constantinople.[35]

However, that was hardly the end of Arianism within early Christianity. Quite simply, despite the verdict of the Council of Nicaea, Arianism was probably the dominant Christology within fourth century Christianity. Many bishops had refused to attend the Council of Nicaea (only about 300 bishops were in attendance, and only three of those represented Western Christianity), because they were wary of being militarily forced into a theological position that they did not hold. Many other bishops, who under force of arms had affirmed the verdict of the Council of Nicaea, recanted their vote at Nicaea once they were safely removed from Constantine's soldiers. In short, the Council of Nicaea had resolved nothing, and the individual bishops, including those who espoused the Arian position, went on preaching as they had previously.[36]

As an example, one can turn to Eusebius of Nicomedia, who was successively the bishop of Berytus and Nicomedia. Eusebius vehemently rejected the doctrine that Jesus and God were of the same substance and led the Arian opposition at the Council of Nicaea before being forced to sign off on the doctrine under force of arms. Safely back home, he renewed his alliance with Arius and was then exiled to Gaul (modern France) by Constantine. However, even in exile, Eusebius continued to lead the Arian charge until his death circa 342.[37]

In response to the continued growth of Arianism, the Council of Antioch in 341 released a new creed that omitted any mention of Jesus and God being of one substance. Apparently, the bishops gathered at the Council of Antioch, while rejecting the earlier findings of the Council of Nicaea, were unable to agree on any formulation regarding the relationship of Jesus Christ to God.

In the middle of the fourth century, a modified form of Arianism (semi-Arianism) was propounded by Macedonius, the bishop and patriarch of Constantinople (339-341 and 351-360). While the formal teachings of Macedonius regarding the nature of Jesus appear to have oscillated somewhat over time, there is little doubt that he did what he could to repress the formulation derived at Nicaea that Jesus and God were of one substance. Macedonius was finally deposed from his episcopacy in 360 and was sent into exile.[38]

Circa 350, Aetius, ordained a deacon of the church at Antioch, taught that God had always existed and that self-existence (*agennesia*) is a part of the very essence of God, while Christ was created by God. Given these premises, Aetius advanced the concept that Jesus Christ was not consubstantial with God and was totally different (*anomoios*) than God, giving rise to the Anomoeist movement in fourth century Christianity. While initially excommunicated for his Arianism, Aetius was later reinstated by Eudoxius, the bishop of Antioch, and was elevated to the episcopacy by Emperor Julian in 361. Aetius died circa 366 in Constantinople.[39]

The Anomoeist teachings of Aetius garnered tremendous support within Syria and the Middle East, in part due to his irrefutable logic as expressed in 300 syllogisms, all but 47 of which were later lost to recorded history. Furthermore, the popularity of Anomoeism was ratified and endorsed by the Council of Sirmium in 357. This council actually endorsed the Anomoeist position that Jesus was "unlike" (*anomoios*) God. In short, based upon the position taken at the Council of Sirmium, the "official" position of Christianity in 357 was that Jesus Christ was "unlike" God and was of a different substance than God![40]

Continuing to gather steam within Middle Eastern Christianity, Anomoeism was further represented in the ecclesiastical hierarchy of Christianity with the appointment of Euzoios as the bishop of Antioch and Eunomius as the bishop of Cyzicus in Mysia, both circa 360. Eunomius had earlier served as a secretary to Aetius, was ordained a deacon in Antioch, and died circa 394. Unfortunately, most of the written works of Eunomius were burned in 398 at the order of Emperor Arcadius, and Anomoeism shortly thereafter began to lose ground rather rapidly.[41]

Only in 381, at the Council of Constantinople, attended by only about 150 bishops, none of whom represented Western Christianity, was the Arian position finally laid to rest within "official" Christendom and repudiated by the ecclesiastical structure of the church with the issuance of the so-called Nicene Creed. Notwithstanding this ecclesiastical dismissal of Arianism, Arianism continued to flourish in many Christian areas and was a potent force within some Germanic tribes until the end of the seventh century. Even today, Arianism continues to be influential in the Unitarian movement and among the Jehovah Witnesses, who regard Arius as a forerunner of their founder, Charles Taze Russell.[42]

By the late fourth century, Adoptionism was still being represented by the Ebionites, the Paulicians of Armenia, the Arians, and the Anomoeists. However, the fifth century saw yet another subordinationist movement gain widespread popular support. Nestorius was born late in the fourth century at Maras, Turkey. He studied under Theodore of Mopsuentia, the bishop of Mopsuentia in Cilicia from 392 to 428, entered the Monastery of St. Euprepius, was ordained a priest, and became a celebrated thinker and theologian. On April 10, 428, he became the bishop of Constantinople, arguably the second highest ecclesiastical position in all of Christendom. On Christmas in 428, Nestorius began a series of sermons that were to rock Christianity to its very foundations. Among other things, Nestorius argued that the Virgin Mary should not continue to be given the title of *theotokos* (literally "God-bearer," but more often translated as "Mother of God"). Nestorius maintained that the use of that title compromised the full humanity of Jesus, whom he apparently saw as being a second Adam. As Adam was vivified by a breath of God, so was Jesus in the womb. In fact, Nestorius refused to call the infant Jesus by the name of God. At the Council of Ephesus in 431, Nestorius's teachings were condemned, and he was deposed from his episcopacy. He later died circa 451 in Panopolis, Egypt.[43]

Despite his death, the subordinationist teachings of Nestorius continued to grow in influence, giving rise to Nestorian Christianity. As such, the Council of Chalcedon in 451 had once again to condemn Nestorius and his teachings and issued a creed that emphasized that the Virgin Mary was the *theotokos* and that Jesus was both God and man simultaneously.

However, this condemnation did little good in suppressing the Nestorian position. In February of 486, Barsumas, the metropolitan of Nisibis, named Theodore of Mopsuestia, the chief Nestorian theologian, as the guardian of right faith of the Persian church, which had been independent of the papacy at Rome since 424. Theodore was later confirmed in this position by the patriarch, Babai, making the Persian Church officially Nestorian. Furthermore, Nestorian Christianity succeeded in gaining control of the theological school at Edessa, which was then closed by imperial order, not by any ecclesiastical structure, in 489. The faculty and students of the school at Edessa then migrated to Persia, where they were welcomed with open arms by the Nestorian Church of Persia.[44]

Preaching a doctrine that presents Jesus as a God-inspired prophet rather than as an incarnation of God, Nestorian Christianity continued to grow and flourish into the sixth century. In fact, by the end of the fifth century, there were seven metropolitan provinces in Persia and several episcopacies in Arabia and India. During the seventh, eighth, and ninth centuries, Nestorian Christianity continued to flourish in China. To this day, there are small pockets of Nestorian Christians to be found in Iraq, Syria, and Iran, although they appear to have compromised their Nestorian roots.[45]

As a final example, consider Clovis I, the Merovingian King of the Salian Franks, who was born in 460 in Rheims, Marne, France, and who died on November 11, 511. Following his military campaign against the Alemanni, and under the influence and guidance of his wife, Clothilda, a princess of Burgundy, Clovis renounced paganism, and accepted Arian Christianity. He then led his entire army and the Salian Frankish kingdom into being baptized into Arian Christianity. Despite the fact that Clothilda was an Arian Christian, she was canonized a saint by the Roman Catholic Church. She died on June 3, 543, in Tours, France, and her feast day is June 3. Of note, Arian Christianity was to remain the dominant religious force within the Frankish people throughout the seventh century.

Summary

In summary, early Christianity was quite conflicted about the issue of the nature of Jesus. The various subordinationist and Adoptionist positions within early Christianity were numerous and at times dominant. One can even speculate that Arian and Nestorian Christianity might well be a very sizable force within Christianity today, if it were not for the fact that these two branches of Christianity were so similar to the Islamic teaching regarding the nature of Jesus that they quite naturally were absorbed into Islam beginning in the first half of the seventh century.

THE NATURE OF GOD

Introduction

Islam and contemporary Christianity also differ concerning the nature of God, although several branches of early Christianity were in substantial agreement with the Islamic and Judaic concept of a strict and uncompromising monotheism, with God being seen as One and Indivisible. The *Qur'an* is most adamant in insisting on *Tawheed* (Oneness of God).

> O People of the Book! Commit no excesses in your religion: nor say of God aught but the truth. Christ Jesus the son of Mary was (no more than) a messenger of God and His word, which He bestowed on Mary, and a spirit proceeding from Him: so believe in God and His messengers, say not "Trinity:" desist: it will be better for you: for God is One God: glory be to Him: (far exalted is He) above having a son. To Him belong all things in the heavens and on earth. And enough is God as a disposer of affairs.(*Qur'an* 4:171)

> In blasphemy indeed are those that say that God is Christ, the son of Mary...They do blaspheme who say: "God is Christ, the son of Mary." But said Christ: "O children of Israel! Worship God, my Lord and your Lord." Whoever joins other gods with God—God will forbid him the garden, and the fire will be his abode. There will for the wrongdoers be no one to help. They do blaspheme who say: God is one of three in a trinity: for there is no god except One God. (*Qur'an* 5:17a, 72-73a)

> They say, "God hath begotten a son!—Glory be to Him! He is self-sufficient! His are all things in the heavens and on earth! No warrant have ye for this! Say ye about God what ye know not? (*Qur'an* 10:68)

> Blessed is He Who sent down the criterion to His servant, that it may be an admonition to all creatures—He to Whom belongs the dominion of the heavens and the earth: no son has He begotten, nor has He a partner in His dominion: it is He Who created all things, and ordered them in due proportion. (*Qur'an* 25:1-2)

> Say: He is God, the One and Only; God, the Eternal, Absolute. He

begetteth not nor is He begotten, and there is none like unto Him. (*Qur'an* 112:1-4)

However and in contrast, when we examine the Christian concept of a triune God, i.e., of a trinity, we find something that is totally foreign to both Judaism and Islam. There is no Islamic or Judaic equivalent to the notion of three persons in one substance. With regard to Judaism, the *Shema* of the *Old Testament* is quite clear in rejecting any concept of the deity other than the Unity of God.

Hear O Israel, the Lord our God, the Lord is One. (*Deuteronomy* 6:4)

A pronounced emphasis on the Unity of God is not limited to the *Old Testament* portion of the *Bible*. Not only does the word "trinity" and its derivations never occur in the *Bible*, but the author of *James* also emphasizes the Unity of God.

You believe that God is one; you do well. Even the demons believe—and shudder.(*James* 2:19)

Furthermore, as reported by the *New Testament,* the Unity of God was also emphasized in the very words of Jesus Christ.

One of the scribes came near and heard them disputing with one another, and seeing that he answered them well, he asked him, "Which commandment is the first of all?" Jesus answered, "The first is, 'Hear, O Israel: the Lord our God, the Lord is one...'" (*Mark* 12:28-29)

Given the above considerations, it is not surprising that the early Apostolic Fathers were typically unwilling or not interested in speculating about the relationship of the Father, Son, and Holy Spirit. Other than directly supporting the divinity of the Son and/or indirectly maintaining the divinity of the Holy Spirit, such early Christian luminaries as Ignatius, Justin Martyr, and Irenaeus were unwilling to proceed in developing any conceptualization of a trinity. Later theologians were more willing to specu-late, with such speculation resulting in the Christian concept of the trinity.

In contrast to the Christian concept of the "Son of God," Islam views Jesus as a resolute prophet of God. In contrast to the Christian concept of the Holy Spirit as the third person of one substance comprising a triune God, Islam sees the Holy Spirit as being a title belonging to the angel Gabriel.

The Trinity

The Christian concept of the trinity is typically expressed as "three in one" and developed over the course of several centuries. In its culmination, it can be seen as having grown out of the concept of the virgin birth of Jesus Christ as the "Son of God."

As noted previously, traditional Christianity portrays the virgin birth of Jesus in terms of Jesus being the "begotten" son of God. For example, *Matthew* 1:18 states that Mary was "with child from the Holy Spirit," and *Luke* 1:35 has an angel telling Mary that the "Holy Spirit will come upon you." While these Biblical verses may be seen as rather ambiguous by some, the Nicene Creed of Christianity allows for no such ambiguity when it states: "We believe in one Lord, Jesus Christ, the only Son of God, eternally begotten of the Father, God from God, Light from Light, true God from true God, begotten, not made, one in Being with the Father." Further, the so-called Apostles' Creed holds that: "I believe in God the Father Almighty; maker of heaven and earth; and in Jesus Christ his only Son, our Lord; who was conceived by the Holy Ghost..."[46]

As can be seen from the above listing of *New Testament* verses and creedal formulations, one of the fundamental problems confronting the Christian concept of the trinity is trying to decide whether the alleged father of Jesus Christ is the Father or the Holy Spirit. *Matthew* 1:18 says that Mary was "with child from the Holy Spirit," not the Father. *Luke* 1:35 says that Mary was told that the "Holy Spirit will come upon you," not the Father. The Apostles' Creed says that Jesus Christ was the Father's only Son, but was "conceived by the Holy Ghost." Even the Nicene Creed, which says that Jesus was "begotten of the Father," goes on to say that Jesus "was incarnate from the Holy Spirit." So who was the father of Jesus Christ? Was it the Father or the Holy Spirit?

Anti-Trinitarian Christian Formulations

However, it is not just Islam and Judaism that reject the traditional Christian formulation of the trinity. The early Christian churches were quite divided with regard to the conceptualized nature of God. To a great extent, these intra-Christian differences were directly related to the intra-Christian differences that existed concerning the nature of Jesus. Thus, the Jesus-as-man proponents within early Christianity, e.g., the Ebionites, Elkasites, Dynamic Monarchianism, Arianism, Anomoeism, and Nestorianism, denied the concept of a trinitarian God and professed the Unity of God and the humanity of a created and finite Jesus. With regard to this issue, these branches of early Christianity were once again basically consistent with Islamic belief, which holds to a strict monotheism in proclaiming the Oneness of God (*Tawheed*).

By way of digression, it should be noted that the Arian position in rejecting the trinity and in espousing the Unity of God found much later expression: (1) in the humanist enlightenment of the 16th century; (2) in the anti-trinitarian movement of the Italian Renaissance; and (3) among the more liberal theologians (e.g., Henry Ware and William Ellery Channing[47]) of the late 18th and early 19th century Congregational Church in America, later resulting in the formation of the Unitarian Church.

However, it was not just the adoptionists within early Christianity who rejected the trinitarian concept. Early Christianity was also character-ized by groups known as subordinationists, who insisted that Jesus Christ was subordinate to God. While all Adoptionists were subordinationists, one could be a subordinationist without being an Adoptionist. Thus, Origen of Alexandria (185-254) is sometimes called the father of Arianism, because he held that Jesus was subordinate to the Father and that the Holy Spirit was subordinate to both the Father and the Son.[48]

Yet another subordinationist group within early Christianity, variously known as Macedonians and Pneumatomachians, believed that the Holy Spirit was essentially inferior to both the Father and the Son. Under the leadership of Macedonius, this group held a middle position between the Arians and those who proclaimed the divinity of Jesus, but were firmly anti-trinitarian when it came to the Holy Spirit.[49]

Rather ironically, the Jesus-as-God branches of early Christianity also tended to reject any trinitarian implications. For example, circa 206, Praxeas, a priest from Asia Minor, taught that God and Jesus were only different names for the same subject, the former being the name by which God formerly interacted with His creation and the latter being the name under which God appeared in humanity. As an additional example, early in the third century, Sabellius, apparently a presbyter at Rome, taught that God was a single monad, which expressed itself in three functions: as the Father in creation, as the Son in redemption, and as the Holy Spirit in sanctification. Sabellius was later excommunicated by Pope Calixtus. Nonetheless, later in the third century, a revival of the Sabellian concept of divine unity became a force in Libya. Circa 375, Sabellian modalism resurfaced in Neocaesarea.[50]

About the same time, Priscillian taught Sabellian modalism in the vicinity of Merida and Cordoba, Spain. His teachings were condemned at the Council of Saragossa in 380, but this condemnation did not stop him from being elected bishop of Avila. In 384, Priscillian was condemned at the Synod of Bordeaux. His teachings were further condemned by the two Councils of Toledo in 400 and 447. However, it was only with the further condemnation of Priscillian's teachings by the Council of Braga in 563 that the Priscillian formulation ceased to have much sway.[51]

Almost a millennium later, Sabellian modalism was reformulated during the Protestant Reformation by Michael Servetus, a Spanish theologian, who died in 1553. It resurfaced once again during the 19th century, when it was promulgated by Emanuel Swedenborg, a Swedish mystic. Even in the early 20th century, Sabellian modalism found expression in John G. Schleppe's "Jesus Only" movement within the Pentecostal branch of American Christianity. The "Jesus Only" movement denies the trinity in asserting that Jesus was and is the one and only person in the nature of God.[52]

Although rarely mentioned, there was a fourth position that was elaborated concerning the nature of Jesus, which also led to a unitarian position regarding the nature of God. So-called angel-Christology surfaced in Rome as early as the first part of the second century. Concerning the nature of

Jesus, this movement taught that a prince of the angels, often equated with Michael, descended to earth and became man in the person of Jesus. This angel-Christology was primarily motivated by a desire to maintain the Oneness of God, while allowing Jesus to be seen as the highest of the created spiritual beings.

Summary

As should be clear by now, the doctrine of the trinity developed gradually over several centuries and not without substantial controversy and rejection.[53] Throughout its first several centuries, early Christianity struggled to maintain a strict monotheistic outlook, while still paying homage to the Father, Jesus Christ, and the Holy Spirit. One solution, represented primarily by the various Adoptionists was to subordinate Jesus to God. A second solution, represented by modalism, was to seek for some way of representing the Father, Jesus, and the Holy Spirit as simply three different functions or modes of self-disclosure of God, with there being no distinctive "persons" within the Godhead. It was only with the Council of Nicaea in 325 that the doctrine that Jesus was of one substance with the Father began to be formulated in any real sense, although even at Nicaea, precious little was said about the Holy Spirit. Furthermore, as previously noted, there was little unity at Nicaea, and what there was occurred only under the force of arms provided by Emperor Constantine. In reality, the Christian doctrine of the trinity was not really accepted until the Council of Constantinople in 381, at which time the Council concluded that the Holy Spirit was not subordinate to the Father and the Son, was a distinct "person" from the Father and the Son, but shared the same divine substance as the Father and the Son. As such, it was only towards the end of the fourth century that the traditional trinitarian concept of Christianity started to become "official" doctrine.

The Athanasian Creed of circa 500 states that God consists of *una substantia—tres personae* (one substance—three persons). However, the controversy was still far from over. As Augustine noted in *De Trinitate* (On the Trinity):

...our Greek friends have spoken of one essence (*ousia*) and three substances (*hypostases*), but the Latins of one essence or substance (substantia) and three persons (*personae*).

The conflict regarding the trinity between Western or Latin Christianity and Eastern or Greek Christianity was not just confined to the issue of whether the trinity was three persons in one substance or three substances in one essence. Beginning in the sixth century, the Western Church gradually began to introduce the *Filioque* (and from the Son) clause into the Nicene Creed, directly following the words "the Holy Spirit...who proceedeth from the Father." While the *Filioque* clause did not become official Roman Catholic doctrine until papal acceptance in the 11th century, the Eastern Church considered this insertion into the Nicene Creed to be a theological error. (The Anglican Church and most Protestant churches have subsequently followed the lead of the Roman Catholic Church in accepting the *Filioque* clause.)

This conflict over the insertion of the *Filioque* clause into Western Christianity's conceptualization of the trinity is not to be minimized. In at least partial response to this conflict, the Photian Schism of 867 divided Western and Eastern Christianity into two warring camps, with Pope Nicholas I refusing to acknowledge Photius as the bishop and patriarch of Constantinople and with Photius declaring Nicholas I deposed from the papacy. In 1054, the war between Western and Eastern Christianity reemerged. Once again, the *Filioque* clause was at least partially to blame. The end result was that Pope Leo IX excommunicated Michael Cerularius, the patriarch of Constantinople, on July 16, 1054. In quick response, Michael Cerularius excommunicated Pope Leo IX. Of note, these excommunications remained in place until lifted on December 7, 1965, by Pope Paul VI and Patriarch Athenagoras I.[54]

Be that as it may, *Insha'Allah* (the One God willing), the above review has illustrated that the early Christian churches were in fundamental disagreement when it came to the issue of the nature of God. Those who stressed the Unity of God via one or another of the subordinationist or Adoptionist positions were generally consistent with the Islamic position of *Tawheed*, i.e., the Oneness of God.

THE PROPHETHOOD OF MUHAMMAD

Introduction

Many contemporary Christians automatically assume that the prophetic office and the age of the prophets came to a sudden end with the fulfillment of the ministry of Jesus Christ. For such Christians, it is just unthinkable that there would be a prophet after Jesus. However, the *New Testament* is replete with references to prophets after the completion of the mission and ministry of Jesus. As the following Biblical references illustrate, it is actually contrary to Christian scriptures to deny the existence of prophets after Jesus.

> At that time prophets came down from Jerusalem to Antioch. One of them named Agabus stood up and predicted by the Spirit that there would be a severe famine over all the world; and this took place during the reign of Claudius. (*Acts* 11:27-28)

> Now in the church at Antioch there were prophets and teachers: Barnabas, Simeon, who was called Niger, Lucius of Cyrene, Manaen a member of the court of Herod the ruler, and Saul. (*Acts* 13:1)

> Judas and Silas, who were themselves prophets, said much to encourage and strengthen the believers. (*Acts* 15:32)

> The next day we left and came to Caesarea; and we went into the house of Philip the evangelist, one of the seven, and stayed with him. He had four unmarried daughters who had the gift of prophecy. While we were staying there for several days, a prophet named Agabus came down from Judea. (*Acts* 21:8-10)

> And God has appointed in the church first apostles, second prophets, third teachers; then deeds of power, then gifts of healing, forms of assistance, forms of leadership, various kinds of tongues. (*I Corinthians* 12:28)

> Let two or three prophets speak, and let the others weigh what is said. If a revelation is made to someone else sitting nearby, let the first person be silent. For you can all prophesy one by one, so that all may learn and all be encouraged. And the spirits of prophets are

subject to the prophets... (*I Corinthians* 14:29-32)

The above verses document numerous individuals whom the *New Testament* claimed were prophets who lived after the end of the earthly ministry of Jesus Christ. These included Agabus, Barnabas, Simeon, Lucius, Manaen, Saul, the four daughters of Philip, and the various, unnamed prophets referred to by Paul in *I Corinthians*. Clearly, there is no Biblical support for Christians to deny the existence of prophets after Jesus. In fact, just the opposite is true. The *New Testament* proclaims a Christian belief in the existence of many prophets after Jesus. Given this understanding, the argument that there were no prophets after Jesus must be rejected by all Christians who adhere to the actual teachings of the *Bible*, and such an argument cannot be used by them to dismiss the prophetic office of Prophet Muhammad.

In contrast to the above sentiments of *Acts* and *I Corinthians*, which indicate that there were many prophets after Jesus Christ, Muslims insist that there was only one prophet after Jesus Christ, i.e., Prophet Muhammad. This belief is based upon a *Hadith* narrated by Abu Huraira and recorded in both *Al-Bukhari* and *Abu Dawud.*

Abu Huraira narrated that: "I heard God's Apostle saying, 'I am the nearest of all the people to the son of Mary, and all the prophets are paternal brothers, and there has been no prophet between me and him (i.e., Jesus)'." (*Al-Bukhari, Hadith* #4:651)

Abu Huraira narrated that the prophet said: "There is no prophet between me and him, that is, Jesus..." (*Abu Dawud, Hadith* #4310)

So far, it has been shown that Christians who adhere to the teachings of the *New Testament* must acknowledge the existence of prophets after Jesus Christ. However, the issue still remains as to whether or not the *Bible* offers any support that Muhammad was a prophet of God. To address this issue, one must begin with the Biblical concept of the prophet yet to come

The Prophet Yet to Come

The Jews at the time of Jesus Christ were awaiting a great prophet that was yet to come. As stated in *Deuteronomy* and as reiterated in *Acts,* this future prophet was believed to be one who would be a lawgiver and temporal ruler like Prophet Moses.

> The Lord your God will raise up for you a prophet like me from among your own people; you shall heed such a prophet...I will raise up for them a prophet like you from among their own people: I will put my words in the mouth of the prophet, who shall speak to them everything that I command. (*Deuteronomy* 18:15, 18)

> Moses said, "The Lord your God will raise up for you from your own people a prophet like me." (*Acts* 3:22)

> This is the Moses who said to the Israelites, "God will raise up a prophet for you from your own people as he raised me up." (*Acts* 7:37)

As shown by the following verses from *John*, which recount a discussion between Prophet John the Baptist and the Jewish priests and Levites, this prophet yet to come had not yet arrived by the time of Prophet John the Baptist. As such, his arrival was yet in the future, i.e., at some time after Prophets John the Baptist and Jesus Christ.

> This is the testimony given by John when the Jews sent priests and Levites from Jerusalem to ask him, "Who are you?" He confessed and did not deny it, but confessed, "I am not the Messiah." And they asked him, "What then? Are you Elijah?" He said, "I am not." "Are you the prophet?" He answered, "No."...They asked him, "Why then are you baptizing if you are neither the Messiah, nor Elijah, nor the prophet?" (*John* 1:19-21, 25)

The above verses clearly demarcate that the prophet yet to come was someone other than the Messiah, i.e., Jesus Christ. This can be shown by Prophet John the Baptist having first denied that he was the Messiah and then still being asked if he were the prophet yet to come. Additionally, it can be illustrated in the phrase "neither the Messiah...nor the prophet," which dramatically contrasts the Messiah with the prophet yet to come, and indicates that they were, in fact, two different people. The fact that the prophet yet to come was not the Messiah, i.e., Jesus Christ, and that the prophet yet to come had not yet arrived during the ministry of Jesus can be illustrated by a second passage from *John*, which narrates the crowd's reaction after having heard Jesus preach.

> When they heard these words, some in the crowd said, "This is really the prophet." Others said, "This is the Messiah." (*John* 7: 40-41b)

By this point, the astute reader may well be wondering what all of this discussion about the prophet yet to come has to do with Prophet Muhammad. After all, the previously cited verses from *Deuteronomy* and *Acts* stated that the prophet yet to come was to be raised up from "your own people," i.e., from among the Israelites. No such prophet emerged from the Israelite people after Jesus Christ, and history has recorded that Prophet Muhammad was an Arab. So what does this whole discussion have to do with Prophet Muhammad? The answer to this question concerns how various *Bible* translators have translated *Deuteronomy* 18:15 and 18 and *Acts* 3:22 and 7:37.

The above cited English translations of *Deuteronomy* 18:15 and 18 and *Acts* 3:22 and 7:37 are from the New Revised Standard Version (NRSV). In rendering these verses into English, the translators have elected to interpret, rather than to offer a literal translation. The words "your own people" in the NRSV is an interpretation of the Hebrew word "*'ach*" (*Deuteronomy* 18:15 and 18) and of the Greek word "*adelphos*" (Acts 3:22 and 7:37). Both words should be literally translated as "brother" or "brethren." As such, versions of the *Bible* that translate these verses in a less interpretive and more literal manner render the verses as saying that a prophet will be raised up from "among your brethren" or "among your brothers." This is the translation found in the King James Version, the Jerusalem Version, the American Standard Version, the New American Version, and the Latin Vulgate. Furthermore, even within the NRSV, footnotes to the text of *Acts* 3:22 and 7:37, which verses quote *Deuteronomy* 18:15, state that the Greek should literally be translated "your brothers," not "your own people."

Given the above discussion, it can be seen that a strong argument can be made that the prophet yet to come was to arise from the brethren of the Israelites and not from the Israelites themselves. As such, the immediate issue becomes one of identifying the brethren of the Israelites.

The Brethren of The Israelites

Who were the brethren of the Israelites? According to *Genesis* 32: 22-32, Prophet Jacob received the name Israel after wrestling with an angel. As such, the Israelites are the descendants of Prophet Jacob, and their "brethren" are to be found among the descendants of Prophet Jacob's brother and uncles, i.e., the descendants of the non-Jacob lines descending from Prophet's Isaac and Abraham.

Who were the non-Jacob line descendants of Prophet Isaac, the father of Prophet Jacob? According to *Genesis* 25:19-26, Prophet Jacob's only brother was his older twin, Esau. Further examination of *Genesis* suggests that Esau was the father of the Edomites (36:9), known as Idumeans in *New Testament* times, through his sons, Eliphaz and Reuel (36:10), as well as through his sons, Jeush, Jalam, and Korah (36:14). In turn, Eliphaz was the father of Teman (father of the Temanites), Omar, Zepho, Gatam, Kenaz, and Amalek (father of the Amalekites) (36:11-12). Further, Reuel was the father of Nahath, Zerah, Shammah, and Mizzah (36:13). These are the tribes and clans of the Edomites and Amalekites from which the prophet yet to come should have arisen at some time after Jesus, if the "brethren" of the Israelites refers to the descendants of Esau. Of note, history records no individual of note who claimed prophethood from these tribes and clans at any point after the life of Jesus.

Well then, who were the non-Jacob line descendants of Prophet Abraham? According to *Genesis* 16:1-16 and 25:1-6, Prophet Abraham had one son out of Hagar, i.e., Prophet Ismail, and six sons out of Keturah, i.e., Zimran, Jokshan, Medan, Midian (father of the Midianites), Ishbak, and Shuah (father of the Shuhites). While *Qur'an* 7:85-93, 11:84-95, and 29: 36-37 refer to Shu'ayb as being a prophet among the Midianites, Shu'ayb lived many centuries before Jesus Christ. Are there any other contenders from among these people? Yes, for Prophet Muhammad was a descendant of Prophet Ismail, through his second son, Kedar. As such, it is only Prophet Muhammad who can be identified as having been a descendant from among these "brethren" of the Israelites who lived after Jesus and whom history acknowledges as a significant individual who claimed the prophetic office.

A Prophet from among the Arabs

Since there has been no prophet yet to come that has emerged from within the Israelite people in the almost 20 centuries since Jesus Christ, and if Prophet Muhammad is the only viable candidate to be the prophet yet to come from among the "brethren" of the Israelites, the question becomes what, if any, evidence exists for considering that a prophet was to arise from the Arab people. That evidence can be found in the *Bible*, as the following example illustrates.

> God came from Teman, the Holy One from Mount Paran. Selah.
> His glory covered the heavens, and the earth was full of his praise.
> (*Habakkuk* 3:3)

"(T)he Holy One" came "from Mount Paran." What was Paran? According to *Genesis* 21:21, it was the home of Prophet Ismail, who lived within "the wilderness of Paran." Well then, if Paran was the home of Prophet Ismail, where was Paran? While Paran is often equated with the Sinai Peninsula in many Biblical atlases, *Numbers* 10:12 clearly differentiated between the wilderness of Sinai and the wilderness of Paran, saying that the Israelites moved in stages from the wilderness of Sinai to the wilderness of Paran. In short, the wilderness of Paran encompassed an area extending from northeastern Arabia down to and including Makkah, and Mt. Paran can be located in the Sirat Mountains that surround Makkah. "(T)he Holy One" was to come "from Mount Paran," i.e., in the vicinity of Makkah, and Prophet Muhammad was born in Makkah.

Was the prophet yet to come to be a prophet from among the "brethren" of the Israelites, i.e., from among the Arab people? The Jews of the sixth century believed the prophet yet to come would be born in Paran in Arabia, a belief consistent with the previously quoted passage from *Habakkuk* 3:3. As such, many of them immigrated to Yathrib, later known as Madinah, which began to host a thriving Jewish community. More specifically, based upon various *Old Testament* passages, many of these Jews believed the prophet yet to come would be born among the Arabs, i.e., the riders on camels, would be an Arab descending from Kedar, would gather all the people (flocks) of Kedar to monotheistic worship, would glorify the "glorious house" (the Ka'ba in Makkah), and would sing "a new song" of revelation.

> For thus the Lord said to me: "Go, post a lookout, let him announce what he sees. When he sees riders, horsemen in pairs, riders on donkeys, riders on camels, let him listen diligently, very diligently." (*Isaiah* 21:6-7)

> Woe is me, that I am an alien in Meshech, that I must live among the tents of Kedar. (*Psalms* 120:5)

> All the flocks of Kedar shall be gathered to you, the rams of Nebaioth shall minister to you; they shall be acceptable on my altar, and I will glorify my glorious house. (*Isaiah* 60:7)

> Sing to the Lord a new song, his praise from the end of the earth! Let the sea roar and all that fills it, the coastlands and their inhabitants. Let the desert and its towns lift up their voice, the villages that Kedar inhabits; let the inhabitants of Sela sing for joy, let them shout from the tops of the mountains. (*Isaiah* 42:10-11)

The Unlettered Prophet

It is a well-known historical fact that Prophet Muhammad was illiterate, neither being able to read or to write, even in his native Arabic. As such, he is referred to as the unlettered prophet. Nonetheless, such issues as personal piety, social justice, and universal and absolute truth became an ever-increasing focus in his already admirable lifestyle. In addition, he began to experience dreams of an intensely spiritual nature. As such, he began to withdraw into periods of isolated and solitary contemplation. He would pack provisions for himself, leave the comfort of his home and family, and spend increasing periods of time in a cave on Mt. Hira, one of the mountains surrounding the valley of Makkah. There, his spiritual retreats were marked by long periods of prayer and fasting.

> Narrated 'Aisha, the wife of the Prophet: "The commencement (of the Divine Inspiration) to God's Apostle was in the form of true

dreams in his sleep, for he never had a dream but it turned out to be true and clear as the bright daylight. Then he began to like seclusions, so he used to go in seclusion in the cave of Hira where he used to worship God continuously for many nights before going back to his family to take the necessary provision (of food) for the stay." (*Al-Bukhari, Hadith* #6:478; see also *Al-Bukhari, Ahadith* #1:3 and 9:111)

Finally, in one of the odd numbered days of the last 10 days of the month of *Ramadan* in 610, Muhammad's spiritual quest began to be fulfilled. He was visited by the angel Gabriel (Jibril) and received his first revelation as a prophet of God.

Narrated 'Aisha, the wife of the Prophet…"He would come back to (his wife) Khadijah again to take his provision (of food) likewise, till one day he received the guidance while he was in the cave of Hira. An angel came to him and asked him to read. God's Apostle replied, 'I do not know how to read.' The Prophet added, 'Then the angel held me (forcibly) and pressed me so hard that I felt distressed. Then he released me and again asked me to read, and I replied, 'I do not know how to read.' Thereupon he held me again and pressed me for the second time till I felt distressed. He then released me and asked me to read, but again I replied, 'I do not know how to read.' Thereupon he held me for the third time and pressed me till I got distressed, and then he released me and said…'" (*Al-Bukhari, Hadith* #6:478; see also *Al-Bukhari, Hadith* #1:3 and 9:111)

Before proceeding to the actual wording of this first revelation to Prophet Muhammad, it is worth pausing briefly to note the remarkable similarity between the above *Hadith* and the following Biblical passage. The latter reports an *Old Testament* vision of a sealed document of revelation being first presented to a literate but unidentified prophet. This prophet is told to read the document of revelation, but correctly replies that the revelation is still sealed, thus implying that this revelation must await the coming of a later prophet. Subsequently, the document is presented to another prophet, who is told to read the revelation, but replies that he cannot read.

> The vision of all this has become for you like the words of a sealed document. If it is given to those who can read, with the command, "Read this," they say, "We cannot, for it is sealed." And if it is given to those who cannot read, saying, "Read this," they say, "We cannot read." (*Isaiah* 29:11-12)

The above verses from *Isaiah* are quoted from the New Revised Standard Version, which inexplicably renders the verses with the plural pronouns "we" and "they." Both the Jerusalem Version and the King James Version use the singular "he" and "I." For comparison sake, the King James Version of the same two verses is quoted immediately below.

> And the vision of all is become unto you as the words of a book that is sealed, which men deliver to one that is learned, saying, "Read this, I pray thee:" and he saith, "I cannot; for it is sealed:" and the book is delivered to him that is not learned, saying, "Read this, I pray thee:" and he saith, "I am not learned." (*Isaiah* 29:11-12, King James Version)

"'Read this, I pray thee': and he saith, 'I am not learned'." Not only is this remarkably consistent with the above quoted *Hadith* narrated by 'Aisha, it is also consistent with the first revelation received by Prophet Muhammad from the angel Gabriel. After squeezing and releasing Prophet Muhammad for the third time, Gabriel pronounced the first words of this new revelation. Of note, the first word of this revelation, i.e., *Iqra'*, can be translated into English as "proclaim," "recite," or "read," and has the same Arabic root as the word *Qur'an*, i.e., "recitation" or "reading."

> Proclaim! (or read!) in the name of thy Lord and cherisher, Who created—created man, out of a (mere) clot of congealed blood: proclaim! And thy Lord is most bountiful—He Who taught (the use of) the pen—taught man that which he knew not. (*Qur'an* 96:1-5)

Ahmad Foretold

The *Qur'an* states that Prophet Muhammad, under a variant form of his name, i.e., Ahmad, was specifically foretold by Jesus Christ.

And remember, Jesus, the son of Mary, said: "O children of Israel!
I am the messenger of God (sent) to you, confirming the law
(which came) before me, and giving glad tidings of a messenger
to come after me, whose name shall be Ahmad." (*Qur'an* 61:6a)

While no Christian scripture from the canonical *New Testament* can be
found that corroborates the above quoted passage from the *Qur'an*, Muslim
students of the *Bible* have frequently offered an explanatory hypothesis
involving *John* 14:26 and 16:7. Both verses contain the Greek word "*parakletos*," which is variously rendered in English translations of the *Bible*
as "comforter," "counselor," "helper," and "advocate." However, if the actual Greek word were "*periklytos*" instead of "*parakletos*," then the translation
of "*periklytos*" into Arabic would be rendered as "Ahmad." Furthermore, a
Christian apocryphal work that is known as the *Gospel of Barnabas* has Jesus
repeatedly referring to a prophet who is yet to come (e.g., 17, 36, 42-43, 72,
and 96-97) and whose name is Muhammad (39, 41, 44, 54, and 97).

Summary

The above discussion has illustrated that Christian scripture suggests
that there would be at least one prophet after Jesus Christ and that this
prophet might well arise from those Arabs who lived in the vicinity of
Makkah and who traced in descent to Prophet Ismail's second son, Kedar.
These findings are consistent with the Islamic belief regarding the prophethood of Muhammad. Further, *Isaiah* appears to foretell the exact circumstances of the first revelation given to Prophet Muhammad, the unlettered
prophet. Finally, an apocryphal Christian writing confirms the Qur'anic
statement that Jesus Christ had directly foretold the coming of Ahmad, i.e.,
a variant of the name Muhammad.

SUMMMARY AND CONCLUSIONS

Whether or not one believes that Jesus's mission and ministry were
limited to the children of Israel; whether or not one believes that Jesus was
crucified; whether one believes that Jesus was man, God, or God and man;
whether one believes that God is trinity or Unity; whether or not one

Religious beliefs aside, the historical record is clear. Throughout the first several centuries of Christianity, one can trace an Islamic or near-Islamic trajectory through all five issues under consideration. Again, whether one chooses to accept or reject such a trajectory as being accurate is a matter of personal religious belief, and, as Muslims, we respect and defend the right of each person to make and formulate his own religious stance regarding these issues.

Chapter

believes that Muhammad was a prophet of God; these are personal religious verdicts that each man and woman must decide for him or herself. As the *Qur'an* says:

> Let there be no compulsion in religion: truth stands out clear from error: whoever rejects evil and believes in God hath grasped the most trustworthy handhold, that never breaks. And God heareth and knoweth all things. (*Qur'an* 2:256)

Islam,
The People of The Book,
and Religious Pluralism

INTRODUCTION

Although often marred and interrupted by religious factionalism, one of the bequests of the 20th century to the contemporary religious landscape of North America was a pronounced emphasis on ecumenism. In 1927, the National Conference of Christians and Jews (NCCJ) was formed to promote interfaith dialogue between these two components of the Abrahamic faiths. In 1950, intra-Christian ecumenism was furthered with the organization of the National Council of Churches, which today includes 36 Protestant, Anglican, and Orthodox denominations within Christianity. In 1962, religious ecumenism reached unprecedented heights when Pope John XXIII called for the Second Vatican Council (1962-1965), which ushered in a new era of Catholic-Protestant dialogue.

Flushed with the success of the Second Vatican Council, many Christian denominations rushed forward to meet in an ecumenical embrace with which they celebrated the commonalities that bound them together as Christians. Catholic priests presided at Protestant worship services, and Protestant ministers were invited to be guest ministers at Catholic Masses. As the immediate aftermath of the Second Vatican Council began to recede somewhat into the pages of history, the initial ardor surrounding the ecumenical movement waned for a while and then began to find new life under the banner of religious pluralism.

At the dawn of the 21st century, the ecumenical movement continues unabated in many quarters and has in fact expanded, as witnessed by the first hesitant steps in a process of Muslim-Jewish and Muslim-Christian dialogues. The three Abrahamic faiths are once again beginning to talk with each other, are finding common ground, and are exploring their differences with tolerance and mutual respect. Given this perspective on the religious history of the last century, it is appropriate to look at the traditional teachings of Islam regarding religious pluralism and at how those teachings have been incorporated into Islamic practice throughout history. This topic is especially relevant in the current temporal context, as certain spokesmen for the Christian Right are busily propagating a totally false view of Islam's teachings and history, in which they try to portray Islam as being intolerant of religious pluralism and as advocating the persecution of non-Muslims. On the one hand, such an erroneous presentation of Islam by the Christian Right is merely a continuation of a longstanding history of Islamophobia in the Christian West, a topic addressed in the following chapter. On the other hand, it is incumbent upon Muslims to set the record straight, which is the topic of the present chapter.

THE TEACHINGS OF THE *QUR'AN*
Freedom of Religion

The respect that Islam affords to religious pluralism is best exemplified in the following Qur'anic injunction, which mandates that there is to be absolutely no compulsion when it comes to religion.

> Let there be no compulsion in religion: truth stands out clear from error: whoever rejects evil and believes in God hath grasped the most trustworthy handhold that never breaks. And God heareth and knoweth all things. (*Qur'an* 2:256)

"Let there be no compulsion in religion..." These words of God are clear and unambiguous. There is to be complete freedom when it comes to an individual's religious choice. He must be free to accept Islam or to reject it. He must be free to accept or reject any religious persuasion whatsoever. Freedom of religious choice is a cardinal tenet of Islam and is a concept that must be upheld by every Muslim. "Truth stands out clear from error," and each individual must have the right to view that dichotomy as he or she wills. As the following verses from the *Qur'an* indicate, not even Prophet Muhammad was allowed to compel non-Muslims to become Muslims, because "(n)o soul can believe, except by the will of God..." Prophet Muhammad was to "admonish with the *Qur'an*," and he was "to proclaim (the message) clearly and openly," but he was not to force any individual to convert to Islam.

> If it had been the Lord's will, they would all have believed—all who are on earth! Wilt thou then compel mankind, against their will, to believe! No soul can believe, except by the will of God... (*Qur'an* 10:99-100a)

> We know best what they say; and thou art not one to overawe them by force. So admonish with the *Qur'an* such as fear My warning. (*Qur'an* 50:45)

> So obey God, and obey His messenger: but if ye turn back, the duty of Our messenger is but to proclaim (the message) clearly and openly. (*Qur'an* 64:12)

> Say: "The truth is from your Lord:" let him who will believe, and let him who will, reject (it)... (*Qur'an* 18:29a)

These same Qur'anic dictates continue to apply to all Muslims for all time. A Muslim is directed to "admonish with the *Qur'an*" and "to proclaim (the message) clearly and openly," but he is never to "compel mankind, against their will, to believe," and he is to "let him who will believe, and let him who will, reject (it)." Correct adherence to Islam demands that Muslims affirm religious freedom for all people.

Islam and Non-Muslims

Religious pluralism does not end with freedom of religion but merely begins with freedom of religion. An added issue is how the adherents of one religion view the followers of a different religion. With regard to addressing how Islam views non-Muslims, the *Qur'an* states that we all, regardless of religious affiliation and practice, belong to God.

> (God) most gracious is firmly established on the throne (of authority). To Him belongs what is in the heaven and on earth, and all between them, and all beneath the soil. (*Qur'an* 20:5-6)

We all belong to God, and we are all creations of God. This is a universal bond that ties together all of humanity. Therefore, it is incumbent upon every Muslim to respect every other person, whatever the other's personal religious affiliation, as a fellow creature of God. Moreover, all of mankind are part of one human family, having been created from a single primal pair of humans. Our individual differences should not be a cause of mutual antipathy and hatred but should serve as a catalyst for interpersonal exploration and for beginning to know and understand each other.

> O mankind! Reverence your guardian Lord, Who created you from a single person, created, of like nature, his mate, and from them twain scattered (like seeds) countless men and women... (*Qur'an* 4:1a)

> O mankind! We created you from a single (pair) of a male and a female and made you into nations and tribes that ye may know each other (not that ye may despise each other). (*Qur'an* 49:13a)

> Mankind was but one nation, but differed (later). (*Qur'an* 10:19a)

A Muslim's obligation to honor and respect other people does not end with the recognition that all people are God's creation and that all people are fellow members of a single human family. In contrast to the traditional teachings of Judaism and Christianity, the *Qur'an* informs Muslims that God has sent a prophet with a divine message to every nation and people.

Before thee We sent (messengers) to many nations, and We afflicted the nations with suffering and adversity that they might learn humility. (*Qur'an* 6:42)

Verily, We have sent thee in truth as a bearer of glad tidings and as a warner, and there never was a people without a warner having lived among them (in the past). (*Qur'an* 35:24)

To every people (was sent) a messenger. When their messenger comes (before them), the matter will be judged between them with justice, and they will not be wronged. (*Qur'an* 10:47)

For we assuredly sent amongst every people a messenger (with the command), "Serve God and eschew evil:" of the people were some whom God guided and some on whom error became inevitably (established). So travel through the earth, and see what was the end of those who denied (the truth). (*Qur'an* 16:36)

Given that Islam maintains that God has sent a prophet with divine revelation to every people, the *Qur'an* directs Muslims to keep that central fact in mind when relating to non-Muslims and to remember that "to each among you have We prescribed a law and an open way." After all, whether consciously realized by each individual or not, "(t)he goal of you all is to God" Who will eventually demonstrate the truth with regard to those religious matters about which the human family disagrees among themselves. In the interim, Muslims are directed to compete with non-Muslims in doing good, i.e., "so strive as in a race in all virtues."

To each among you have We prescribed a law and an open way. If God had so willed, He would have made you a single people, but (His plan is) to test you in what He hath given you; so strive as in a race in all virtues. The goal of you all is to God; it is He that will show you the truth of the matters in which ye dispute. (*Qur'an* 5:48b)

"(S)o strive as in a race in all virtues." A Muslim is to relate to a non-Muslim as though each were in a race to perform good works. The earthly sojourn of mankind is the universal race in which all of humanity is engaged, and men and women should compete with one another in the performance of "all virtues." This is the healthy competition prescribed by Islam—a competition to do good for the sake of God.

The *Qur'an* also admonishes Muslims not to be too quick in labeling others as non-believers and reminds Muslims of their own religious status before they accepted the revelation contained in the *Qur'an*.

> O ye who believe! When ye go abroad in the cause of God, investigate carefully and say not to anyone who offers you a salutation: "Thou art none of a believer!"…Even thus were ye yourselves before till God conferred on you His favors: therefore carefully investigate. For God is well aware of all that ye do. (*Qur'an* 4:94)

How is a Muslim to relate to those who hate him and to those who hate Islam? Even in such an extreme situation, God instructs all Muslims to stand for "fair dealing" and to make sure that they do not "swerve to wrong and depart from justice." Further, God reminds all Muslims that even those people who are one's enemies today may be one's friends tomorrow and that one should act accordingly. "It may be that God will grant love (and friendship) between you and those whom ye (now) hold as enemies." Still further, contrary to the Islamophobic propaganda one often encounters, the *Qur'an* states that there is absolutely no prohibition on Muslims from seeking and maintaining friendly relations with non-Muslims, so long as those non-Muslims are among those who do not actively engage in a religious war against Islam, and as long as they do not drive Muslims out of their own homes.

> O ye who believe! Stand out firmly for God, as witnesses to fair dealing, and let not the hatred of others to you make you swerve to wrong and depart from justice. Be just: that is next to piety: and fear God. For God is well-acquainted with all that ye do. (*Qur'an* 5:8)

> It may be that God will grant love (and friendship) between you and those whom ye (now) hold as enemies. For God has power (over all

things), and God is oft-forgiving, most merciful. God forbids you
not, with regard to those who fight you not for (your) faith nor
drive you out of your homes, from dealing kindly and justly with
them: for God loveth those who are just. God only forbids you,
with regard to those who fight you for (your) faith, and drive you
out of your homes, and support (others) in driving you out, from
turning to them (for friendship and protection). It is such as turn
to them (in these circumstances), that do wrong. (*Qur'an* 60:7-9)

Taken together, the above passages from the *Qur'an* form a model
textbook of ecumenical fellowship and religious pluralism, the main points
of which can be summarized as follows. (1) We are all creations of God.
(2) We all belong to the same human family. (3) All people have at one time
or another had a prophet within their midst who came with divine revelation from God. (4) As such, every people have received a divine law and an
"open way" to God, whether or not they have preserved that way and law in
a reasonably uncorrupted form. (5) Therefore, be careful and cautious in saying that someone else is a non-believer. (6) Given the above considerations,
all religious communities should view themselves as being tested by God in
this life and should engage in friendly competition with one another in the
performance of "all virtues" and in doing good. (7) Always remember that
today's enemies may be tomorrow's friends and act accordingly. (8) Do not
eschew friendly and just relations with those of a different faith merely
because they adhere to a different religion. Only if the others actively make
war against one's religious faith and drive one from his own home is one to
avoid them. (9) In the end, God "will show you the truth of the (religious)
matters in which ye dispute."

Islam and the People of The Book

A phrase that occurs with some frequency in the *Qur'an* is *Ahl Al-Kitab*,
i.e., People of the Book. This phrase refers to those religious communities
who have at one time or another received an actual book of revelation from
God. The *Qur'an* specifically mentions four such books prior to the *Qur'an*.
These are the books of revelation given to Prophets Abraham, Moses,
David, and Jesus. The first such book, i.e., that given to Prophet Abraham,

is no longer existent. Muslims believe that the latter three books have been corrupted and contaminated over time and that the contemporary *Torah, Psalms*, and various gospels are no longer the same pristine books of revelation originally sent to Prophets Moses, David, and Jesus. Nonetheless, as all of these prior books of revelation that are specifically mentioned in the *Qur'an* are claimed by the Judaeo-Christian tradition, Muslims typically use People of the Book as a designation for Christians and Jews.

The *Qur'an* addresses the issue of the People of the Book and of Jews and Christians in several different passages. For example, the *Qur'an* affirms that the Israelites were originally a "chosen people," in that they were blessed with a large number of prophets, i.e., "I preferred you to all others (for My message)."

> O children of Israel! Call to mind the (special) favor which I bestowed upon you, and that I preferred you to all others (for My message). (*Qur'an* 2:47; repeated in *Qur'an* 2:122)

> We did deliver aforetime the children of Israel from humiliating punishment, inflicted by Pharaoh, for he was arrogant (even) among the inordinate transgressors. And We chose them aforetime above the nations knowingly and granted them signs in which there was a manifest trial. (*Qur'an* 44:30-33)

However, the *Qur'an* also suggests that the Israelites forfeited their status as a chosen people by failing to uphold their end of the divine covenant. With regard to this point, it should be noted that a covenant is merely a type of contract. When one party to a contract defaults on that contract, the contract can become null and void, and the other party to that contract is no longer bound by the contract. As such, the following passage from the *Qur'an* is highly relevant.

> God did aforetime take a covenant from the children of Israel...But because of their breach of their covenant, We cursed them and made their hearts grow hard: they change the words from their (right) places and forget a good part of the message that was sent them, nor wilt thou cease to find them—barring a few—ever bent on (new)

deceits: but forgive them, and overlook (their misdeeds): for God loveth those who are kind. (*Qur'an* 5:12a, 13)

Does the above mean that the *Qur'an* and Islam condemn all Jews? Does it suggest that all People of the Book are cursed by God? Does it in anyway justify a view that Islam encourages violence against Jews and Christians? The answers to all of these questions are found in the above quoted passage, and those answers are all, "No." With regard to the first question, the passage informs that "nor wilt thou cease to find them (the Jews)—barring a few—ever bent on (new deceits)." Two points emerge from a proper understanding of this passage. Firstly, there are those people among the Jews who do not engage in deceits, which is a point that will be elaborated in the next paragraph. Secondly, the Arabic language is very specific when it comes to use of the second person pronoun. In English, "you" or "thou" can refer to one person, to two people, and to a multitude of individuals. However, in Arabic, which is the original language of the *Qur'an*, the second person pronoun is very specific as to number. A different second person pronoun is used for when "you" refers to one person, refers to two people, and refers to three or more people. In the above quoted passage, the "thou" in "nor wilt thou cease to find them—barring a few—ever bent on (new) deceits" is in the singular form[55], i.e., this is a statement that appears to be directed to Prophet Muhammad, who is the "thou" in the quoted verse. As such, the passage is historically and geographically specific to the environs of seventh century Madinah. (Ibn Kathir's classic commentary on the *Qur'an* notes that the "deceits" referenced in *Qur'an* 5:13 refer to an assassination plot against Prophet Muhammad by members of the Jewish tribes of Madinah.[56]) It is not a passage that can be applied to all Jews for all times. Thirdly and quite importantly, even with regard to those Jews who are "ever bent on (new) deceits," the passage ends with a direction to "forgive them, and overlook (their misdeeds)."

Picking up on the first point made in the immediately preceding paragraph, the *Qur'an* reiterates on numerous occasions that not all People of the Book are alike. There are good Jews and bad Jews and good Christians and bad Christians. There are People of the Book who are "on the right course," who "have faith," who honor their commitments, and who "stand (for the right)…rehearse the signs of God all night long…prostrate themselves in adoration (of God)…(and) enjoin what is right and forbid what is wrong." With regard to these People of the Book, "(o)f the good that they do, nothing will be rejected of them." The following passages from the *Qur'an* clearly illustrate these points.

> If only the People of the Book had believed and been righteous, We should indeed have blotted out their iniquities and admitted them to gardens of bliss. If only they had stood fast by the law, the gospel, and all the revelation that was sent to them from their Lord, they would have enjoyed happiness from every side. There is from among them a party on the right course, but many of them follow a course that is evil. (*Qur'an* 5:65-66)

> If only the People of the Book had faith, it were best for them. Among them are some who have faith, but most of them are perverted transgressors. (*Qur'an* 3:110b)

> Among the People of the Book are some who, if entrusted with a hoard of gold, will (readily) pay it back; others, who, if entrusted with a single silver coin, will not repay it unless thou constantly stoodest demanding, because, they say, "There is no call on us (to keep faith) with these ignorant (pagans)." But they tell a lie against God and (well) they know it. Nay—those who keep their plighted faith and act aright—verily God loves those who act aright. (*Qur'an* 3:75-76)

> Not all of them are alike: of the People of the Book are a portion that stand (for the right); they rehearse the signs of God all night long, and they prostrate themselves in adoration. They believe in God and the last day; they enjoin what is right and forbid what is wrong, and they hasten (in emulation) in (all) good works. They are in the ranks of the righteous. Of the good that they do, nothing will be rejected of them, for God knoweth well those that do right. (*Qur'an* 3:113-115)

> And there are certainly among the People of the Book those who believe in God, in the revelation to you, and in the revelation to

them, bowing in humility to God. They will not sell the signs of God for a miserable gain! For them is a reward with their Lord, and God is swift in account. (*Qur'an* 3:199)

The *Qur'an* states, and Islam thus holds, that there are good People of the Book and bad People of the Book, i.e., good Jews and bad Jews and good Christians and bad Christians. To this I must sadly add that there are good Muslims and bad Muslims. However, as a general rule, the *Qur'an* does state that the Jews as a group will typically be "(s)trongest among men in enmity to the believers," while the Christians as a group will be "nearest among them in love to the believers." This sentiment is illustrated in the following Qur'anic passage, where the second person pronoun, i.e., "thou," is in the singular form in the original Arabic[57], indicating Prophet Muhammad is being directly addressed and thus suggesting a specific historical and geographical context for understanding this passage.

> Strongest among men in enmity to the believers wilt thou find the Jews and pagans; and nearest among them in love to the believers wilt thou find those who say, "We are Christians:" because amongst these are men devoted to learning and men who have renounced the world, and they are not arrogant. (*Qur'an* 5:82)

Within Islam, all Muslims are seen as belonging to a common religious family. As such, all adult Muslims address adult Muslim males as "brother," and adult Muslim females as "sister." Further, all Muslim children address adult Muslim males as "uncle" and adult Muslim females as "aunt." Given this understanding of the relationship of one Muslim to another, it is not too much of a stretch to suggest that the People of the Book, including all Jews and Christians, are the "cousins" of all Muslims. This close "familial" relationship between Muslims and the People of the Book is suggested in the following verse from the *Qur'an*, where Muslims are informed that the food of the People of the Book is acceptable in meeting Islamic dietary restrictions and that Muslim men may marry Jewish and Christian women. With regard to this last point, it must be emphasized that Muslim men are not allowed to marry women who are neither Muslims nor People of the

Book. As such, the following verse of the *Qur'an* dramatically illustrates the special relationship that is to exist between Muslims and the People of the Book.

> This day are (all) things good and pure made lawful unto you. The food of the People of the Book is lawful unto you and yours is lawful unto them. (Lawful unto you in marriage) are (not only) chaste women who are believers, but chaste women among the People of the Book, revealed before your time... (*Qur'an* 5:5a)

In summarizing the Qur'anic perspective, and thus the Islamic perspective, on the People of the Book, the following two verses from the *Qur'an* are definitive.

> Those who believe (in the *Qur'an*), and those who follow the Jewish (scriptures), and the Christians and the Sabians[58]—any who believe in God and the last day and work righteousness, shall have their reward with their Lord; on them shall be no fear, nor shall they grieve. (*Qur'an* 2:62)

> Those who believe (in the *Qur'an*), those who follow the Jewish (scriptures), and the Sabians and the Christians—any who believe in God and the last day and work righteousness—on them shall be no fear, nor shall they grieve. (*Qur'an* 5:69)

Islam and taking non-Muslims as friends

The issue of how Islam views non-Muslims, as well as the special relationship that exists between Muslims and People of the Book, has been presented previously in this chapter. Nonetheless, the claim is often made by non-Muslims, frequently by quoting the *Qur'an* out of context, that Muslims are forbidden to take Jews and Christians as friends and protectors. As this fallacious claim is heard so commonly, it is presented as its own distinct topic.

There are really two issues here, and each needs to be dealt with separately. The first issue deals with "friends," and the second with "protectors." With regard to taking others, whether Muslims or non-Muslims, as protectors, Islam teaches that the only real protector is God. For example, *Qur'an* 2:257 states: "God is the protector of those who have faith." Additionally, *Qur'an* 3:150 declares: "Nay, God is your protector, and He is the best of helpers." Finally, *Qur'an* 7:3 states: "Follow (O men!) the revelation given unto you from your Lord, and follow not, as friends or protectors, other than Him." *Qur'an* 22:78 proclaims: "And hold fast to God! He is your protector—the best to protect and the best to help!"

It is hard to imagine that any conscientious Christian or Jew would dispute the fact that God is one's only real protector. As such, one should not take men, however powerful and whatever their religion, as personal protectors in place of God. The only real protector is God. Any other conviction represents a form of idolatry and polytheism, however subtly expressed and however unconscious it may be. As such, it is within the above context that one must understand any Qur'anic verses that bar Muslims from taking Christians and Jews as protectors.

As to the issue of friendship, there are many Muslims, myself included, who have Christian and Jewish friends. In fact, the *Qur'an* specifically allows Muslims to have non-Muslim friends, so long as those non-Muslims are not fighting Muslims or driving them out of their homes.

> It may be that God will grant love (and friendship) between you and those whom ye (now) hold as enemies. For God has power (over all things); and God is oft-forgiving, most merciful. God forbids you not, with regard to those who fight you not for (your) faith nor drive you out of your homes, from dealing kindly and justly with them: for God loveth those who are just. God only forbids you, with regard to those who fight you for (your) faith, and drive you out of your homes and support (others) in driving you out, from turning to them (for friendship and protection). It is such as turn to them (in these circumstances) that do wrong. (*Qur'an* 60:7-9)

The above having been said, the *Qur'an* does instruct Muslims that they are not to take as friends those who make "a mockery or sport" of Islam, whether or not they are Christians or Jews.

O ye who believe! Take not for friends and protectors those who take your religion for a mockery or sport—whether among those who received the scriptures before you (e.g., Christians and Jews), or among those who reject faith; but fear ye God, if ye have faith (indeed). (*Qur'an* 5:57)

What devout Christian takes as a friend someone who constantly ridicules Christianity? What conscientious Jew numbers among his close companions those people who incessantly mock Judaism? The answers are obvious: no one. As such, it is not at all surprising that the *Qur'an* directs Muslims to avoid socializing with individuals who consistently "take your religion (i.e., Islam) for a mockery or sport."

In addition, several passages in the *Qur'an* state that a believer should not take unbelievers as friends "rather than" believers. In these verses, the key operative phrase is "rather than." The Muslim is certainly not prohibited from having non-Muslim friends, but he is directed not to take non-Muslim friends "rather than" Muslim friends. It is within this context that the following Qur'anic verses should be understood.

Let not the believers take for friends or helpers unbelievers rather than believers: if any do that, in nothing will there be help from God: except by way of precaution, that ye may guard yourselves from them. But God cautions you (to remember) Himself; for the final goal is to God. (*Qur'an* 3:28)

Yea, to those who take for friends unbelievers rather than believers: is it honor they seek among them? Nay—all honor is with God. Already has He sent you word in the book, that when ye hear the signs of God held in defiance and ridicule, ye are not to sit with them unless they turn to a different theme: if ye did, ye would be like them. For God will collect the hypocrites and those who defy faith—all in hell...O ye who believe! Take not for friends unbelievers rather than believers: do ye wish to offer God an open proof against yourselves? (*Qur'an* 4:139-140, 144)

It is only natural that members of one religion should seek out their co-religionists for friendship and fellowship. Such behavioral patterns will, God willing, help to strengthen one's own faith and spirituality. Even common sense suggests that one is more likely to find a deeper, more satisfying, and more intimate friendship with one's co-religionist than with someone from a different faith and religious background. The former is more likely to reinforce one's faith, while the latter is more likely to introduce an element of doubt into one's faith.

> Your (real) friends are (no less than) God, His messenger, and the (fellowship of) believers—those who establish regular prayers and regular charity, and they bow down humbly (in worship). (*Qur'an* 5:55)

> O ye who believe! Take not into your intimacy those outside your ranks: they will not fail to corrupt you. They only desire your ruin: rank hatred has already appeared from their mouths: what their hearts conceal is far worse. We have made plain to you the signs if ye have wisdom. Ah! Ye are those who love them, but they love you not... (*Qur'an* 3:118-119a)

Muslims are not to take non-Muslims as friends if those non-Muslims attack Islam, drive Muslims out of their homes, or ridicule Islam. Further, Muslims are not to take non-Muslims as friends "rather than" Muslims. As is the case for all adherents to any given religion, one's closest and most intimate friends are likely to be one's co-religionists. With the above in mind, a Muslim may have Jewish and Christian friends. In fact, *Qur'an* 5:82 declares that Christians are nearest to Muslims in love. Additionally, it should be noted that the *Qur'an* 5:5 expressly permits Muslim men to marry Christian and Jewish women, a permission that would be unthinkable if Muslims actually were prohibited from having Christian and Jewish friends.

> ...and nearest among them in love to the believers wilt thou find those who say, "We are Christians:" because amongst these are men devoted to learning and men who have renounced the world, and they are not arrogant. (*Qur'an* 5:82b,c)

> This day are (all) things good and pure made lawful unto you.

The food of the People of the Book is lawful unto you and yours is lawful unto them. (Lawful unto you in marriage) are (not only) chaste women who are believers but chaste women among the People of the Book…(*Qur'an* 5:5a)

Islam and Prosletizing

As previously noted, Prophet Muhammad was directed by God to "admonish with the *Qur'an*" (*Qur'an* 50:45) and to "proclaim (the message) clearly and openly" (*Qur'an* 64:12). By extension, all Muslims have a religious duty to proclaim the message of Islam as encapsulated within the revelation of the *Qur'an*. However, the *Qur'an* gives very explicit instructions about how that duty is to be performed. Muslims are directed to "(i)nvite (all) to the way of thy Lord with wisdom and beautiful preaching." Muslims are to refrain from heated argument and unworthy disputation but are to present their arguments "in ways that are best and most gracious." Muslims are only to "dispute…with means better (than mere disputation)." Having witnessed in a gracious and beautiful way, Muslims are then to allow non-Muslims to make their own choice as to their religious beliefs and affiliations.

Invite (all) to the way of thy Lord with wisdom and beautiful preaching; and argue with them in ways that are best and most gracious: for thy Lord knoweth best who have strayed from His path, and who receive guidance. (*Qur'an* 16:125)

And dispute ye not with the People of the Book, except with means better (than mere disputation), unless it be with those of them who inflict wrong (and injury); but say, "We believe in the revelation which has come down to us and in that which came down to you; our God and your God is One; and it is to Him we bow (in Islam)." (*Qur'an* 29:46)

Say: "O People of the Book! Come to common terms as between us and you: that we worship none but God; that we associate no partners with Him; that we erect not, from among ourselves, lords and patrons other than God." If then they turn back, say ye:

"Bear witness that we (at least) are Muslims (bowing to God's will)."
(*Qur'an* 3:64)

The Issue of the *Dhimmi* and *Jizyah*

Before leaving the discussion of how the *Qur'an* refers to non-Muslims, it is important to introduce the topic of the *Dhimmi* and the *Jizyah*. A *Dhimmi* is a non-Muslim who is living as a protected person in a Muslim state. As a *Dhimmi* or protected person, the non-Muslim: enjoys the full services and protection of the state; may practice his own religion according to his faith; is governed by his own religious law when it comes to such areas as dietary rules and regulations, marriage, divorce, and inheritance; has autonomy of local government within his own community; and is free of certain obligations to the state. With regard to the latter point, the *Dhimmi* is not subject to military service and is not subject to the religiously mandated charity (*Zakat*) that is levied against every Muslim who has an agricultural income or who has an economic surplus that he has been able to hold for one year.

The *Jizyah* is a tax levied against male *Dhimmi* who have reached the age of puberty in exchange for his protected status within the Muslim state and in exchange for the various services that he and his family receive from the state. No *Jizyah* is levied against women and children. In principle, the *Jizyah* paid by a *Dhimmi* can be compared to the income tax paid by most inhabitants of any Western country, although the *Jizyah* is typically far less expensive than any income tax and no more demanding than the *Zakat* paid by Muslims.

Unfortunately, many Western commentators on Islam present the *Jizyah* as though it were a repressive and punitive fine imposed upon non-Muslims for the benefit of Muslims. In doing so, they grossly distort the concept of *Dhimmi* and *Jizyah*, and often quote and misinterpret the following verse   of the *Qur'an*.

Fight those who believe not in God nor the last day, nor hold that forbidden which hath been forbidden by God and His messenger, nor acknowledge the religion of truth, from among the People of the Book, until they pay the *Jizyah* with willing submission and feel themselves subdued. (*Qur'an* 9:29)

In considering the above verse, it should be noted that the verse is specific to non-Muslims living in a Muslim state. The verse does not apply to non-Muslims living in a non-Muslim state. Thus, this verse's injunction to fight non-Muslims is limited to those non-Muslims who are living in a Muslim state and who refuse to pay the *Jizyah*. Just as the United States or any other Western country would prosecute any citizen who refused to pay his income tax and just as the Muslim state would prosecute any Muslim who refused to pay the *Zakat*, so the Muslim state is directed in this verse to prosecute any non-Muslim who refuses to pay the *Jizyah*. A specific historical example of how the *Jizyah* has been imposed on *Dhimmi* in the past will be explored later in this chapter.

THE EXAMPLE OF THE PROPHET

There are two religiously authoritative sources in Islam. The first is the *Qur'an*, and the second is the *Sunnah* or example of Prophet Muhammad. With regard to relations between Muslims and non-Muslims, the teachings of the *Qur'an* have already been presented. However, it is still necessary to consider how Prophet Muhammad related to non-Muslims, and the clearest example of this can be found in the Prophet's issuance of the Covenant of Madinah.

In the year 622, Prophet Muhammad and the Muslims of Makkah migrated to Madinah in order to secure freedom of religious practice and freedom from religious persecution. With the Prophet's arrival in Madinah, the first Islamic state was born. From this point on in his life, Prophet Muhammad was not only the messenger of God, but he was also the head of state. One of his first acts as head of state was his issuance of the Covenant of Madinah (*Sahifat Al-Madinah*), which specified the nature of the interrelations that were to exist among the Muslims who emigrated from Makkah to Madinah, the Muslims who were indigenous to Madinah, the pagans who were indigenous to Madinah, and the Jews who were indigenous to Madinah. The various articles of the Covenant of Madinah are highly instructive in demonstrating the Prophet's stipulations regarding relations between Muslims and non-Muslims in an Islamic state.

The Covenant of Madinah specifically stipulated that the Jews of Madinah were one community with the Muslim believers, that they were free to profess and practice their own religion, and that they were entitled to all the rights pertaining to a Muslim believer. The Covenant of Madinah bound the Jews and Arabs of this initial Islamic state together in a mutual defense pact, prohibited both parties from committing sins to the prejudice of the other party, and mandated that their relations with each other were to be based on mutual advice, consultation, and righteousness. Should a member of either party wrong a member of the other party, the wronged party had legal redress and was to be aided by the entire community. In short, all people, regardless of ethnic or religious identity, were to be treated equally under a system of universal law, justice, and morality.[59]

While almost 1,400 years old, the Prophet's Covenant of Madinah is still a model of religious tolerance and pluralism. However, the Covenant of Madinah is hardly the only example of Prophet Muhammad's conduct when it comes to relations between Muslims and non-Muslims. The following sayings of Prophet Muhammad are also relevant to the discussion.

> Al-'Irbad ibn Sariyat Al-Sulami said...the Prophet...said...: "God has not permitted you (the Muslims) to enter the houses of the People of the Book without permission (from them), or to beat their women, or to eat their fruits when they give you what is imposed (the Jizyah) on them." (*Abu Dawud, Hadith* #3044)

> Ibn 'Umar narrated that God's Apostle said: "Gabriel kept on recommending to me about treating neighbors in a kind and polite manner, so much so that I thought that he would order (me) to make them (my) heirs." (*Al-Bukhari, Hadith* #8:44; see also *Al-Bukhari, Hadith* #8:43)

As the above narrations illustrate, Prophet Muhammad specifically prohibited Muslims from acting unjustly towards the People of the Book and taught that a Muslim should always treat his neighbors, whether Muslim or non-Muslim, in an exemplary manner. However, the following statement is perhaps the clearest example of the Prophet's teaching when it comes to relations between Muslims and non-Muslims. In it, Prophet Muhammad clearly instructed all Muslims that all people are God's children, and should be treated as such.

> Anas and 'Abd Allah ibn Mas'ud reported that the Messenger of God said: "All creatures are God's children, and those dearest to God are the ones who treat His children kindly." (*Mishkat Al-Masabih*, page 1039)

THE ISLAMIC CONQUEST

With the dramatic increase in Islamophobia after September 11, 2001, there have been those among the religious right of Christianity who have attempted to rewrite the history of Islam in order to smear Islam as a religion of war. In doing so, these verbal gladiators of the religious right have often focused on the so-called "Islamic Conquest" and have insisted that the dramatic spread of Islam after Prophet Muhammad's death in 632 demonstrates a religious mentality characterized by violence, war, and conquest. However, the reality is that even a cursory perusal of the context of the "Islamic Conquest" demonstrates just the opposite.

At the time of Prophet Muhammad's death in 632, Islam was still basically confined to what is today Saudi Arabia. By 711 and after the passage of only 79 years, the Islamic state had expanded throughout western Asia, northern Africa, and parts of Europe, and included the geographic area represented by the following contemporary countries and islands: Afghanistan, Algeria, Armenia, Azerbaijan, Bahrain, Cyprus, Egypt, Eritrea, Georgia, Iran, Iraq, Israel, Jordan, Kyrgyzstan, Kuwait, Lebanon, Libya, Morocco, Oman, Pakistan, Palestine, Portugal, Qatar, Rhodes, Spain, Syria, Tajikistan, Tunisia, Turkmenistan, United Arab Emirates, Uzbekistan, and Yemen. Superficially, this might appear to be indicative of the erroneous claim that Islam has historically been a religion of war and conquest. However, this "Islamic Conquest" can only be properly understood within the context of relevant population figures. Using Western, non-Muslim population estimates that are current in scholarly academic circles, it has been estimated that the total population of the Islamic state in 632 was only about 2.5 million people, while the population of the so-called "conquered" countries was about 35.6 million people circa 700.[60] In other words, the proponents of the fallacious theory of an "Islamic Conquest" of militaristic subjugation would have one believe that an Islamic state of only 2.5 million people, not all of whom were Muslim, was able to conquer by outside force of arms a population that was over 14 times as large as that of the Islamic state!

At a time when warfare was limited to swords and spears and when no one side had a marked superiority over any other side in military technology, the proposal that an Islamic state of only 2.5 million people, not all of whom were Muslim, could run roughshod over lands numbering about 35.6 million people is too ludicrous to countenance. Clearly, some other explanation is necessary to explain the so-called "Islamic Conquest." With that in mind, only two explanations are really possible: (1) the "Islamic Conquest" resulted from divine intervention and thus represented divine will; and (2) the "Islamic Conquest" happened because the indigenous and subjugated people of the "conquered" lands rose up in revolt against their tyrannical overlords and actively aided the Muslims, whom the indigenous masses correctly perceived to be liberators who would insure fair and impartial government. Chroniclers who were writing during the seventh through ninth centuries give ample support for the latter explanation and document numerous examples of native populations siding with their Muslim liberators and rising up in revolt against their local oppressors. For example, history documents that the Jewish tribes of North Africa, no doubt aware of the precedents embodied in the Covenant of Madinah, actively allied with the Muslim armies during the conquest of North Africa.

As an additional example, one can turn to the Byzantine Empire that sprawled across what is today Greece, Turkey, Syria, and Palestine. Ostensibly a Christian government, the Byzantine Empire severely persecuted Jews and dissident Christian groups such as Nestorian and Jacobite Christians. Compared to the tyranny that they had been experiencing under Christian rule, such religious communities saw Muslim government as a liberating, tolerant, and flexible alternative, which assured their freedom of religious faith and practice. Additionally, the *Jizyah* collected by Muslim governments from these People of the Book was often considerably less oppressive and onerous than the taxes formerly exacted by the Christian governments. As such, many Jewish and Christian communities actively allied with the Muslims in taking over large areas of the Byzantime Empire.[61]

That the hopes and dreams of the persecuted religious minorities, both Jews and dissident Christians, of the ostensibly Christian Byzantine Empire were not abused by their Muslim liberators can be illustrated as follows. (1) When Palestine entered into the Islamic state led by 'Umar ibn Al-Khattab, the second Caliph of Islam, 'Umar specifically guaranteed the safety of the lives and property of those Christians living in Jerusalem, Lod, and Bethlehem, declared their churches and monasteries inviolate, and prohibited Muslims from taking over Christian churches as places for Muslim worship. (2) When Al-Madain, in what is now Iraq, became part of the Islamic state, a declaration of protection was given to the Nestorian patriarch, Yeshuyab III (650-660), by the Islamic government. Once again, Christian people, churches, and monasteries were protected by the Muslim liberators, and Muslims were forbidden from confiscating any existing building or structure, whether to serve as a mosque or as a dwelling. Thus the Nestorian patriarch would later write to the bishop of Persia that the Muslims "have not attacked the Christian religion, but rather they have commended our faith, honored our priests...and conferred benefits on churches and monasteries."[62]

In short, any fair-minded assessment of the so-called "Islamic Conquest" must begin with the realization that the Muslim armies coming out of the Arabian Peninsula were the liberators of oppressed and subjugated peoples who were actively crying out for the social justice embodied in Muslim leadership. As such, the Muslims were actively aided by the people they were liberating.

THE CRUSADES

Introduction

The Crusades offer a rather unique opportunity to witness Muslim behavior towards non-Muslims within the context of a war of aggression, which was initiated and waged by the non-Muslims of Western Europe against the Muslims of the Middle East. Responding to Pope Urban II's call in 1095 at the Council of Clermont for a genocidal war against the Muslims of the Middle East (more on this topic in the subsequent chapter), Western and ostensibly "Christian" Europe responded with a series of military invasions of the Middle East over the next few centuries. Within this specialized context of being attacked by foreign aggressors bent on the wholesale destruction of the Muslim people, history documents that Muslims continued to practice the dictates of Islam when it came to how they treated their non-Muslim oppressors, i.e., the Christian Crusaders.

The Second Crusade

Odo de Diogilo, a monk of St. Denis, was the private chaplain to King Louis VII during the Second Crusade. In writing about his experiences, this Christian monk commented in some detail about the conduct of his Muslim opponents during this war, specifically noting the manner in which these Muslim soldiers treated the surviving Crusaders of the Second Crusade. He noted that the Muslims were moved to pity at the sight of the Crusaders' misery, tended the sick, lavishly gave money to the poor, and fed the starving. De Diogilo elaborated on the compassionate and merciful help given by the Muslim soldiers to their Crusader antagonists and contrasted that aid and comfort with how these Crusaders had been afflicted with oppression, beatings, robbery, and involuntary servitude by their Christian co-religionists of the Byzantine Empire. As a result of the caring and loving conduct of the Muslims towards the captured and defeated Crusaders, de Diogilo reported that over 3,000 of the surviving Crusaders converted to Islam and actually joined the Muslim army. This is not conversion-by-the-sword but conversion by means of mercy, humane treatment, and love of fellow man![63]

It should also be noted that adherents to the Orthodox Catholic denominations frequently allied with the Muslims against the Roman Catholic invaders from Europe, precisely because these Orthodox Catholic Christians received better treatment from the Muslims than they did from their Roman Catholic counterparts.

The Third Crusade

An even more striking example of Islamic conduct towards non-Muslims who are attacking Muslims in a war of aggression is exemplified in the pattern of conduct of Al-Malik Al-Nasr (the victorious king) Salah Al-Din (prosperity of the religion) Abu Al-Mozaffer (father of Al-Mozaffer) Yusef (Joseph) ibn Ayub (son of Ayub) ibn Shadhi (son of Shadhi) Al-Rawadiya (clan to which he belonged) Al-Hadaniya (Kurdish tribe to which he belonged), the sultan and military leader of the Muslims during the Third Crusade, who is better known in the West as Saladin. A few specific vignettes regarding Salah Al-Din's treatment of his non-Muslim attackers follow.

At one point during the course of the Third Crusade, King Richard I of England was stricken with a fever and was ingloriously confined to his sickbed within a city besieged by the forces of Salah Al-Din. Hearing of the king's plight, Salah Al-Din kept daily runners scurrying to the besieged city with baskets of snow from the mountains to lower Richard's temperature and with baskets of fresh fruit to nourish his ravaged body. It is not too much to conclude that Salah Al-Din's generosity and mercy were directly responsible for saving the life of Richard the Lionheart.[64]

On another occasion, King Richard I lost his horse during a day's battle against the army of Salah Al-Din. Before hostilities began again the next morning, Salah Al-Din sent a soldier under a flag of truce to the Crusader lines. The soldier was bringing an Arabian horse as a gift from Salah Al-Din to King Richard I in order to make sure that the English king was properly and suitably mounted for the day's approaching battle.

Once, after a battle at Beirut, 45 prisoners were taken by the army of Salah Al-Din. Among the 45 prisoners was an old man who had trouble moving. Salah Al-Din saw the old man and inquired as to why he had come to the Holy Land from so far away. The old man replied that his home was several months' journey away and that he had merely come to make a pilgrimage to the Basilica of the Holy Sepulchre. Salah Al-Din immediately had the man released and supplied him with a horse so that he could continue his pilgrimage.[65]

In 1187, Salah Al-Din defeated the Crusaders at the Battle of Hattin and took many prisoners, including King Guy and Reynald of Chatillon. While Reynald was executed for a pattern of particularly egregious and heinous war crimes, including the chronic breaking of truces, the torture and killing of civilian non-combatants, etc., King Guy and several other

Crusaders were granted clemency and released.[66]

On October 2, 1187, Salah Al-Din wrested Jerusalem away from the Crusaders. Given the fearful slaughter perpetrated by the Crusaders when they had taken Jerusalem 88 years previously, in which as many as 40,000 to 70,000 inhabitants were summarily slaughtered by the Crusaders, many must have anticipated that they would be killed in fearful revenge. However, this was not the teaching of Islam, and thus it was not the practice of Salah Al-Din. The Christian Crusaders were merely expelled from Jerusalem, each being allowed to take his wealth and possessions with him. In fact, the very wealthy Crusaders were provided with armed escorts to insure the safety of their possessions. The Orthodox Catholic Christians who were not Crusaders were allowed to continue living in Jerusalem in peace. Jews, who had been incinerated in their own synagogue by the Crusaders only 88 years previously, were once again allowed to live in Jerusalem. With regard to the latter point, a Jewish poet, Yuda Al-Harizi, memorialized Salah Al-Din's conquest of Jerusalem by noting that Salah Al-Din accepted back to Jerusalem all the children of Israel and that the Jews were now allowed to live in peace.[67]

As a final example, it is noted that while it had been the habit of King Richard I of England to execute his captives rather than to be burdened by their care, Salah Al-Din had a different strategy to avoid being bogged down by the care and policing of large numbers of prisoners of war. In short, his strategy was to release them upon their word that they would cease taking up arms against him.[68]

Summary

Admittedly, the context of war is an extreme situation. However, even within those specifics in which the Muslims of the Middle East were the targets of attempted genocide by the Western Crusaders, history records the exemplary conduct of Muslims to their Crusader foes in the Second and Third Crusades. Such behavior illustrates that the Islamic teachings regarding how a Muslim is to treat a non-Muslim are not merely empty rhetoric but are part and parcel of the very lifeblood of what it means to be a Muslim.

JEWISH-MUSLIM RELATIONS IN MUSLIM SPAIN

Prior to the expulsion of Muslim rule by Ferdinand and Isabella, Muslim Spain was a beacon of enlightenment regarding Jewish-Muslim relations. Jewish, Christian, and Muslim scholars and theologians would regularly meet in Cordova to discuss theological and philosophical issues that concerned the three great monotheistic religions. The scholarly atmosphere was one of mutual respect that encouraged scholars of all three faiths to learn from each other.

In support of the above proposition, it is perhaps sufficient to note that Maimonides, the great Jewish philosopher and theologian, was actually a student of Ibn Rushid (Averroes), the great Muslim scholar. After leaving Muslim Spain for Egypt, Maimonides worked as the personal physician to Sultan Salah Al-Din (Saladin). Further, in writing about this period of Jewish-Muslim relations, Abba Eban, the Israeli scholar and former foreign secretary of Israel, has opined that Muslim-Jewish relations in Muslim Spain was one of only two times in the history of the Jewish people in which the Jews were treated justly.[69]

THE EXPULSION OF THE JEWS FROM CHRISTIAN SPAIN

Beginning in the 15th century, Jews living in Christian Europe began to be increasingly ostracized and persecuted. In rapid succession, the Jews were expelled and deported from Vienna and Linz in 1421, from Cologne in 1424, from Augsburg in 1439, from Bavaria in 1442 and 1450, from Perugia in 1485, from Vicenza in 1486, from Parma in 1488, from Milan and Lucca in 1489, and from Tuscany in 1494. In his 1524 publication, ominously entitled *On the Jews and Their Lies*, Martin Luther, one of the most revered leaders of the Protestant Reformation, directly advocated that: Jews should be completely segregated from Christians, Jewish homes should be destroyed, Jews should be made to do forced labor, and Jewish synagogues and prayer books should be burned.[70]

However, such Christian persecution of Jews was of little consequence compared to the Christian persecution of Jews and Muslims that unfolded during the Spanish Inquisition. In 1478, their Catholic Majesties, King Ferdinand and Queen Isabella of Spain, received a papal bull from Pope Sixtus IV that authorized the Spanish Inquisition. With papal support, the Christian monarchs of Spain then initiated the Spanish Inquisition in 1483 with the expressed goal of either rooting out all Jews from Spain or forcing the Jews to convert to Christianity. During the next 12 years, approximately 13,000 Jews died as martyrs secondary to the torture and execution meted out by the Spanish Inquisition. Finally, in 1492, the Jews of Spain were met with a royal decree from their Catholic Majesties that stipulated that all Jews must either convert to Christianity and undergo baptism or be forcibly deported from Spain. While some Jews succumbed to this religious blackmail and accepted Christianity, at least outwardly, approximately 100,000 to 170,000 Jews refused to convert and were expelled from Spain.[71]

Hearing of the plight of the persecuted Jews and Muslims in Christian Spain, Sultan Beyazid II, the Muslim ruler of the Ottoman Empire, sent the Ottoman fleet under the command of Kemal Reis to evacuate the oppressed and persecuted Jews and Muslims from Christian Spain. He then settled these homeless Jews within the confines of the Ottoman Empire, many around the area of Edirne and Thessalonica, in the spring of 1492. There, within the confines of a Muslim state and government, these Jews were allowed the freedom to practice their religion and occupations and to practice a limited self-autonomy in government. In referring to his resettlement of these Jews from Spain, Sultan Beyazid II reportedly stated, "They (Ferdinand and Isabella) impoverished their kingdom and enriched mine."[72] Most of the 25,000 Jews of modern Turkey are the descendants of those Jews who were initially rescued from Christian persecution by the Muslims of the Ottoman Empire.[73]

THE *DHIMMI* DURING THE 19TH CENTURY

The concepts of the *Dhimmi* (protected person) within a Muslim state and of the *Jizyah* (payment to a Muslim state made by a *Dhimmi*) were previously introduced in this chapter. It is now time to turn to an examination of the practical application of these concepts. In so doing, I have elected to present an example that is taken from the 19th century in an area that is now part of Uzbekistan but was then known as the Khanate of Khiva. The selection of this example is based solely on personal reasons that follow from the fact my great grandparents (Abraham and Maria Dyck Dirks) and great, great grandparents (Benjamin H. and Aganetha Schartner Dirks) were *Dhimmi* in the Khanate of Khiva from 1882-1884.

The story of how my ancestors came to be *Dhimmi* in the Khanate of Khiva stretches back in time to the Protestant Reformation in the Netherlands. One of the Protestant movements in the Netherlands of the late 15th and early 16th centuries was an Anabaptist sect that later coalesced into the various Mennonite denominations found in modern Christianity. Central to the tenets and practices of these Anabaptists were absolute pacifism and a rejection of infant baptism, the latter of which was based upon a belief that an individual should make a reasoned choice to be baptized and thus should be of a reasoning age, usually defined as adulthood or post puberty.

Just as the Jews and Muslims of Spain had been persecuted throughout the Spanish Inquisition, so the Mennonites of the Netherlands were persecuted by the Netherlands' own version of the Inquisition. Many Mennonites were tortured, burned at the stake for being heretics, and drowned. To escape this persecution, these Dutch Mennonites fled to Prussia, where they were well established by early in the 18th century. However, even in German Prussia, more subtle forms of persecution and discrimination began to develop. As such, late in the 18th centuries, many Mennonites emigrated from Prussia to the Russian-controlled Ukraine under a grant of religious freedom from Empress Catharine the Great. This grant of religious freedom, given in return for the Mennonites settling and farming previously untilled agricultural land, supposedly guaranteed these Mennonite colonists that they would be forever free from military conscription and that they could establish their own churches and schools free from Russian Christian interference.

In 1871, rumors began to sweep through the Karlswalde Mennonite Colony in Volhynia, Russia, (now in northwestern Ukraine) that the Russian czar had revoked the privileges originally granted to the Mennonites by Catherine the Great. Later, it was confirmed that a decree of 1870 had stipulated that certain aspects of the Mennonites' religious freedom were to be revoked in 1880. In response, many Mennonites emigrated from Russia to the United States beginning in 1874. However, some Mennonites chose to remain in Russia until the 1880 deadline approached and then chose to emigrate to the Khanate of Khiva, which was a Muslim country. My ancestors were among this latter group.

The bedraggled and impoverished Mennonite caravans on the way to the Khanate of Khiva were forced to spend the winter of 1881-1882 in the all-Muslim town of Sirbulak, Russia. Fleeing from persecution by their fellow Christians in Russia, the Mennonites in Sirbulak were overcome by Muslim kindness and generosity. The Muslims of Sirbulak gave the Mennonites permission to conduct weekly worship services in the local mosque and prepared food for the hungry and impoverished Mennonites, even during the Islamic month of *Ramadan* (July of 1882) when Muslims fast from sunup to sunset. Even though the Muslims were denied all food and drink throughout the daylight hours of this month, they made sure that their Christian "guests" were properly fed throughout the day.

Finally, in late July of 1882, the Mennonite refugees received permission to enter the Khanate of Khiva. However, to reach the Khanate of Khiva, the Mennonite colonists had to travel through another Muslim country, the Khanate of Bukhara. To insure their safety during their journey through Bukhara to Khiva and presumably knowing that the Mennonites were pacifists whose religious beliefs prohibited them from defending themselves, the *Khan or 'Amir* of Bukhara assigned an escort of Bukharan soldiers to accompany the Mennonite refugees to Bukhara's border with Khiva. These Muslim soldiers not only provided protection but also arranged for food for the Christian refugees, repaired bridges for the caravan wagons to cross, and even tore down fences and led the refugee caravan across cultivated land in order that the journey for the caravan members would be as short and as comfortable as possible. All of this was consistent with Islamic law, which specifies that a Christian family in a Muslim country must be protected by the Muslim government.

Upon finally reaching the Khanate of Khiva at the end of September of 1882, these Christian refugees who had fled from Christian persecution to find religious freedom in a Muslim land were welcomed with open arms by the *Khan* of Khiva. The *Khan* offered them legal residency, freedom of religious faith and practice, exemption from military service according to their religious beliefs, and as much free land as they might want for their agricultural pursuits in a previously unproductive area on the west bank of the Amu Darya River in Lausan, about 85 miles north of the city of Khiva and about 95 miles south of the Aral Sea, near Nukus. Of note, this land was easily irrigated by digging trenches from the nearby river, and the Mennonites quickly established a system of irrigation trenches. In exchange, the *Jizyah* set by the *Khan* was 05% of the yearly harvest of the Mennonites and 12 days of free labor from each adult Mennonite male per year. In appreciation for this most generous offer, the Mennonites also promised that they would not raise pigs, an animal considered to be unlawful by both Muslims and Orthodox Jews.

In considering the *Jizyah* (05% of the yearly harvest and 12 days of free labor per year per adult male) imposed on these Mennonite refugees in the Khanate of Khiva, it is instructive to compare this *Jizyah* with the *Zakat* (obligatory charity) imposed on Muslim subjects in a Muslim state. A Muslim resident of the state, who may not have been given any free land by the state, would have still been required to give 05% of the produce from his irrigated land in *Zakat* and would still have been liable for military conscription etc.[74] As can be seen, the Mennonite refugees from Christian persecution in Russia were not only granted religious freedom and free agricultural land by the Muslim state but were actually taxed at a rate comparable to that paid by a Muslim resident of the state.

The Mennonite colony in the Khanate of Khiva collapsed in 1884, secondary to crop failure caused by a grasshopper infestation. These Christian refugees then left for the United States. However, the short life of the Mennonite colony in Khiva does not invalidate or alter the examples of religious pluralism and of Islamic conduct towards Christian refugees that are embedded within this history.

SUMMARY AND CONCLUSIONS

The foregoing discussion has examined the Qur'anic precepts governing Muslim relations with non-Muslims, Prophet Muhammad's example of how Muslims should interact with non-Muslims, and several historical examples of good and wholesome relations between Muslims and non-Muslims. Within all three categories of information, one finds a shining paradigm for ecumenism and religious pluralism. In presenting these illustrious examples of Muslim interaction with non-Muslims, I do not pretend to be so naïve or so misleading as to maintain that some deviant examples of Muslim conduct towards non-Muslims cannot be found within the pages of recorded history. Sadly, there are historical examples of some Muslims treating non-Muslims in a way that is forbidden by Islam. However, such deviant examples are not representative of the religious teachings of Islam and of true Islamic conduct.

Islamophobia in the Christian West

INTRODUCTION

Any cursory perusal of the American media's coverage of Islam reveals a consistent pattern of misrepresentation and distortion. The American media erroneously and rather systematically portrays Islam as being a primitive, backwards, and third-world religion of violence, militaristic subjugation, oppression of women, sexual exploitation, erotic harem life, and fanaticism. However, these egregious misrepresentations and malicious distortions of Islam in Western circles do not begin with the modern American media and have had a long, slanderous, and defamatory history, which stretches back in time at least 900 years into the dimly lit recesses of European art and literature. While current limitations of space and time preclude a thorough analysis and review of the history of Islamophobia in the Occident, the following milestones are worthy of mention.

A BRIEF TOUR OF HISTORY

Clermont and the Crusades

At the Council of Clermont on November 25, 1095, Pope Urban II sanctified the Christian concept of *sacrum bellum* (Holy War) when he offered plenary indulgence (forgiveness of all past sins) for any person willing to join the First Crusade and wage Holy War against the Muslims in the Middle East. In making his plea, Pope Urban II branded all Muslims as "an accursed race, a race utterly alienated from God, a generation, forsooth, which has neither directed its heart nor entrusted its spirit to God." He further urged his soon-to-be Crusaders to "exterminate this vile race from our lands." He closed his rallying cry for this so-called Holy War by emoting, "*Deus volt*" (God wills it).[75]

Pope Urban II's statements at the Council of Clermont are all the more egregious in that he should have known better than to utter such religious bigotry and hatred. After all, only 19 years previously, Urban II's predecessor, Pope Gregory VII, had written the following words to Al-Nasir, the Muslim ruler of Bijaya (modern Algeria).

> Almighty God, who wishes that all should be saved and none lost, approves nothing in so much as that after loving Him one should love his fellow man, and that one should not do to others what one does not want done to oneself. You and we owe this charity to ourselves, especially because we believe in and confess one God, admittedly, in a different way, and daily praise and venerate Him, the creator of the world and ruler of this world.[76]

Despite the ecumenical fellowship implied in Pope Gregory VII's missive, Pope Urban II cried out for a genocidal war against all Muslims, and the resulting barbarities and atrocities of the so-called "Christian" Crusaders cannot easily be overlooked. In a complete negation of the Biblical message of Jesus Christ, these "Christian" Crusaders from the West committed one outrage after another against Muslims, as well as against Eastern Christians and Jews. The following list serves only to highlight some of the more odious Islamophobic atrocities committed by these so-called Crusaders for Christ.

In late 1168, Bilgays fell to the conquering army of King Amalric of Jerusalem and his army of self-avowed Christian Crusaders. The entire population of the city was put to death after the city fell. Men, women, and children were all slaughtered indiscriminately and without regard for such distinctions as military combatants vs. civilian non-combatants. Further, as religious bigotry often knows no limits, the Crusaders made no distinction between Muslims and Coptic Christians in their fearful onslaught on the city's inhabitants. Both Muslims and non-Western Christians were victims of that awful slaughter.[77]

In 1194, during the Third Crusade, approximately 3,000 civilian non-combatants (including women and children) and prisoners of war were summarily executed in Castle Acre under the orders of Richard the Lionheart, King of England and Duke of Normandy. At the time of their execution, these individuals were completely defenseless. Approximately 2,700 of these victims were soldiers who had been taken captive and made prisoners of war, while almost 300 victims were women and children. When burdened by Muslim prisoners of war, King Richard's solution was simply to have them executed.[78]

However, the atrocity perpetrated at Castle Acre was nothing compared to those that had happened ninety-five years previously during the First Crusade. On July 15, 1099, Muslim Jerusalem fell to a conquering army of Christian Crusaders. The atrocities committed over the next two days were almost beyond comprehension. (1) The victorious and Christian conquerors slaughtered between 40,000 and 70,000 people in Jerusalem, most of whom were civilian non-combatants and many of whom were women and children. (2) In their desperation to escape the fearful slaughter, the Jews of the city barricaded themselves inside a synagogue, hoping that the conquerors would respect their house of worship. However, there was no sanctuary to be found from the Crusaders in the synagogue, and the victorious Christian soldiers promptly set the synagogue afire, incinerating the Jewish population of Jerusalem. (3) The Eastern Christian priests of the Basilica of the Holy Sepulchre were driven from their church, and many were tortured in order to get them to confess where they had hidden their religious relics. (A fact often not recounted by Western historians is that the Eastern Christians of the various Orthodox Catholic denominations frequently allied with the Muslims against their Western Christian co-religionists over the course of the Crusades, because these Orthodox Catholics knew that they would receive better treatment and greater religious freedom from the Muslims than from their Christian counterparts from the West.) (4) In another house of worship within Jerusalem, i.e., the Dome of the Rock, the third holiest site in Islam, the conquering Christian Crusaders completely vandalized and desecrated the building. They stole everything of value, including: 40 large, silver candelabra; 150 smaller, silver candelabra; a great silver lamp; and more than 20 gold candelabra.[79]

One of the victorious combatants, i.e., Raymond of Aguiles, memorialized his participation in these atrocities at Jerusalem, and his comments are quoted immediately below.

> Wonderful sights were to be seen. Some of our men (and this was more merciful) cut off the heads of their enemies; others shot them with arrows, so that they fell from the towers; others tortured them longer by casting them into the flames. Piles of heads, hands and feet were to be seen in the streets of the city. It was necessary to pick one's way over the bodies of men and horses. But these were small matters compared to what happened at the Temple of Solomon, a place where religious services are normally chanted…in the Temple and porch of Solomon, men rode in blood up to their knees and bridle reins."[80]

According to Raymond, a stalwart Christian Crusader, "(p)iles of heads, hands and feet," the torturing of Muslims by burning them alive, and riding horses in rivers of Muslim blood were "(w)onderful sights to be seen." The brutality and barbarity of the above can hardly be imagined by any civilized man or woman. However, even these heinous actions of the Christian Crusaders during their sacking of Jerusalem paled beside the events following the First Crusade's fall of Ma'arra beginning on December 12, 1098. For three days, the victorious Crusader army slaughtered every man, woman, and child of the city. The death toll was enormous, and thousands upon thousands were put to the sword. However, the unimaginable atrocities did not stop at that point. The conquering Crusaders actually practiced mass cannibalism upon the former inhabitants of Ma'arra. Two, independent, eyewitness accounts from the ranks of the Christian victors are worth noting. The first was penned by Radulph of Caen, who referred to Muslims as pagans, and the latter was written by Albert of Aix.

> In Ma'arra our troops boiled pagan adults in cooking pots; they impaled children on spits and devoured them grilled.[81]

> Not only did our troops not shrink from eating dead Turks and Saracens; they also ate dogs![82]

History has seldom recorded such brutalities and barbarities committed against the adherents of one religion (Islam) by the self-confessed proponents of another religion (Christianity).

The *Chanson de Geste*

Circa 1100, what is presumed to be the earliest of the *chanson de geste* (song of deeds) was penned in France. The 4,000-line *La Chanson de Roland* (*Song of Roland*), presumably written by Turold, an otherwise obscure Norman poet, ushered in the age of French epic poetry, which was later popularized by the *trouveres* (troubadours) of the 13th century, and which continued unabated until the dawn of the 17th century. *La Chanson de Roland* presents a highly fictionalized and historically inaccurate rendition of the Battle of Roncevaux in 778, a largely insignificant skirmish between the Franks and the Basques. However, as transformed by the pen of Turold, the Battle of Roncevaux becomes an epic confrontation between the rear guard of Charlemagne's victorious army and the Muslims of Andalusia, who are portrayed as having treacherously and immorally broken their terms of surrender as hammered out in a formal treaty with Ganelon, the authorized representative of Charlemagne. Of note, Ganelon is represented in the song as being a co-conspirator with the Muslims. According to the ongoing fictions of *La Chanson de Roland*, as Charlemagne's army crossed the Pyrenees in its return to France, the rear guard under the command of Roland, Duke of the Marches and Brittany, was surrounded by the "treacherous" Muslims of Andalusia at the Pass of Roncevaux, and was exterminated in a "heroic last stand" worthy of the most exaggerated accounts of the Spartans at Thermopylae, the Texans at the Alamo, or the U.S. Seventh Cavalry at the Little Bighorn.[83]

Not withstanding the undisputed historical fact that the Muslims of

Andalusia were not even present at the Battle of Roncevaux, under the influence of the *La Chanson de Roland*, the French *chanson de geste* quickly became a literary art form that specialized in Islamophobia. Stretching the boundaries of "artistic license" beyond all finite limits, the historical saga of Charlemagne was transformed into a cosmic conflict between good and evil. It should come as no surprise that the forces of good were represented in these *chanson* by Charlemagne and the "Twelve Noble Peers" of Christendom. In marked contrast, evil was personified in the form of a "polytheistic" and "idolatrous" Muslim enemy, who regularly bowed down to worship idols of Prophet Muhammad and Apollo, the latter having somehow been magically transformed from being one of the deities among the fabled pantheon of Greek and Roman mythology atop Mt. Olympus into being a god in the non-existent pantheon of Islam.[84]

Dante

The next stop on our brief historical tour of Islamophobia in the Christian Occident takes us from early 12th-century France to early 14th-century Italy. Dante Alighiere (1265-1321) was a famed Florentine poet, whose most famous work was *La Commedia*, which was later renamed *La Divina Commedia* (*The Divine Comedy*). Presumably written between the years 1307 and 1321, *The Divine Comedy* offers the reader successive tours of hell, purgatory, and paradise. For our purposes, it is the journey through hell that is most illustrative, for it is in the deeper recesses of hell that Dante assigns Prophet Muhammad and identifies him as being "chief among the damned souls who have brought schism into religion."[85] Within hell, Prophet Muhammad is portrayed as being split from head to waist and as tearing apart his own breast with his bare hands.[86]

Chaucer

Moving along in our literary review from early 14th-century Italy to late 14th-century England, we are immediately confronted by the classic writings of Chaucer, an English court poet. His *Canterbury Tales* is a classic of English literature, to which countless generations of American high school students have been exposed, albeit often against their will. Comprised of 24 tales told by a group of fictitious individuals making a pilgrimage to

Canterbury Cathedral, eight of the tales take place outside of the Christian Occident, and one of those, i.e., the Man of Law's Tale, is of particular interest in charting the history of Islamophobia in Christendom.

According to Chaucer's Man of Law, Muslims were worse than pagans. In support of this Islamophobic propaganda, the Man of Law maintained that pagans had the potential to be eventually converted into and absorbed by Christendom.   In contrast, Muslims were presented as a treacherous people who comprised a barbarous nation, who committed abominations, who engaged in behavior that is anathema to civilized society, and who were completely beyond divine redemption. If that weren't enough, the tale propagated the myth that Muslims automatically kill all individuals who convert from Islam to Christianity. Still further, the tale associated Islam with the Assyrian queen Semiramia, thus building an association to legalized incest and erotic decadence. In short, Muslims were portrayed as being evil incarnate.[87]

Voltaire

Journeying from late 14th-century England to the "Enlightenment" of 18th-century France, we encounter Voltaire's tragedy,[88] *Mahomet le Prophete, ou le Fanatisme*. In *Mahomet*, Voltaire described Prophet Muhammad as being a rebellious and seditious camel-dealer, who fabricated a series of revelations to produce a *Qur'an* in which "every page does violence to sober reason,"[89] and who murdered men and abducted women in order to force conversion upon his peers. First presented in 1742, the play's Islamophobia exceeded even that permitted during 18th-century France, and the play was banned. In his later writings, Voltaire softened his criticism ever so slightly, apparently being satisfied to label Prophet Muhammad as being cruel and brutal.[90]

The Modern Era and The Christian Right

Unfortunately, such blasphemous distortions of Islam are not confined to the literary arts of Europe in the bygone days of the medieval era and the so-called Enlightenment. During the 19th century, Occidental artists created numerous paintings that depicted Muslims as bloody-sword-wielding warriors and as overindulging in the erotic enticements of sultry harems.[91]

By the dawn of the 20th century, Western art and literature had indelibly engrained in the Occidental mind a picture of Islam as a polytheistic religion of idolatry and of Prophet Muhammad as the Antichrist and as a blood-thirsty, hyper-libidinous epileptic with delusions of religious grandeur. Within the last year, such fallacious images have become regular propaganda pronouncements by the ministerial representatives of the religious right of American Christianity. Unfortunately, these pronouncements of, dare one say it, militant Christian extremists have received extensive media coverage without the media giving Muslims equal time to respond to the malicious distortions of Islam embedded in these propaganda attacks. The following examples of the Islamophobia of the militant Christian extremists are especially noteworthy.

On an October 6, 2002, broadcast of *Sixty Minutes* and contrary to all historical evidence, Jerry Falwell, a ministerial spokesman for the religious right of Christianity, claimed that Prophet Muhammad was a terrorist. His statement that Prophet Muhammad was a terrorist was repeated on the November 18, 2002, edition of *ABC News*. However, the Christian Right's relentless attack against Islam does not end with Jerry Falwell.

Comments from other ministerial spokesmen of the Christian Right were also carried on the November 18, 2002, edition of *ABC News*. Pat Robertson was shown saying that what the Muslims wanted to do to the Jews was even worse than what Adolf Hitler had done to them. Jimmy Swaggert opined that America should ship "every single Muslim student in every college in this nation…back to where they came from." However, the prize for vitriolic hatred and slander went to Jerry Vines, who pronounced that Prophet Muhammad was "a demon-possessed pedophile," apparently because one of Prophet Muhammad's wives was just past puberty at the time of their marriage. In making this charge, Mr. Vines conveniently ignored the fact that the marriage of females shortly after attaining puberty was a marital custom that was common throughout most of history up until the last century.

With regard to Mr. Vines's comments, it should be noted that many Biblical scholars place the age of the Virgin Mary upon giving birth to Jesus Christ at about 14 years. If Mr. Vines were to apply contemporary American standards, as they are currently codified in the laws of many states, to his understanding of the conception and birth of Jesus Christ, i.e., that Jesus is the begotten son of "God the Father," in a manner consistent with his applying contemporary American standards to Prophet Muhammad's marriage to 'Aisha, then he should conclude that his "God the Father" was guilty of statutory rape against the Virgin Mary. While no Muslim, myself included, would ever make such a slanderous charge against God, the comparison shows the ludicrous results that can be obtained by anachronistically applying current standards to situations that existed over 1,300 years ago. One only wishes that Mr. Vines had considered this before making his heinous accusations.

However, the Islamophobic attacks of the militant Christian extremists were only just beginning. Additional charges against Islam and against Prophet Muhammad were quickly uttered by Pat Robertson on the November 24, 2002, edition of ABC's *This Week with George Stephanopoulos*. During this broadcast, Mr. Robertson leveled the following accusations: (1) Prophet Muhammad was a warrior; (2) Prophet Muhammad preached a doctrine of "*Jihad* against the infidels;" (3) Islam fosters a view that Jews   are the descendants of apes and pigs, calls for the destruction of all Jews, and propagates a virulent hatred of Jews; (4) Islam is violent at its core, as attested to by the so-called Islamic Conquest; (5) "the people of Madinah   were Jews, and he (Prophet Muhammad) killed everyone of them;" and   (6) Muslims are the "kind of people" that "murder their enemies."

With regard to the first accusation leveled by Mr. Robertson, it is sufficient to examine the life of Prophet Muhammad. Despite the seemingly unbearable persecution and assassination attempts leveled against him during a time and setting marked by incessant tribal warfare, Prophet Muhammad's entire life record reveals only 82 battles fought under his command or sanction. The duration of most of these battles was only a single day in length, and, if one were to add up all of these battles, they would occupy far less than one of the Prophet's approximately 62 years of life. Furthermore, throughout these 82 battles, only 1,018 people (259 Muslims and 759 non-Muslims) were actually killed. On the average, only 12.4

individuals lost their lives in each battle, demonstrating quite convincingly that it is quite misleading simply to characterize Prophet Muhammad as a warrior. Clearly, the Prophet's life serves as a superlative model of restraint in warfare, not as a model of an aggressive warrior.[92]

With regard to Mr. Robertson's second accusation, it is noted that *Jihad* means "striving" or "effort" and does not mean "Holy War." This point will be elaborated later on in this chapter (see pgs. 180-182). Further, the call to wage war against infidels was specific to those infidels who had treasonously broken their peace treaties with the early Muslim community, who had actively attacked the Muslim community, or who had actively abetted the attackers of the Muslim community. This point is also elucidated further on pgs. 180-182 in this chapter. Mr. Robertson's third accusation, i.e., that Islam fosters a view that all Jews are the descendants of pigs and apes, calls for the destruction of all Jews, and propagates a virulent hatred of Jews, was previously refuted in the preceding chapter, which documents the enormous fallacy of Mr. Robertson's charge. As demonstrated in the prior chapter, the *Qur'an* teaches that all humans descend from a common ancestor and that there are righteous Jews and unrighteous Jews. Further, the historical examples illustrated in the prior chapter document how Muslims frequently saved the Jews from their Christian oppressors and persecutors.

With regard to Mr. Robertson's fourth accusation, i.e., that Islam is inherently violent, as supposedly attested to by the Islamic Conquest, the true facts regarding the so-called Islamic Conquest were elucidated on pgs. 156-158 (*The Islamic Conquest*) of the preceding chapter. However, even if Mr. Robertson's highly distorted views of the Islamic Conquest were accepted as fact, it would hardly make Islam any more violent than the violence committed by the Christian Crusaders and more recently by Christian Serbia (see pgs. 168-170, 179 of this chapter). Why is Mr. Robertson not bewailing the violent history that is Christianity? Given the historical record documenting unending Christian violence and torture during the Crusades, the Spanish Inquisition, and the genocidal wars launched against Muslims in modern Bosnia and Kosovo by Christian Serbia, one would think that Mr. Robertson would want to get his own religious house in order before misrepresenting the religious beliefs of others.

Mr. Robertson's fifth accusation, i.e., that the people of Madinah were Jews and that Prophet Muhammad killed everyone one of them, is a complete distortion of history. At the time that Prophet Muhammad moved to Madinah, the people of Madinah consisted of two Arab tribes and three Jewish tribes. Although some Jewish males, not females or children, were executed for treason against the Islamic state of Madinah, it is a complete fabrication to say that Prophet Muhammad killed all the Jews of Madinah or to say that all the people of Madinah were Jews. As to Prophet Muhammad's conduct towards the Jews of Madinah, one needs only to turn to pgs. 154-155 in the preceding chapter.

With regard to Mr. Robertson's sixth accusation, i.e., that Muslims are the kind of people that murder their enemies, one need only consider the following verses from the *Qur'an*.

> Nor take life—which God has made sacred—except for just cause. And if anyone is slain wrongfully, we have given his heir authority (to demand retribution or to forgive): but let him not exceed bounds in the matter of taking life: for he is helped (by the law). (*Qur'an* 17:33)

> On that account: We ordained for the children of Israel that if anyone slew a person—unless it be for murder or for spreading mischief in the land—it would be as if he slew the whole people: and if anyone saved a life it would be as if he saved the life of the whole people. Then although there came to them Our messengers with clear signs, yet, even after that, many of them continued to commit excesses in the land. (*Qur'an* 5:32)

20th Century Academia

Even within the hallowed and ivy-covered walls of 20th-century academia, the misrepresentation and distortion of Islam have been something of a cottage industry. In particular, Islam has often been poorly represented and understood in the 20th-century writings of academically sanctioned Orientalists and reputed scholars of comparative religion. A brief sampling of their errors and misrepresentations should suffice to illustrate this point.

(1) With regard to the Battle of Badr, the Battle of Uhud, and the Battle of the Trench, John Hardon, a Jesuit priest and recognized "expert" on comparative religion, has written that all three battles were "provoked by Mohammed."[93]

(2) W. Montgomery Watt has written of Prophet Muhammad's "connivance at assassinations,"[94] a charge that was also maintained by Alfred Guillaume.[95]

(3) John Wansbrough and his academic followers have written and taught that the text of the *Qur'an* was not standardized until almost 150 years after the death of Prophet Muhammad, that there are no reliable sources on the historical life of Prophet Muhammad to be found in Muslim literature, and that the religion of Islam was originally called Hagarism.[96]

(4) Alfred Guillaume has also written that: (A) the *Qur'an* was written by Prophet Muhammad with help from non-Arabs who had access to and borrowed heavily from the *Bible* and *Talmud*; and (B) in Islam, "(a) woman cannot sue for divorce, on any grounds, and her husband may beat her,"[97] fabrications that will be debunked later in the following chapter.

(5) Lars Qualben, whose specialty was Christian church history, appears to have gone out of his way to demonstrate his Islamophobia, his gross misunderstanding of Islam, and his absolute intolerance of many branches of early Christianity.

Mohammed, epileptic in childhood...The religion of his people was heathenism, but Mohammed and his tribe came in frequent contact with Judaism and degenerate forms of Christianity (Ebionism, Arianism, and Sabellianism)...(In Islam) there are two classes of angels: good and bad...No atonement is necessary... the best of all (good works) is war—even to death—against the unbelievers...Polygamy and concubinage are encouraged... Islam is a strange admixture of heathenism, Judaism, and Ebionite Christianity...the "holy war" of the spread of Islam.[98]

In response, one can only note that: (1) Prophet Muhammad was not an epileptic; (2) Arianism and the religion of the Ebionites were closer to the teachings of Jesus Christ and his actual disciples than was Pauline Christianity, which was the foundation of contemporary Christianity; (3) there are no "bad" angels in Islamic angelology, because Islam holds that angels have no free will and can therefore never go astray; (4) Islam actually put limits and conditions on polygamy and concubinage, something the *Bible* never did; and (5) there is no "Holy War" concept in Islam.

Bosnia and Kosovo

The last decade of the 20th century witnessed massive carnage in the Balkans, as Christian Serbia conducted genocidal wars against the Muslims of Bosnia and Kosovo. Euphemistically billed as "ethnic cleansing," the Christian Serbian onslaught against Muslim Bosnia resulted in at least 200,000 fatalities and in more than two million individuals being driven from their homes by the end of 1994, and it was only terminated secondary to markedly belated NATO intervention.[99] However, the Balkan conflict was not yet over. Christian Serbia then proceeded to attack Kosovo. By June of 1999, the "ethnic cleansing" of Kosovo had resulted in an untold number of deaths and in hundreds of thousands of refugees being driven out of Kosovo. The Kosovo conflict, like the conflict in Bosnia, was also ended only through NATO military intervention.[100]

Summary and Conclusions

It is a well known fact that it takes substantially longer to rebut a charge than it does to make one. Ten or more fallacious statements can be made against Islam in a matter of a minute or two of media coverage or within the confines of a few simple sentences of printed text. In contrast, to thoroughly rebut those charges in a scholarly manner with hard evidence could take multiple volumes of books. To illustrate this, consider the following theoretical charge against Christianity: most Biblical scholars claim that Mary was only about 14 years old at the time of giving birth to Jesus Christ, therefore, under the laws of many of the individual states comprising the United States, God the Father committed statutory rape against Mary. To thoroughly rebut the charge, one would have to: (1) examine and present all the evidence, circumstantial and otherwise, concerning Mary's age; (2) analyze and present the statutory rape statutes of all 50 states; (3) deal with the issue of the begotten vs. the created "sonship" of Jesus; (4) discuss and define the concept of God the Father; and (5) etc.

It is obviously easier to attack than to defend. As such, and given the enormous expenditure of time and space that would be required to defend Islam from each of the attacks against it that have been detailed on pages 174-178 of this chapter, I am left with having simply to make a blanket denial of the accuracy of all of the Islamophobic attacks delineated above, whether such attacks have come from ancient literary sources, from the militant Christian extremists of the present moment, or from those 20th-century Orientalists and academicians whose own Islamophobia fuels their tainted scholarship.

THE AMERICAN MEDIA AND ISLAM

Introduction

Given the preceding history of the presentation of Islam in Occidental art, literature, Christendom, and academia, it is small wonder that the American media exhibits all the external symptoms of full-fledged Islamophobia. However, it is not now my intention to excuse or to rational-ize the prevalence of Islam-bashing in the American media. Rather, I wish to look at some of the characteristic ways in which the American media continues to distort Islam into the worst possible caricature of itself. The following list is hardly exhaustive, but it does highlight some of the more typical ways in which Islam is demonized in the American media.

Mistranslation of Arabic Words

In the wake of September 11, 2001, the American media has inundated the reading and viewing public with the word "*Jihad*." Unfortunately, the American media appears to delight in mistranslating *Jihad* as "Holy War," thus creating an almost automatic reflex of fear and disgust among non-Muslims whenever they hear that term.

The noun "*Jihad*" is from the verb "*Jahada*," which means "to strive" or "to exert." Thus, the correct translation of *Jihad* is "striving, exertion, or effort." Within the Islamic context, *Jihad* means "striving for the sake of God." Thus, any activity in which one strives for the sake of God is *Jihad*. Given that understanding, it is noted that the most prevalent form of *Jihad* is preaching or religious and moral exhortation. *Jihad*-as-exhortation may take the form of: inviting non-Muslims into the fold of Islam, and offering verbal disapproval of the traditional worship of non-Muslims; firmness in presenting the truth, especially as it relates to issues of religion, morality, and justice; and enlightening others as to the *Qur'an* and its message of divine revelation. It is this last form of *Jihad* that is enjoined upon Muslims in the following passage from the *Qur'an*.

> Therefore listen not to the unbelievers, but strive (*Jihad*) against them with the utmost strenuousness with the (*Qur'an*). (*Qur'an* 25:52)

As the above should illustrate, *Jihad*-as-exhortation is a far cry from "Holy War." Furthermore, it should be noted that God's words "with the utmost strenuousness" suggest that *Jihad*-as exhortation may well be the greatest of all kinds of *Jihad*. This conclusion is echoed in the following *Hadith*, in which Prophet Muhammad emphasized the superiority of *Jihad*-as-exhortation.

> Abu Sa'id Al-Khudri reported the Apostle of God as saying: "The best striving (*Jihad*) in the path of God is (to speak) a word of justice to an oppressive ruler." (*Abu Dawud, Hadith* #4330)

Jihad means "effort" or "striving" or "exertion," and perhaps the highest form of *Jihad* is *Jihad*-as-exhortation. *Jihad* may also refer to an individual's struggle against his own base instincts or to any other effort engaged in for the sake of God, including marriage, parenting, being a good neighbor, etc. *Jihad* does not mean "Holy War," although it is possible that *Jihad* might include fighting for the sake of God. However, fighting or war is only one small aspect of *Jihad*, and the Prophet clearly stated that *Jihad*-as-war is not the highest form of *Jihad*.

Nonetheless, the American media continues to insist on translating *Jihad* as "Holy War" despite the fact that the Arabic equivalent of

"Holy War" appears nowhere in the *Qur'an*, despite the fact that the term "Holy War" owes its popularity and conceptual foundation to its use by Christians in justifying the *Reconquista* (Christian conquest of Andalusia) and the Occidental barbarisms of the Christian Crusades, and despite the fact that Islam has no equivalent concept to the medieval Christian belief in *sacrum bellum* (Holy War).

As can be seen, the concept of Holy War is a Western Christian term, not an Islamic term. Distortion of Islam is inherent whenever the media applies Christian concepts, such as Holy War, in translating Islamic terms from Arabic. Without going into detail, words such as "fundamentalist" and "fundamentalism" are further examples of the misrepresentation of Islam by utilizing Christian-based concepts to describe Muslims and their religion.

Quoting The *Qur'an* and *Ahadith* out of context

A second technique used by the media to misrepresent Islam is to quote verses of the *Qur'an* and various portions of the *Ahadith* out of context, thus distorting their original meaning beyond all recognition. As an example, in mid-October of 2001, a commentator on a national network television show in the United States maintained that Islam was a religion of war, which preaches that all Muslims are directed to kill all non-Muslims. He then proceeded to confront a panel of several young Muslims with the following passage from the *Qur'an*.

> But when the forbidden months are past, then fight and slay the pagans wherever ye find them, and seize them, beleaguer them, and lie in wait for them in every stratagem (of war)... (*Qur'an* 9:5a)

Unfortunately, the panel of young Muslims failed to respond directly to the passage being quoted. Had they done so, they might have pointed out that the commentator had quoted a passage that had been ripped totally out of its context within the *Qur'an*. The appropriate context for the passage in question is established merely by quoting the four verses preceding this verse, the remainder of this verse, and the immediately subsequent verse.

> A (declaration) of immunity from God and His messenger, to those of the pagans with whom ye have contracted mutual alliances—go

ye, then, for four months, backwards and forwards, (as ye will), throughout the land, but know ye that ye cannot frustrate God (by your falsehood) but that God will cover with shame those who reject Him. And an announcement from God and His messenger, to the people (assembled) on the day of the great pilgrimage—that God and His messenger dissolve (treaty) obligations with the pagans. If, then, ye repent, it were best for you; but if ye turn away, know ye that ye cannot frustrate God. And proclaim a grievous penalty to those who reject faith. (But the treaties are) not dissolved with those pagans with whom ye have entered into alliance and who have not subsequently failed you in aught, nor aided anyone against you. So fulfill your engagements with them to the end of their term: for God loveth the righteous. But when the forbidden months are past, then fight and slay the pagans wherever ye find them, and seize them, beleaguer them, and lie in wait for them in every stratagem (of war); but if they repent, and establish regular prayers and practice regular charity, then open the way for them: for God is oft-forgiving, most merciful. If one amongst the pagans asks thee for asylum, grant it to him, so that he may hear the word of God; and then escort him to where he can be secure. That is because they are men without knowledge. (*Qur'an* 9:1-6)

Read within its context, it is clear that the passage in question is not advocating the wholesale destruction of pagan people or of any other people. Rather, *Jihad*-as-war is prescribed only against those pagans who are actively fighting against the Muslim *Ummah* (nation or community). In other words, the passage in question prescribes war in cases of self-defense. This is amply demonstrated by the injunctions to: honor prior treaties, if they have been upheld by the other side; accept any repentance and conversion to Islam that the pagans offer; and grant asylum and safe escort to a place of security to any combatant who asks for it. Muslims are to grant safe refuge when asked for it by any combatant who ceases to fight against them, and they should take that opportunity to practice *Jihad*-as exhortation, i.e., "so that he may hear the word of God." Whether or not the asylum-seeker accepts Islam, Muslims are then to "escort him to where he can be secure."

Seen within this context, the Qur'anic passage quoted by the television commentator is anything but an injunction to kill all non-Muslims. Rather, the passage permits Muslims to wage *Jihad*-as-war against those who are actively fighting against them, i.e., to fight a war of self-defense, but then directs Muslims to give asylum, religious exhortation, and safe conduct to anyone who surrenders his arms. This is not religion by the sword, but a religion of mercy, for "God is oft-forgiving, most merciful."

Quite frankly, examples such as the above begin to strain the imagination of those charitable souls who would like to attribute the media's quoting out of context to sloppy and negligent research.

Confusing Culture with Religion

A third way in which the American media distorts Islam is by attempting to merge the worst features of certain third world cultures with the religion of Islam. As one example, I refer you to a PBS special entitled *Murder in Purdah*, which aired in my home area a couple of years ago. Focusing on the plight of our Muslim sisters in the hinterlands of Pakistan, the program systematically served up the worst cultural abuses of women in rural Pakistan as though these heinous actions were inherently symptomatic of Islam, even though in reality they were obvious violations of Islam. Involuntary and forced marriages, blatant subjugation of women, spousal abuse, and murder of sisters, daughters, and wives were all portrayed as being examples of Islamic teaching. Cultural psychopathology was erroneously labeled as being the religious standards of Islam. Packaged as an informative and newsworthy documentary, the program was nothing more than Islamophobic propaganda.

Confusing Islam with other Religions

Following the arrest of John Allen Williams, a.k.a. John Allen Muhammad, the Beltway Sniper who terrorized Maryland and Virginia in October of 2002, both print and TV media outlets were quick to inform the world that Mr. Williams was a Muslim. This religious identification seemed to be repeated with every mention of Mr. Williams by the media, as though to make sure that the American public identified the Beltway killings with

Islam. To further aid in that identification, the media constantly referred to Mr. Williams by his adopted name of John Allen Muhammad. Having heard literally scores of times from news reporters and TV anchormen that Mr. Williams was a Muslim, what other conclusion could the American public draw than that Mr. Williams was a Muslim. But, was he?

The fact is that Mr. Williams is not a Muslim and apparently has never been a Muslim. Mr. Williams is, however, a member of the Nation of Islam, a religious group headed by Louis Farakhan, which is not part of Islam, despite its self-chosen name. The Nation of Islam was not even founded until the 20th century and is indigenous to the United States. The Nation of Islam religion was created by W.D. Fard, a.k.a. Wali Fard Muhammad, in Detroit, Michigan, in 1930. The movement then came under the leadership of Elijah Poole, a.k.a. Elijah Muhammad, in the mid-1930s, and he continued to lead the movement until his death in 1975. For an older generation of Americans, the Nation of Islam is synonymous with the so-called Black Muslim movement of the 1960s.

A simple recounting of three of the articles of belief of the Nation of Islam should make it abundantly clear to non-Muslim readers that the Nation of Islam is a totally distinct and separate religion from Islam. Firstly, within the Nation of Islam, it is accepted that W.D. Fard, the founder of the religion, was God. Secondly, within the Nation of Islam, it is accepted that Elijah Muhammad was a prophet and messenger of God. Thirdly, the Nation of Islam preaches the separation of the races and the racial superiority of Blacks, while traditionally claiming that Caucasians are literally the devil.[101]

All three of the above beliefs of the Nation of Islam are anathema to Muslims and to the religion of Islam. The Islamic religion absolutely forbids associating a human being, e.g., W.D. Fard, as a partner of God or as an incarnation of God. Islam maintains that humanity is a creation of God and that no human being can be God. Islam also maintains that Prophet Muhammad was the last of the prophets and messengers of God. Finally, Islam explicitly prohibits racism in all forms.

While a number of African-American Muslims have used the Nation of Islam as a stepping stone in their personal religious transition between

Christianity and Islam, including such notables as Muhammad Ali and Malcolm X, the fact remains that the Nation of Islam is not and never has been a branch of Islam. As isolated print and TV reports have occasionally referred to Mr. Williams participation in the Nation of Islam's Million Man March, as Mr. Williams was correctly identified as being a member of the Nation of Islam within days of his capture, and as any responsible and well-informed newspaper reporter, TV pundit, or news anchor should be acutely aware of the fact that Islam and the Nation of Islam are two different religions, it is inexcusable that the media continues to identify Mr. Williams as being a Muslim and as being an adherent to Islam. Such identifications are nothing less than a complete fabrication and distortion of the truth. Yet, as I write this line in December of 2002, the American media appears to be continuously engaging in the misrepresentation of Mr. Williams's religious identity long after the true facts of the matter have come to light.

Classical Conditioning Paradigm

In presenting yet a fourth way in which the American media distorts and misrepresents Islam, it is necessary to digress slightly into the history of psychology. Beginning in 1901, Ivan Petrovich Pavlov initiated a series of studies on classical conditioning, i.e., a form of learning in which an old response is evoked by a new stimulus. In his classic experiment, Pavlov repeatedly paired the ringing of a bell with giving food to hungry dogs. A hungry dog naturally salivates when presented with food, i.e., this is an unconditioned reflex. The genius of Pavlov's experiment was that he was able to demonstrate that after sufficient pairings of bell ringing and food presentation, the dogs would begin to salivate at the mere ringing of the bell, i.e., a conditioned reflex had been established in which the "learned stimulus" (the ringing of the bell) could now evoke the same response as the "unlearned stimulus" (the presentation of the food). In follow-up studies, Pavlov successfully demonstrated that classical conditioning is not an artifact of the laboratory setting, but is one of the primary ways in which humans and animals learn. Of great importance for our present discussion, he also demonstrated that words could serve as learned stimuli.[102]

With this background in mind, I would like to direct your attention to two examples of classical conditioning that have been part and parcel of the message of the American news media for over 10 years. The first is the phrase "Muslim terrorist" and the second is the phrase "Muslim extremist." Both phrases have become an almost nightly mantra on network news shows. Both are rather obvious examples of a classical conditioning experiment, regardless of whether that experiment has been intentional or inadvertent.

Almost all Americans have a negative, visceral reaction to the words "terrorist" and "extremist." Their reaction of disgust and antipathy to these words is comparable to the hungry dog's salivation when confronted by food. Given this paradigm, the insertion of the word "Muslim" as a modifier of the words "terrorist" and "extremist" is directly comparable to Pavlov's ringing of a bell immediately before presenting the food to the hungry dogs. Over the course of hundreds and thousands of repetitious associations of "Muslim" with "terrorist" and "extremist," our nightly news shows have made the very word "Muslim" a learned stimulus for the worst sorts of visceral reactions from the American psyche. By this time, it is no longer even necessary to use the words "terrorist" and "extremist." Merely using the word "Muslim" is a sufficient stimulus in and of itself to elicit hostility and loathing.

It would be nice to think that this classical conditioning paradigm regarding the word "Muslim" was a happenstance or inadvertent accident of fate. Yet, as I watch the nightly news shows, as I listen to the various talking heads pontificate, and as I read my daily newspaper, I find no other consistent pattern in which a person's self-professed religion is being used as a verbal modifier to describe his crimes. Why is it that I do not read of "Christian profiteers and embezzlers" when reading about Enron and other corporate collapses? In the wake of the sexual scandals rocking the Roman Catholic Church in America, why am I not inundated with the repetitious association of "Christian pedophile" and "Christian child molester?" Why do I not hear the nightly news programs talking about "Jewish sadists" when they briefly report on the abuses of the Israeli occupation? Why was the modifying adjective "Christian" not used repeatedly in reporting on the Branch Davidian cult at Waco, Texas? Why were we not informed about the "Christian suicides" at Jonestown? Why does our local newspaper coverage not inform us about "Christian rapists," "Jewish thieves," and "atheist burglars?" If a self-professed Muslim's religious affiliation is to be considered a newsworthy aspect of that person's crime, then let the playing field be leveled and let every criminal's crime be modified by his or her self-professed religious affiliation.

Admittedly, the American media may wish to offer up the defense that the self-professed Muslim's crime was inherently tied to and motivated by his own idiosyncratic and highly distorted vision of Islam. They might further wish to argue that a religious motivation cannot be found for the corporate embezzler, the thief, the burglar, the rapist, the drive-by murderer, etc. In all fairness, their defense may have some merits in many cases. However, it falls flat when it encounters the Jonestown suicides, and the sexual atrocities perpetrated on young girls and women by David Koresh, the self-described prophet of the Branch Davidians. I might also add that it fails to satisfy when it is applied to various Israeli abuses, most of which are carried out under the psychological justification, whether conscious or unconscious, that the Israelis are the divinely sanctioned "chosen race" to whom all others are inferior and that the reestablishment of the Solomonic Empire is a God-given right of the Jews.

The Internet

So far, I have been confining my remarks to the traditionally defined media, i.e., newspapers, magazines, books, television, and radio. However, in our modern technological age, the contemporary media has outstripped its traditional definition. In particular, I would turn your attention to the Internet.

There is no doubt that the Internet offers Muslims and Islam the potential of great blessings. I can turn on my computer, log on to the Internet, and download all manner of books and material on Islam that would otherwise be unavailable to me. On-line, I can perform word searches of the *Ahadith* literature, consult the writings of the great scholars of the past, and keep abreast of the latest in Islamic thought and literature. These blessings are enormous.

However, the Internet is merely a tool. Like any tool, it can be used constructively or destructively. A hammer may be used to drive in the nail that stabilizes two parts of a house. It can also be used to bludgeon someone to death. At the present time, the Internet offers anyone with computer literacy the opportunity to create a so-called Islamic web page and to promote all manner of obscenities in the name of Islam. Here, we begin to confront the curses of the Internet. However, those curses are not limited to bogus Islamic web sites. They also include the instant reporting of unsubstantiated rumor and gossip, often with an Islamophobic element, that would never make its way into publication by the traditional media. Yet, on the Internet, such reports are readily available at the touch of one's computer keyboard.

Hollywood and Islam

Let us now consider another aspect of our expanded definition of the media. I refer to the movies of Hollywood and to the publication of novels. Both purport to be providing fiction. Yet, the psychological truth of the matter is that fiction can often lead to greater emotional involvement and to stronger identifications than can fact.

With the ending of the Cold War, the writers of so-called thrillers and the producers of action films have needed a new set of villains. President Reagan's "Evil Empire" no longer exists, and the consuming public needs a new villain that has at least a patina of reality about it. Enter Islam, stage left.

Movies such as *Executive Decision, Iron Eagle,* and *True Lies* have made millions by marketing Islam as the newly found enemy of the American people. Relying on erroneous stereotypes and caricatures, the fiction of Hollywood and the major publishing houses is beginning to feed Islamophobia more fully and more insidiously than even the traditional media.

Fiction tends to bypass human reason and evaluation and speaks directly to the emotional psyche of the consumer. When one reads or views a good yarn, one's analytical facilities and critical judgments are semi-suspended, and one simply gets caught up with the story. The consumer of fiction seldom stops to ask himself whether the presentation of Islam and Muslims that he is receiving has any semblance to reality. Nonetheless, his image of

Islam and Muslims is indelibly marked by the emotional associations he has while imbibing in this recreational pastime. If fiction consistently portrays Islam and Muslims as the contemporary enemy, the consuming public will inevitably respond to Islam and to Muslims just as it did to the fictional enemies found in its reading and viewing material.

So, where are the major novels and motion picture films that give the American public an opportunity to identify with a warm, caring, righteous, sympathetic, and godly Muslim man or woman?

CONCLUSIONS

How does the history of Islamophobia in the Christian West translate into modern reality? How do the Islamophobic pronouncements of the militant Christian extremists influence American behavior? How does the media's Islamophobic coverage of contemporary events influence the mindset of the American public? Perhaps, the answer is to be found in the federal government's crime statistics.

> The FBI's annual hate crimes report found that incidents targeting people, institutions and businesses identified with the Islamic faith increased from 28 in 2000 to 481 in 2001—a jump of 1,600 percent.[103]

In considering the above quotation, two points should be kept in mind. Firstly, one should realize that many hate crimes against Muslims go unreported. Thus, the above figures are extremely conservative in documenting the enormous rise in recent hate crimes against Muslims. Secondly, over 70% of 2001, the year in which hate crimes against Muslims so drastically escalated, occurred before the September 11th attacks.

Chapter 7

Original Sin and the role of Women: Comparing the Abrahamic Faiths

INTRODUCTION

While the history of Islamophobia in the Christian West was sketched out in the previous chapter, the role and status of women in Islam are frequently encountered themes in Islamophobic propaganda that deserve their own separate and specific discussion. This Islamophobic propaganda regarding women typically maintains that Muslim women are unconscionably oppressed by a patriarchal society. As examples of this alleged oppression, the Islamophobic propagandists point, as if by innate reflex, to the typically modest dress of most Muslim women, to the fact that many Muslim women do not work outside the home, to the limited role of polygamy in a few Muslim families, and to so-called "arranged" marriages.

In making these accusations, those who bewail the status of women in Islam ignore the age-old adage that "people who live in glass houses shouldn't throw stones." The wisdom of that proverb is amply demonstrated by examining the role and status of women in the Judaeo-Christian tradition, as illustrated by relevant passages from the *Bible*, by the writings of the so-called Apostolic Fathers of early Christianity, and by the traditional practices of Judaism and Christianity. The knowledge to be gleaned from such an analysis may be deeply disturbing to some Jews and Christians who are less familiar than they thought with the teachings of their own religions. Nonetheless, such an analysis is necessary to provide a suitable context for examining the role and status of women in Islam. Once the stage has been set by examining the traditional teachings about women to be found within the Judaeo-Christian tradition, the discussion will then turn to the role and status of women in Islam.

WOMEN IN THE *OLD TESTAMENT*
Introduction

While there are many issues that could be addressed regarding the role and status of women as portrayed by the *Old Testament*, the present discussion is limited to ten discrete topics: (1) women and ritual purity, (2) women and virginity, (3) women and rape, (4) women and spoils of war, (5) women and inheritance, (6) women and vows, (7) women and involuntary marriage, (8) women and the marital dowry, (9) women in relation to their husbands, and (10) women and fighting. An examination of the Biblical texts regarding these ten issues reveals a consistent pattern of relegating women to second-class status, spurning the basic human rights of women, and treating women as the mere chattel or property of some male relative, whether by birth or by marriage. Such is the *Old Testament* legacy regarding women, and such is the "divine" teachings about women that must be acknowledged and embraced by any Jew or Christian who perceives the *Old Testament* to be the word of God.

Women and Ritual Purity

Like Islam, the Judaeo-Christian tradition teaches that women are ritually impure and ceremonially unclean during menstruation and for a set time following childbirth. However, there are differences between the two traditions regarding the details of such ritual impurity. Within the context of the current discussion, it should be noted that Islam makes no distinction regarding the ritual impurity of the postpartum mother that is based upon the sex of the baby. As the following *Old Testament* passage indicates, this is decidedly not the case in the Judaeo-Christian tradition, where the period of ritual impurity is twice as long following the birth of a girl as it is following the birth of a boy.

> Speak to the people of Israel, saying: If a woman conceives and bears a male child, she shall be ceremonially unclean seven days; as at the time of her menstruation, she shall be unclean. On the eighth day the flesh of his foreskin shall be circumcised. Her time of blood purification shall be thirty-three days; she shall not touch any holy thing, or come into the sanctuary, until the days of her purification are completed. If she bears a female child, she shall be unclean two weeks, as in her menstruation; her time of blood purification shall be sixty-six days. (*Leviticus* 12:2-5)

What does this say about the status of women in the Judaeo-Christian tradition? Why does the birth of a daughter necessitate a period of ritual impurity and of being ceremonially unclean that extends for twice the time as does the birth of a son? Is this not a blatant, Biblically-based statement supporting a second-class status for women? Isn't the mother being "punished" for having given birth to a daughter instead of a son?

Women and Virginity

As noted above, the status of a woman within the *Old Testament* scriptures is denigrated by having given birth to a daughter instead of a son. However, that is just the beginning of the humiliation and abuse that the *Old Testament* specifies should be heaped upon women. For example, consider the case of a previously unmarried bride, whose husband accuses her of not having been a virgin at the time of marriage.

> Suppose a man marries a woman, but after going in to her, he dislikes her and makes up charges against her, slandering her by saying, "I married this woman; but when I lay with her, I did not find evidence of her virginity." The father of the young woman and

her mother shall then submit the evidence of the young woman's virginity to the elders of the city at the gate. The father of the young woman shall say to the elders: "I gave my daughter in marriage to this man but he dislikes her; now he has made up charges against her, saying, 'I did not find evidence of your daughter's virginity.' But here is the evidence of my daughter's virginity." Then they shall spread out the cloth before the elders of the town. The elders of that town shall take the man and punish him; they shall fine him one hundred shekels of silver (which they shall give to the young woman's father) because he has slandered a virgin of Israel. She shall remain his wife; he shall not be permitted to divorce her as long as he lives. If, however, this charge is true, that evidence of the young woman's virginity was not found, then they shall bring the young woman out to the entrance of her father's house and the men of her town shall stone her to death, because she committed a disgraceful act in Israel by prostituting herself in her father's house. So you shall purge the evil from your midst. (*Deuteronomy* 22:13-21)

There are two main points to be made regarding the above *Old Testament* passage. Firstly, if accused of not being a virgin by her husband, the previously unmarried bride's parents must publicly "spread out the cloth before the elders of the town" at the gate of the city. The cloth in question refers to the bedding from the marriage night, presumably blood-stained.[104] If the cloth is bloody, thus supposedly indicating bleeding from the hymen having been ruptured during intercourse on the wedding night, then the bride was found innocent of the charge made against her by her husband, but at the cost of her public humiliation in having her parents have to display the bloody cloth publicly. However, what vindication did the bride attain? She had to remain married to the man who falsely accused her, and she received absolutely nothing in exchange for having been slandered by her husband. However, her husband did have to pay the bride's father 100 shekels of silver, because the father's honor had been falsely damaged. (At 0.33 ounce of silver per shekel,[105] that translates into a fine of only 33 ounces of silver, or about $162.00 in today's currency!) Recompense was only given to the bride's father, not to the bride. It was only the bride's father's honor that deserved recompense, not the bride's honor. Secondly, with regard to the cloth from the wedding night, if "evidence of the young woman's virginity was not found," then "the men of her town shall stone her to death." Notice that the bride was deemed guilty unless she could establish her innocence by a properly bloody cloth from her wedding night bed. A variety of strenuous physical activities besides intercourse can rupture a hymen. The hymen may even have been ruptured during childhood. Nonetheless, if the hymen was not intact at the start of the wedding night for any of a number of reasons having nothing to do with sexual intercourse, there would be no bloody cloth, and the bride would then be killed by stoning.

The conclusions to be drawn about the role and status of women from these *Old Testament* verses are chilling and beyond comprehension to any reasonably educated person of the modern world. Such conclusions include: (1) a previously unmarried bride is guilty of prior illicit sexual conduct unless she can prove otherwise; (2) a bride has no recourse against the groom's false claims of her prior sexual promiscuity, and must remain married to him; and (3) only the bride's father's honor is worthy of recompense, not the bride's honor. As noted by at least one Biblical authority, the above indicates that the only operative consideration in the above laws governing sexual conduct is a concern for the rights of the male in a male-dominated family and that a blatant double standard exists in this text regarding the relative rights of males and females.[106]

Women and Rape

Issues regarding ritual impurity and the status of a previously unmarried bride who is accused of prior sexual misconduct by her husband are only the tip of the iceberg when it comes to how the *Old Testament* treats women. As the following Biblical verses indicate, an even more powerful example concerns the issue of rape.

> If a man is caught lying with the wife of another man, both of them shall die, the man who lay with the woman as well as the woman. So you shall purge the evil from Israel. If there is a young woman, a virgin already engaged to be married and a man meets her in the

town and lies with her, you shall bring both of them to the gate of that town and stone them to death, the young woman because she did not cry for help in the town and the man because he violated his neighbor's wife. So you shall purge the evil from your midst. But if the man meets the engaged woman in the open country, and the man seizes her and lies with her, then only the man who lay with her shall die. You shall do nothing to the young woman; the young woman has not committed an offense punishable by death, because this case is like that of someone who attacks and murders a neighbor. Since he found her in the open country, the engaged woman may have cried for help, but there was no one to rescue her. If a man meets a virgin who is not engaged, and seizes her and lies with her, and they are caught in the act, the man who lay with her shall give fifty shekels of silver to the young woman's father, and she shall become his wife. (*Deuteronomy* 22:22-29a)

As the above verses indicate, the punishment decreed by the Deuteronomic Law for adultery was death. However, the punishment for rape varied substantially, depending on whether or not the woman was married. If she was married or engaged, the man who raped her was put to death, because "he violated his neighbor's wife." Notice that the rapist of a married or engaged woman was condemned to death not because he had raped a woman, but because he had infringed on the property rights of another man, i.e., "he violated his neighbor's wife," indicating that the status of the woman was nothing more than chattel or property. That this is the correct interpretation can be seen by contrasting the above scenario with the punishment of a man who rapes a woman who is not married or engaged. In this latter case, he need only pay the victim's father 50 shekels of silver, apparently in recompense for having sullied the honor of the victim's father, and then marry the victim. Not only is the unmarried victim of rape not recompensed in any manner for having been raped, she is forced to marry the rapist!

The above verses leave no doubt concerning the *Old Testament* teachings regarding the role and status of a woman. Unless she is widowed or divorced, she is the mere property of her father or her husband. As such, in the case of her having been raped, the rapist is: (1) killed if his victim is married or engaged, because he has infringed on and abused the husband's property, i.e., his wife or fiancée; and (2) forced to pay the victim's father 50 shekels of silver, if the victim is unmarried and still living in her father's house, because he has sullied the honor of and shamed the victim's father. At 0.33 ounce of silver per shekel,[107] the total fine for raping an unmarried woman was only 16.5 ounces of silver or about $81.00 in today's currency. As to the   victim herself, if she is neither married nor engaged, she then has to marry the very man who raped her! Could the regard accorded to a woman in the *Old Testament* teachings be any clearer? Yet, these teachings must be held   to be divine laws by any Christian or Jew who holds the *Old Testament* to be the divinely inspired words of God.

However, there is yet another issue to be considered regarding the Deuteronomic Law governing cases of rape. If a married or engaged woman is raped within a town or city, she is also to be put to death, because she did not yell loudly enough or fight fiercely enough to prevent the rape from occurring. Thus, an engaged or married woman who is raped at knifepoint within a town has the unenviable choice among three heinous alternatives: (1) yelling and being killed by her assailant's knife before being raped; (2) saving her life by not yelling, being raped, and then not reporting the crime; and (3) saving her life by not yelling, being raped, reporting the crime, and then being killed for having been raped.

Women and Spoils of War

The *Old Testament* also condones, and in fact decrees, that women who are captured in times of war are the booty and spoils of the victors and that the victors are to "enjoy the spoil of your enemies" as a gift given unto them by God. Any such woman whom a victor desires should be kept as a slave for one month while she mourns the deaths of her family members. As soon as that month has passed, she forcibly becomes the wife of the victor who desires her.

> When you draw near to a town to fight against it, offer it terms of peace. If it accepts your terms of peace and surrenders to you, then all the people in it shall serve you at forced labor. If it does not

submit to you peacefully, but makes war against you, then you shall besiege it; and when the Lord your God gives it into your hand, you shall put all its males to the sword. You may, however, take as your booty the women, the children, livestock, and everything else in the town, all its spoil. You may enjoy the spoil of your enemies, which the Lord your God has given you. (*Deuteronomy* 20:10-14)

When you go out to war against your enemies, and the Lord your God hands them over to you and you take them captive, suppose you see among the captives a beautiful woman whom you desire and want to marry, and so you bring her home to your house: she shall shave her head, pare her nails, discard her captive's garb, and shall remain in your house a full month, mourning for her father and mother; after that you may go into her and be her husband, and she shall be your wife. (*Deuteronomy* 21:10-13)

Women and Inheritance

An additional example of how the *Old Testament* relegates women to a second-class status can be seen in the laws of inheritance. As indicated by the following verses, a daughter could inherit from her father only if the father had no surviving sons. If there were at least one surviving son, the daughters were barred from all inheritance.

Then the daughters of Zelophehad came forward...and they said, "Our father died in the wilderness...and he had no sons. Why should the name of our father be taken away from his clan because he had no son? Give to us a possession among our father's brothers. Moses brought their case before the Lord. And the Lord spoke to Moses, saying: The daughters of Zelophehad are right in what they are saying; you shall indeed let them possess an inheritance among their father's brothers and pass the inheritance of their father on to them. You shall also say to the Israelites, "If a man dies, and has no son, then you shall pass his inheritance on to his daughter..." (*Numbers* 27:1a, 2b-3a, 3c-8)

If the above laws governing inheritance were not bad enough, these laws were soon amended to restrict a daughter's right to inherit from her father. Even in the case in which a daughter could inherit because there wasn't a surviving son, the new amendment specified that the inheritance could only occur if the daughter married a man from the clan of her father's tribe. In short, if she were to inherit in the case where she did not have at least one paternal brother, her inheritance was contingent upon her marrying a man from the clan of her father's tribe, in which case the inheritance actually passed to her husband. Quite clearly, patriarchal property rights trumped a daughter's right to inherit from her father, even in the situation where she had no paternal brother. The following *Old Testament* verses delineate this further restriction on a woman's ability to inherit.

> Then Moses commanded the Israelites according to the word of the Lord, saying, "The descendants of the tribe of Joseph are right in what they are saying. This is what the Lord commands concerning the daughters of Zelophehad, 'Let them marry whom they think best; only it must be into a clan of their father's tribe that they are married, so that no inheritance of the Israelites shall be transferred from one tribe to another; for all Israelites shall retain the inheritance of their ancestral tribes. Every daughter who possesses an inheritance in any tribe of the Israelites shall marry one from the clan of her father's tribe, so that all Israelites may continue to possess their ancestral inheritance...'" (*Numbers* 36:5-8)

Women and Vows

Not only did a woman not have rights to her own body (as in the prior example of rape) and inheritance, she also had no rights when it came to making vows, promises, and pledges. This is dramatically illustrated in the following *Old Testament* verses where the so-called Mosaic Law allows a father to negate his unmarried daughter's vows and allows a husband to nullify his wife's vows and pledges. In short, the unmarried daughter is the property of her father, the married woman is the property of her husband, and the "property owner" can negate and nullify any vow, promise, or pledge rendered by the "property." As specified in *Numbers* 30:9, only in the case of a widow or divorcee was a woman's vow or oath considered to be legally binding in its own right.

> When a woman makes a vow to the Lord, or binds herself by a pledge, while within her father's house, in her youth, and her father...expresses disapproval to her at the time that he hears of it, no vow of hers, and no pledge by which she has bound herself, shall stand...If she marries, while obligated by her vows or any thoughtless utterance of her lips by which she has bound herself, and her husband hears of it and...expresses disapproval to her, then he shall nullify the vow by which she was obligated, or the thoughtless utterance of her lips, by which she bound herself...And if she made a vow in her husband's house, or bound herself by a pledge with an oath, and her husband...nullifies them at the time that he hears them, then whatever proceeds out of her lips concerning her vows, or concerning her pledge of herself, shall not stand. Her husband has nullified them...Any vow or any binding oath to deny herself, her husband may allow to stand, or her husband may nullify. (*Numbers* 30:3-4a, 5b, 6-7a, 8b, 10-11a, 12b, 13)

Women and Involuntary Marriage

It has previously been shown that the *Old Testament* dictates that a woman who is neither married nor engaged must marry her rapist if she is raped. Further, a woman who stands to inherit because there is no male heir can only inherit if she marries within her father's clan. To these examples of involuntary marriage being forced on a woman, one can now add two more such examples from the pages of the *Old Testament*. The first such example consists of the *Old Testament* concept of Levirate Marriage, while the second concerns a specific historical situation involving the Israelite tribe of Benjamin.

As specified in the Deuteronomic Law, the widow of a man who has not yet fathered a son must marry one of the brothers of her deceased husband, whether or not that is her choice, in order that the deceased's brother may father a son in the name of the deceased husband.

When brothers reside together, and one of them dies and has

no son, the wife of the deceased shall not be married outside the
family to a stranger. Her husband's brother shall go in to her, taking her in marriage, and performing the duty of a husband's brother to her, and the firstborn whom she bears shall succeed to the
name   of the deceased brother, so that his name may not be
blotted out   of Israel. (*Deuteronomy* 25:5-6)

As specified in the subsequent verses to those quoted immediately
above, the deceased husband's brother may, however, decline to marry the
widow. In such a case, the widow may publicly humiliate her brother-in-law
by pulling off his sandal and spitting in his face. While the deceased
husband's brother may escape a forced marriage in this manner, no such
escape exists for the widow who must meekly comply with the dictates of
the Levirate Marriage code and marry her brother-in-law regardless of her
personal preferences and choice.

The second example of women being given in forced marriage revolves
around a specific historical circumstance concerning the Israelite tribe of
Benjamin. According to *Judges* 19-21, a certain Levite was traveling from
Bethlehem to his home in the hill country of Ephraim. Along the way,
he and his concubine stopped for the night in Gibeah, where they were
sheltered in the house of an elderly man. That night, the Benjaminites of the
town surrounded the house and demanded from the elderly man that he
turn out his Levite guest that they might engage in the homosexual rape of
the Levite. The elderly man refused, and in an effort to appease the crowd
the Levite's concubine was shoved out the door to the ravages of the mob.
The Benjaminite men repeatedly gang-raped the concubine and left her
dead on the threshold to the door of the house.

The next morning, the Levite packed the corpse of his concubine on
a donkey and returned home. Upon arriving back at home, he cut the body
of his concubine into 12 pieces, sending one piece to each of the 12 tribes
of Israel. In this way, he demanded vengeance against the tribe of Benjamin.
Excluding the tribe of Benjamin, the 11 remaining tribes of Israel gathered
together at Mizpah and decided on a course of action. Initially, they merely
sent emissaries to the tribe of Benjamin, demanding that the tribe hand over
the perpetrators of the crime. However, the tribe of Benjamin refused this

request, and the 11 other tribes of Israel first swore that none of them would ever give one of their daughters to be the wife of a Benjaminite and then attacked the tribe of Benjamin. After a multi-day battle, the entire tribe of Benjamin was reduced to just 600 men, with all their women and children having been slaughtered.

Thereafter, the remaining 11 tribes of Israel began to grieve that the tribe of Benjamin was doomed to extinction because the entire tribe was reduced to just 600 people, all of them male. To complicate matters, they had all sworn at Mizpah not to give any of their daughters to the Benjaminites as wives, so the tribe could not be perpetuated in this manner. However, the Israelites of Jabesh-gilead had not been present at Mizpah and had therefore not taken the oath not to give their daughters to the Benjaminites. Therefore, the rest of the Israelites attacked Jabesh-gilead for no other reason than to capture 400 virgins that could be given to the tribe of Benjamin as wives. In order to do so, they ended up killing every other person at Jabesh-gilead, including all the men, the non-virgin women of marital age, and all the children. The Israelites then gave these 400 virgins to the 600 Benjaminites to take as wives in forced marriage.

However, the tribe of Benjamin was still 200 wives short to give each man one wife. Therefore, the elders of the tribes of Israel devised the following plan. They instructed the Benjaminites who did not yet have wives to wait in ambush in the vineyards of the town of Shiloh at the time of a religious festival. When the young women of Shiloh came out to dance in the festival dances, the Benjaminites were simply to abduct 200 of the women and take them forcibly as wives. In this way, each male of the tribe of Benjamin had a wife, but no Israelite had given a daughter to the tribe of Benjamin in marriage. Rather, the daughters had been taken by brute force.

The debased morality to be repeatedly found in the above scenario from *Judges* 19-21 is almost beyond comprehension. While there are certainly more ethical issues involved than the ones specific to the forced abduction, rape, and marriage of 600 young women, it is that aspect of the story that is once again graphically illustrative of the demeaning *Old Testament* view regarding the rights of and personhood of women.

Women and the Dowry

It was the *Old Testament* custom that a dowry (*mohar* in Hebrew; *Mahr* in Arabic) was paid by the husband or the husband's family. However, the dowry was not given to the bride but to the bride's father or nearest male relative, as demonstrated in *Genesis* 29:15-30, 31:15, 34:12, *Exodus* 22:16, and *I Samuel* 18:25. It was this situation that reportedly led to the complaint of Rachel and Leah, the wives of Prophet Jacob.

> Then Rachel and Leah answered him, "Is there any portion or inheritance left to us in our father's house? Are we not regarded by him as foreigners? For he has sold us, and he has been using up the money given for us..." (*Genesis* 31:14-15)

Could the complaints of Rachel and Leah be any more graphic in their description of being treated by their father as mere property in having been "sold" into marriage? Not only were they "sold," but they didn't even receive the proceeds from their "sale!"

Women in Relation to their Husbands

Several passages within the *Old Testament* address the status of a woman in relation to her husband, but many of these obscure the issue in translating from Hebrew to English. The following passages are representative of this tendency.

> But God came to Abimelech in a dream by night, and said to him, "You are about to die because of the woman whom you have taken; for she is a married woman." (*Genesis* 20:3)

> When people who are fighting injure a pregnant woman so that there is a miscarriage, and yet no further harm follows, the one responsible shall be fined what the woman's husband demands, paying as much as the judge determines. (*Exodus* 21:22)

> ...discard her captive's garb, and shall remain in your house a full month, mourning for her father and mother; after that you may go in to her and be her husband, and she shall be your wife. (*Deuteronomy* 21:13)

> If a man is caught lying with the wife of another man, both of them shall die, the man who lay with the woman as well as the woman.

So you shall purge the evil from Israel. (*Deuteronomy* 22:22)

Suppose a man enters into marriage with a woman, but she does not please him because he finds something objectionable about her, and so he writes her a certificate of divorce, puts it in her hand, and sends her out of his house; she then leaves his house... (*Deuteronomy* 24:1)

When the wife of Uriah heard that her husband was dead, she made lamentation for him. (*II Samuel* 11:26)

What all of the above verses have in common is the use of the Hebrew word "*ba'al*" or one of its derivatives or alternate forms. In each case, the *Bible* translators have elected to translate "*ba'al*" or its alternate form as "husband" or some wording signifying "to marry," "marriage," "wife of another man," etc. However, the literal meaning of "*ba'al*" is "owner," "master," or "possessor." In short, if translated literally, each of the above verses would signify that a wife was the possession or slave of her husband/master/owner!

"*Ba'al*" is not the only Hebrew word that is being misleadingly translated in English versions of the *Bible*. Another example would be the Hebrew word "'*adon*" and its cognates. "'*Adon*" is from a root word that means "to rule" and is literally translated as "lord" or "sovereign." In the two following verses, it has been misleadingly translated as "husband" or "husbands." (Note that in the latter of the two verses, the author of *Amos* refers to women as "cows.")

So Sarah laughed to herself, saying, "After I have grown old, and my husband is old, shall I have pleasure?" (*Genesis* 18:12)

Hear this word, you cows of Bashan who are on Mount Samaria, who oppress the poor, who crush the needy, who say to their husbands, "Bring something to drink!" (*Amos* 4:1)

Summing across all the above verses, it is clear that the *Old Testament* portrayal of a woman's role in relationship to her husband is either that of a slave or possession to her *ba'al* (master, owner, and possessor) or of a subject to her '*adon* (ruler or sovereign lord). The former relationship, i.e., that of being the property or possession of one's husband, is also signified in the wording to be found in the Decalogue or Ten Commandments, where a wife is merely included as one object in a list of property (slaves, livestock, and inanimate objects) belonging to her husband.

You shall not covet your neighbor's house; you shall not covet your neighbor's wife; or male or female slave, or ox, or donkey, or anything that belongs to your neighbor. (*Exodus* 20:17)

Neither shall you covet your neighbor's wife. Neither shall you desire your neighbor's house, or field, or male or female slave, or ox, or donkey, or anything that belongs to your neighbor. (*Deuteronomy* 5:21)

Women and Fighting

In a peculiar passage from the Deuteronomic Law, there are two verses that relate to the issue of a woman who rushes to help her husband when her husband is in the middle of a fight with another man. These two verses specify that if in her fighting to help her husband the woman grabs the genitals of her husband's antagonist, a non-negotiable punishment befalls the woman, i.e., "you shall cut off her hand: show no pity."

If men get into a fight with one another, and the wife of one intervenes to rescue her husband from the grip of his opponent by reaching out and seizing his genitals, you shall cut off her hand: show no pity. (*Deuteronomy* 25:11-12)

Consider this passage for a moment in the light of the following hypothetical example. A woman sees another man wantonly attack her husband, resulting in her husband's life being in imminent danger. Being physically much smaller and weaker than her husband's attacker and having no weapons available to her, she nonetheless rushes forward at considerable personal risk and saves her husband's life by the expedient of grabbing and squeezing the attacker's genitalia as hard as she can. What is the Biblically mandated reward for this heroine who has saved her husband's life against tremendous odds? According to the Deuteronomic Law, her reward is that the "offending hand" is to be amputated, because she has dared to threaten damage to the masculinity of her husband's attacker.

Summary

The preceding examples provide numerous illustrations of the teachings of the *Old Testament* regarding the demeaned role and status of women. Summarizing across these ten examples, the common thread appears to be that women are basically to be treated as chattel or property. Women had no inherent rights as human beings, could be forced into marriages to which they objected, and even when some recompense was due for slandering or raping a woman, the recompense was due to the woman's father or husband, because his honor or "property rights" had been violated. According to almost any viable moral and ethical system, this scriptural legacy within the Judaeo-Christian tradition is a shameful and sorry state of affairs.

WOMEN IN THE *NEW TESTAMENT*
Introduction

Some Christians may attempt to disavow the *Old Testament* legacy regarding the role and status of women and to insist that such treatment of women was superceded by the new covenant ushered in with Jesus Christ. Yet before blithely consigning the depersonalization of women and the systematic violation of their basic human rights to the *Old Testament* period, such Christians would do well to consider the teachings regarding women that are to be found within the pages of the *New Testament*. In what follows, the *New Testament* perspective on four issues is examined. These issues are: (1) women and veiling; (2) the role of women in the church; (3) the role of a woman in marriage; and (4) the role of women compared to men.

Women and Veiling

The Islamophobia of the Christian West frequently centers on the modest dress of Muslim women. In particular, one hears frequent criticism of the custom of veiling that has been adopted by some Muslim women. However, the *New Testament* also dictates that women "should dress themselves modestly and decently," should not braid their hair, and should not attract attention to themselves by wearing "gold, pearls, or expensive clothes." Furthermore, as illustrated in the third of the following passages,

Paul specifically instructs women to veil their heads, especially if they are praying.

> ...women should dress themselves modestly and decently in suitable clothing, not with their hair braided, or with gold, pearls, or expensive clothes, but with good works, as is proper for women who profess reverence for God. (*I Timothy* 2:9-10)

> Wives...Do not adorn yourselves outwardly by braiding your hair, and by wearing gold ornaments or fine clothing; rather, let your adornment be the inner self with the lasting beauty of a gentle and quiet spirit, which is very precious in God's sight. (*I Peter* 3:1a, 3-4)

> Any man who prays or prophesies with something on his head disgraces his head, but any woman who prays or prophesies with her head unveiled disgraces her head—it is one and the same thing as having her head shaved. For if a woman will not veil herself, then she should cut off her hair; but if it is disgraceful for a woman to have her hair cut off or to be shaved, she should wear a veil. (*I Corinthians* 11:3-6)

In the immediately preceding passage, the Greek word "*katakalupo*" and its associated forms have been rendered as "veil" by the translators of the New Revised Standard Version of the *Bible*. Other acceptable translations would substitute the concept of covering the head for the concept of veiling, the former of which is the translation offered by the King James Version and several other translations.

Women in the Church

Paul, the initial architect of what has become Pauline Christianity, offered explicit instructions about the role of women in the Christian church. These instructions on the status of women in Christian worship are strict and unambiguous, and they clearly define a "subordinate" and second-class status to all women. Paul informs the reader that "it is shameful for a woman to speak in church" and that women "are not permitted to speak," even to the point of being allowed to ask a question. Instead, women are meekly to "ask their husbands" once they are "at home."

> As in all the churches of the saints, women should be silent in the churches. For they are not permitted to speak, but should be subordinate, as the law also says. If there is anything they desire to know, let them ask their husbands at home. For it is shameful for a woman to speak in church. (*I Corinthians* 14:33b-35)

The basic gist of the above *New Testament* verses is that women are to be denied at least one important aspect of a religious education, i.e., the right to question and to engage in dialogue with the religious leader. In short, the true fulfillment of their religious education becomes totally dependent upon what their husbands are willing to tell them and upon what their husbands are willing to have them learn.

Women in Relation to their Husbands

The above instructions that women are not even to ask a question in church but are to wait and "ask their husbands at home" imply that wives are subordinate to their husbands. This implication becomes explicit in several other *New Testament* passages.

> Wives, be subject to your husbands as you are to the Lord. For the husband is the head of the wife just as Christ is the head of the church, the body of which he is the Savior. Just as the church is subject to Christ, so also wives ought to be, in everything, to their husbands. (*Ephesians* 5:22-24)

> Wives, be subject to your husbands, as is fitting in the Lord. (*Colossians* 3:18)

> Wives, in the same way, accept the authority of your husbands, so that, even if some of them do not obey the word, they may be won over without a word by their wives' conduct, when they see the purity and reverence of your lives...It was this way long ago that the holy women who hoped in God used to adorn themselves by accepting the authority of their husbands. Thus Sarah obeyed Abraham and called him lord. (*I Peter* 3:1-2, 5-6a)

But I want you to understand that Christ is the head of every man, and the husband is the head of his wife, and God is the head of Christ. (*I Corinthians* 11:3)

As the above passages from the various epistles demonstrate, the *New Testament* position is that women are to be subordinate to their husbands. "Wives, be subject to your husbands...accept the authority of your husbands...the husband is the head of his wife..." Furthermore, wives are to be subordinate and subject to their husbands "even in" the case where their husbands "do not obey the word" of God. In marked contrast, I know of no Muslim woman who would even begin to consider accepting such a dehumanizing position of servitude.

As a brief addendum, the reference in *I Peter* 3:6a to Sarah calling Prophet Abraham her lord is a reference to *Genesis* 18:12, where the Hebrew word typically translated as husband is actually "*adon*," which literally means "lord."

Women in Relation to Men

However, the *New Testament* does not restrict a woman to being in a second-class status merely to her husband. Indeed, Paul and the anonymous author of *I Timothy* rather graphically and dramatically define the second-class status of women in relation to all men.

For a man ought not to have his head veiled, since he is the image and reflection of God; but woman is the reflection of man. Indeed, man was not made from woman, but woman from man. Neither was man created for the sake of woman, but woman for the sake of man. (*I Corinthians* 11:7-9)

Let a woman learn in silence with full submission. I permit no woman to teach or to have authority over a man; she is to keep silent. (*I Timothy* 2:11-12)

Note the words of Paul that claim that man "is the image and reflection of God; but woman is the reflection of man...(n)either was man created for the sake of woman, but woman for the sake of man." Man is the glorious reflection of God, but woman is only the reflection of man. Man was *not* created for the sake of lowly woman, but woman was created for the sake and pleasure of man. As noted by the author of *I Timothy*, no woman is to be permitted to teach or to have authority over a man. She is to know her place, to keep silent, and to learn in silence with full submission, presumably to a man. Can the teachings of any religion be more sexist than this? With this scriptural legacy, how can any Christian in good conscience cast aspersions upon the role and status of women in Islam, especially since, as will be seen later, Islam categorically rejects the blatant sexism embedded in the above passages from the *New Testament* epistles being quoted?

Summary

If the sum total of the above passages from the *New Testament* were not bad enough, it must be emphasized that the *Old Testament* passages quoted earlier were never specifically and unambiguously abrogated by the *New Testament*. In short, the Christian who adheres to the *Bible* as the divine and literal word of God must affirm the blatant sexism and gender prejudice embedded in both the *Old Testament* and the *New Testament*. However, the worst is still yet to be seen. It is only when considering the traditional Christian concept of Original Sin that one confronts the fullness and vastness of the bigoted sexism lurking throughout the Christian tradition.

ORIGINAL SIN AND THE ROLE OF WOMEN
Introduction

It should be stated at the outset that the Christian concept of Original Sin is totally foreign to both contemporary Judaism and Islam, as well as to Eastern Christianity. In short, the doctrine of Original Sin is a completely Western Christian invention and innovation, which is primarily drawn from a rather idiosyncratic interpretation of *Romans* 5:12-19, and which is based on the assumption that every human inherits the sin of "Adam's initial fall from grace" through conception via the act of sexual intercourse, an act that according to Augustine was contaminated by "concupiscence." Thus, according to traditional Western Christianity, the whole of mankind inherits Adam's original sin in eating of the forbidden fruit through being conceived through the sexual act. Once again, it should be emphasized that such an inheritance of and concept of Original Sin are completely contrary to the religious teachings of Judaism, Islam, and Eastern Christianity, but are indigenous to Western Christianity.[108]

As typically portrayed in Western Christian literature, "Adam's initial fall from grace" was a cataclysmic event, resulting in the following severe punishments that have accrued upon all humans ever since. (1) Adam and Eve were thrown out of the Garden of Eden and were forever barred from returning to it (*Genesis* 3:22-24). (2) Adam and his male descendants were specifically punished by being forced to till the "cursed" ground in order to find sustenance through "toil" and "the sweat of your face" (*Genesis* 3: 17-19). (3) Eve and her female descendants were punished by the physical pain of childbirth and by having their husbands forever rule over them (*Genesis* 3:16). (4) All of humanity is punished by having to undergo death at the end of their lives in the earthly world (*Genesis* 3:22-24).

Original Sin and the Role of Women

How does this Western Christian concept of Original Sin relate to the role and status of women? According to traditional Christian doctrine, "Adam's initial fall from grace" was not directly attributable to any moral or spiritual failing in Adam but was specifically secondary to the ethical and religious turpitude of Eve, who having been deceived by Satan, then deceived her husband. Had it not been for Eve, Adam would never have fallen from grace. Thus, all the toil and suffering of humanity ever since that first fateful bite of the forbidden fruit can be laid directly at the doorstep of Eve and through her to all women. With regard to that point, the following passage from *I Timothy* becomes directly relevant.

> For Adam was formed first, then Eve; and Adam was not deceived, but the woman was deceived and became a transgressor. Yet she will be saved through childbearing, provided they continue in faith and love and holiness, with modesty. (*I Timothy* 2:13-15)

Eve deceived Adam, who was her moral and spiritual superior. It was Eve who succumbed to the temptations of Satan, not Adam. As such, Eve's only hope for salvation, and after Eve for all women, was through undergoing the penance of the aforementioned physical pain of childbirth. However, the above verses from *I Timothy* are only the start of the process by which Western Christianity has traditionally attempted to lay the blame for all of the sins of humanity upon women. The Western Christian concept of women being to blame for Original Sin was further elaborated by the so-called Apostolic Fathers of early Western Christianity.

The unique role of women in the Western Christian concept of Original Sin is encountered as early as the end of the second century or the very beginning of the third century in Tertullian's *De Cultu Feminarum* (Concerning the Dress of Women).[109] Writing as an early Christian theologian and moralist, Tertullian's view of women in the role of Original Sin is blatant and bigoted sexism at its very worst. As an illustration, one need only quote the following passage from Tertullian.

> Do you (women) not know that you are each an Eve? The sentence of God on this sex of yours lives in this age. The guilt must of necessity live, too. You are the devil's gateway. You are the unsealer of that forbidden tree. You are the first deserter of the divine law. You are she who persuaded him (Adam) whom the devil was not valiant enough to attack. You so carelessly destroyed man, God's image. On account of your desert, even the son of God had to die. (*De Cultu Feminarum*)

To take Tertullian at his written word, women as a sex are responsible not only for "Adam's initial fall from grace" but also for the alleged crucifixion of Jesus Christ, whose alleged agonies on the cross were necessitated by the state of Original Sin in which all of humanity has lived ever since Adam and Eve ate of the forbidden fruit in the Garden of Eden. In short, Tertullian blamed the female sex for Adam's fall, Original Sin, the toil and suffering of all of humanity (the punishment for Adam's fall), and for the alleged crucifixion of Jesus Christ (the alleged redemption for Original Sin). He referred to them as "the devil's gateway."

However, Tertullian was not the only Apostolic Father to lay the burden of Original Sin on the female sex. Over 140 years after Tertullian's libel of all women, Augustine,[110] the bishop of Hippo from circa 395 to 430, joined the fray, jumping in with hobnailed boots. Summing across several of his written works, the following quotation regarding Augustine's view of the role of women in Original Sin can be constructed.

> Through Adam's sin, all of his posterity were corrupted, and were born under the penalty of death, which he had incurred. Thence, after his sin, he was driven into exile, and by his sin the whole race of which he was the root was corrupted in him, and thereby subjected to the penalty of death. And so it happens that all descended from him, and from the woman who had led him into sin, and was condemned at the same time with him—being the offspring of carnal lust on which the same punishment of disobedience was visited—were tainted with the original sin...What is the difference whether it is in a wife or a mother, it is still Eve the temptress that we must beware of in any woman...if it was good company and conversation that Adam needed, it would have been much better arranged to have two men together as friends, not a man and a woman. (*Enchyridion*, chapter 26; Letter #243; and *The Literal Meaning of Genesis*)

Jewish Postcript

As previously noted, the concept of Original Sin and of woman's supposed responsibility for Original Sin is a conceptual construct of Western Christianity. However, Judaism does not get completely off the hook when it comes to these notions. For example, an early formulation of Original Sin can be found in the Jewish writings of *II Esdras*, which is also occasionally known as *IV Esdras*. (*II Esdras* is one of the books of the *Old Testament* Apocrypha, was written late in the first century, and has some Christian interpolations.[111]) Additionally, *Ecclesiasticus*, which is also known as *Sirach*, *Wisdom of Bar Sirach*, and *The Wisdom of Jesus Ben-Sirach*, specifies that all sin originated from Eve, i.e., woman. (*Ecclesiasticus* is also one of the books of the *Old Testament* Apocrypha and dates to the second century BCE.[112])

> ...and to him (Adam) thou commanded one only observance of thine, but he transgressed it. Forthwith, thou appointed death for him and for his generations, and from him were born nations and

tribes, peoples and clans innumerable. And every nation walked after their own will, and behaved wickedly before thee, and was ungodly... (*II Esdras* 3:7-8)

From a woman did sin originate, and because of her "we all must die." (*Ecclesiasticus* 25:24)

One cannot help but wonder how much effect the above verses had on Philo, the first century Alexandrian Jew and philosopher. Certainly, Philo drew a sharp distinction between men, whom he characterized as *nous* (mind or the higher intellectual capacity), and women, whom he characterized as *aisthesis* (sense-impression or the lower form of perception). Philo further emphasized that men were immortal and in the image of God, while women were mortal and connected with *soma* (the body). Therefore, Philo concluded that women as a gender should be considered as belonging to a category of things that is undesirable and wrong. As can be seen, sexism and misogyny run rampant in Philo's writings.[113]

Summary

The legacy of Western Christianity's concept of the role of women in Original Sin was to bedevil women into the 20th century. As noted by Augustine, Western Christianity traditionally viewed Eve as "the cause of his (Adam's) sin" and viewed each and every woman within the following framework: "it is still Eve the temptress that we must beware of in any woman."

POLYGAMY AND THE JUDAEO-CHRISTIAN TRADITION
Introduction

The very limited practice of polygamy in Islam is one of the favorite whipping boys of Islamophobia in the Christian West. It appears that Islam-bashers never tire of grossly exaggerating and distorting the role of polygamy in Islam. As such, the true facts of the matter regarding the highly circum-scribed role of polygamy in Islam will be covered later in this chapter. However, before turning to that discussion and to an examination of the issue of the role of women in Islam, the record needs to be set straight about the role of polygamy in the Judaeo-Christian tradition.

Technically speaking, polygamy can take either of two forms: (1) one man married to more than one woman, which is known as polygyny; and (2) one woman married to more than one man, which is known as polyandry. Throughout history, polyandry has been quite rare, resulting in polygamy often being used interchangeably with polygyny. As such, the current discussion of polygamy in the Judaeo-Christian tradition, as well as the subsequent discussion of polygamy in the Islamic tradition, will employ the more frequently encountered term "polygamy," even though polygyny is the technically more precise term in both instances.

Polygamy in the *Bible*

Although it is seldom mentioned in Judaeo-Christian circles, the institution of polygamy is well established in the *Bible*. The so-called Mosaic Law of Judaism recognized polygamy, gave it divine sanction, and even went so far as to specify: (1) the rights of a first wife when her husband later took a second wife, and (2) the inheritance rights of the various male descendants resulting from a polygamous marriage.

> If he takes another wife to himself, he shall not diminish the food, clothing, or marital rights of the first wife. (*Exodus* 21:10)

> If a man has two wives, one of them loved and the other disliked, and if both the loved and the disliked have borne him sons, the first-born being the son of the one who is disliked, then on the day when he wills his possessions to his sons, he is not permitted to treat the son of the loved as the firstborn in preference to the son of the disliked, who is the firstborn. He must acknowledge as firstborn the son of the one who is disliked, giving him a double portion of all that he has; since he is the first issue of his virility, the right of the firstborn is his. (*Deuteronomy* 21:15-17).

In an *Old Testament* passage that prohibits a man from having two sisters as wives simultaneously, the so-called Mosaic Law again implies that polygamy is acceptable in other circumstances.

> And you shall not take a woman as a rival to her sister, uncovering her nakedness while her sister is still alive. (*Leviticus* 18:18)

In addition, the Deuteronomic Law of Levirate Marriage (see pages 200-201of this chapter) could actually force a man into polygamy unless he was willing to be publicly shamed and humiliated.

Furthermore, it appears that certain *New Testament* passages recognize polygamy. Thus, *I Timothy* 3:2 and 3:12 make a point of emphasizing that bishops and deacons should have only one wife. The fact that these two church officials are singled out as having to be monogamous inevitably implies that other early Christians could be and often were polygamous.

Over and above the preceding Biblically-based laws that acknowledge and ratify polygamous marriage, the *Bible* repeatedly refers to different individuals who were polygamous. Cain's descendant, Lamech, had two wives (*Genesis* 4:19). Prophet Abraham was simultaneously married to Sarah and to Hagar (*Genesis* 16:1-4). Prophet Abraham's brother, Nahor, had both a wife and a concubine (*Genesis* 22:20-24). Prophet Jacob was simultaneously married to Rachel and Leah and used their two female slaves as concubines (*Genesis* 29:21-30:22). Esau, the brother of Prophet Jacob was polygamous, having at least three wives. (*Genesis* 26:34; 28:6-9).

Well after the patriarchal age, polygamy continued to be practiced among the children of Israel. Ashhur, a descendant of Judah, had two wives (*I Chronicles* 4:5). Shaharaim, a descendant of Benjamin, had at least three wives simultaneously (*I Chronicles* 8:8-9). Gideon, one of the judges of pre-monarchial Israel had multiple wives and at least one concubine (*Judges* 8:30-31). Other judges of Israel appear to have been polygamous, for the *Bible* records that Jair the Gileadite had 30 sons (*Judges* 10:3-4), Ibzan of Bethlehem had 30 sons and 30 daughters (*Judges* 12:8-9), and Abdon had 40 sons (*Judges* 12:13-14). Elkanah, the *Bible's* father of Prophet Samuel, had two wives (*I Samuel* 1:1-2).

Polygamy was especially prevalent among the various kings of Israel and Judah. King Saul had multiple wives, which were later given to Prophet David (*II Samuel* 12:7-8). Not counting the women given to him who had formerly been wives of King Saul, Prophet David had at least eight wives and 10 concubines (*I Samuel* 25:39-44, *II Samuel* 5:13-16, and *I Chronicles* 3: 1-9 and 14:3). Prophet Solomon reportedly had at least 700 wives and 300 concubines (*I Kings* 11:1-3). Rehoboam, the son of Prophet Solomon and a king of Judah, had 18 wives and 60 concubines (*II Chronicles* 11:18-21). Abijah, king of Judah, had 14 wives (*II Chronicles* 13:21). Jehoram, king of Judah, had multiple wives simultaneously (*II Chronicles* 21:16-17). Joash, king of Judah, had two wives simultaneously (*II Chronicles* 24:1-3). King Ahab of Israel had multiple wives simultaneously (*I Kings* 20:1-7). Jehoiachin, king of Judah, had multiple wives (*II Kings* 24:15). King Zedekiah of Judah also had multiple wives simultaneously (*Jeremiah* 38: 14-24).

Having noted all of the above instances of Biblically sanctioned polygamy, it now needs to be emphasized that there is no record in the *Bible* of Jesus Christ or any other of the prophets of God forbidding the practice of polygamy.

Polygamy in Post Biblical Judaism

Given the above Biblical basis for polygamy, Judaism continued to sanction polygamy throughout the first few centuries, as witnessed by the writings of Josephus in the first century, the writings of Justin Martyr in the second century, and in the Roman law of 212 that legalized Jewish polygamy. Additionally, the *Talmud* specifically allowed up to four wives for commoners and up to 18 wives for kings.[114] In fact, Judaism did not abrogate the right of a man to have multiple wives simultaneously until the famous ruling of Rabbi Gershom bar Judah[115] in the 11th century. However, even after that ruling, some Jews continued to practice polygamy.

Polygamy in Post Biblical Christianity

Within the early Christian churches, polygamy continued to be practiced for several centuries after the earthly ministry of Jesus Christ and was even supported by some of the so-called Apostolic Fathers. To illustrate this latter point, one can profitably turn to the writings of Augustine, the bishop of Hippo and a canonized saint of the Roman Catholic Church.

Since it was in order to provide sufficiently numerous descendants, the practice of one man having several wives at the same time was unobjectionable...When men, ignorant of any other manner of living, happen to read about these deeds, unless they are deterred

218 THE ABRAHAMIC FAITHS

by an authority, they consider them sins. They cannot understand that their own entire mode of living, in connection of marriage, banqueting, dress, and the other necessities and refinements of human life, seems sinful to people of other nations at other times. (*Christian Instruction*)

...we read that many females served one husband, when the social state of that nation allowed it, and the purpose of the time persuaded it: for neither is it contrary to the nature of marriage. (*De Bono Conjugal*)

In addition, numerous examples of polygamy being sanctioned by Christianity can be cited. (1) Muqawqas (Cyrus),[116] the Christian bishop and patriarch of Alexandria, actually sent Maryam bint Shim'un to Prophet Muhammad as a slave and concubine in the year 629 or 630. (2) In 726, Pope Gregory II reportedly told a missionary to the Germanic tribes that if a man had an infirm wife who was not able to have sexual intercourse, the husband could be allowed to take a second wife if he otherwise could not contain himself sexually. (3) Charlemagne (circa 742-814), the Holy Roman Emperor, had two wives and numerous concubines and instituted a law which appears to have made polygamy legal even for priests. (4) Further, the Protestant Reformation brought new instances of church-sanctioned polygamy into Christianity. As one example, one can point to the Anabaptist rule in Munster, Germany, circa 1531-1534, where polygamy was not only countenanced, but where it was taught that any man who wanted to be a true Christian must practice polygamy. As a second example, one notes the preaching of Bernardino Ochino in 16th-century Poland. As yet a third example, Martin Luther acknowledged that he could find no scriptural prohibition against polygamy, countenanced the polygamous marriage of Philip of Hesse, and advised King Henry VIII simply to take a second wife rather than to divorce his then current wife. Furthermore, Luther's associate, Philipp Melanchton (1497-1560), wrote to King Henry VIII, stating: "(I)t is certain that polygamy is not forbidden by divine law, nor is it a thing altogether without precedent. Abraham, David, and other holy men had several wives; hence it is obvious that polygamy is not against the divine law." (5) It wasn't until November 11, 1563, at the Council of

Trent, that the Roman Catholic Church barred polygamy without exception. (6) In 1650, following the Thirty Years War, the Christian government of Nuremberg (Germany) passed a law that said that every man was allowed to have two wives. (7) In 19th-century America, polygamy was practiced by the Joseph Smith and his followers and continues to be practiced to the current time by certain splinter groups from this movement. (8) Even today, at least two Christian denominations in Africa recognize polygamy, including the Legion of Mary Church and the African Orthodox Autonomous Church South of the Sahara.[117]

Summary

In summarizing the Judaeo-Christian tradition regarding polygamy, the following points need to be emphasized. (1) The *Bible* specifically sanctioned the institution of polygamy, going so far as to specify the individual inheritance rights of the sons resulting from a polygamous marriage. (2) The *Bible* places no conditions or limitations on polygamy, allowing a man to have as many wives as he wanted under any and all conditions. (3) The early Christian churches did not even begin to prohibit polygamy until many centuries after Jesus Christ, and Judaism did not get around to banning polygamy until the 11th century. (4) Further, these later prohibitions against polygamy were the rulings of organized religion, not the rulings of the *Bible*, a consideration that came to the fore during the Protestant Reformation,when various Protestant reformers and communities reinstituted the right of Christian men to be polygamous. (5) In short, polygamy is an inherent part of the Judaeo-Christian tradition.

A FINAL WORD ON WOMEN IN
THE JUDAEO-CHRISTIAN TRADITION

It must be acknowledged that most branches of contemporary Judaism and Christianity do not endorse the blatantly sexist positions embedded in the previously quoted passages from the *Old Testament, New Testament,* and Apostolic Fathers. However, they can do so only at the risk of maintaining that the *Bible* is not the divine and literal word of God. Without in some way disavowing the *Bible* as the word of God, the Judaeo-Christian tradition is stuck with affirming all the blatant and bigoted sexism embedded in the previously quoted passages of the *Bible*.

THE LIBERATION OF WOMEN IN ISLAM

Introduction

Against the backdrop of the role and status of women within the Judaeo-Christian tradition, the culmination of Islam in the revelation of the *Qur'an* and in the teachings of Prophet Muhammad liberated women from the bondage of being considered no more than a father's or husband's property or chattel and ennobled women with such basic human rights as inheritance, freedom of choice regarding marriage, and equality with men in the pursuit of knowledge, in freedom of speech and expression, within the bonds of marriage, and with regard to vows and contracts. These concepts were not only revolutionary in seventh-century Arabia, but they were also a cataclysmic change from how women were viewed in most other parts of the seventh-century world, including in Western and Eastern Christendom. In what follows, the role and status of women in Islam are drawn from the *Qur'an* and the sayings of Prophet Muhammad.

Equality of the Sexes in Creation

As noted previously, the Judaeo-Christian tradition has typically portrayed women as being an inferior to men. This portrayal is especially blatant in certain *New Testament* writings (see, for example, *I Corinthians* 11:7-9, which was quoted in "Women in relation to Men" on page 209 of this chapter) and in the writings of the so-called Apostolic Fathers (see "Original Sin and Role of Women" on pages 211-213 of this chapter). In marked contrast, Islam affirms the equality of the sexes within creation and emphasizes that men and women are of "like nature."

> O mankind! Reverence your Guardian-Lord, Who created you from a single person, created of like nature his mate and from them twain scattered (like seeds) countless men and women— (*Qur'an* 4:1a)

> It is He Who created you from a single person and made his mate of like nature, in order that he might dwell with her (in love). (*Qur'an* 7:189a)

And God has made for you mates (and companions) of your own nature and made for you out of them sons and daughters and grandchildren. (*Qur'an* 16:72a)

According to the *Qur'an*, Eve was made of "like nature" as Adam. Here we find a complete rejection of the Christian concept that man is the glorious "reflection of God; but woman is (only) the reflection of man" (*I Corinthians* 11:7-9).

Equality of the Sexes in Society

The equality of the sexes in Islam is not limited to equality in creation and to men and women being of "like nature." There is also equality of the sexes in human society. Thus, the *Qur'an* enjoins that men and women are "protectors, one of another," that men and women have their "mutual (rights)" through God, and that women "have rights similar to the rights against them, according to what is equitable."

The believers, men and women, are protectors one of another: they enjoin what is just, and forbid what is evil... (*Qur'an* 9:71a)

O mankind! Reverence your Guardian-Lord, Who created you from a single person, created of like nature His mate and from them twain scattered (like seeds) countless men and women—fear God, through Whom ye demand your mutual (rights), and (reverence) the wombs (that bore you): for God ever watches over you. (*Qur'an* 4:1)

And women shall have rights similar to the rights against them, according to what is equitable; but men have a degree (of advantage) over them. And God is exalted in power, wise. (*Qur'an* 2:228b)

With regard to the last quoted verse's statement that men have a degree of advantage over women, this refers to innate physical differences between the sexes and to certain economic advantages and responsibilities that fall to men. As a group, men tend to have greater physical strength and speed than women, thus giving them a "degree (of advantage)" over women in certain areas. Furthermore, as men do not bear children, they have certain "advantages" when it comes to surviving and to the ability to do strenuous labor without interruption during the late stages of pregnancy. The more primitive the society, the more important those physical advantages become for survival. In modern, technological societies, that "degree (of advantage)" becomes miniscule. Additionally, within Islam, men have certain economic responsibilities and liabilities that women do not have. These economic differences are discussed on pages 227-229 in this chapter.

However, before leaving the current discussion of the equality of the sexes in society that is provided by Islam, it is instructive to contrast the Islamic with the Judaeo-Christian position when it comes to making charges of sexual impropriety against women. As illustrated earlier in this chapter, the Deuteronomic Law of the *Old Testament* provided that a bridegroom could accuse his new bride with not having been a virgin at the time of the wedding. Unless the bride's parents could present a bloodied cloth from the wedding night bed, thus supposedly indicating a ruptured hymen and virginity, the bride would be put to death by stoning. As such, the bride was guilty unless "proven" innocent by the bloodstained cloth. Even if the bride was found innocent of the charge, she had to remain married to her accuser, and the most that happened to her accusing husband was that he had to pay the bride's father 100 shekels of silver and could never divorce his bride.

The situation within Islam is far different than that prescribed by the Deuteronomic Law. Within Islam, a woman accused of sexual infidelity is innocent unless proven guilty by four eyewitnesses to her sexual indiscretion. Additionally, a baseless charge of sexual infidelity is dealt with harshly, with the husband having to undergo 80 lashes and being barred from giving evidence in the future. Still further, such a baseless charge provides the woman with grounds for divorce.

And those who launch a charge against chaste women and produce not four witnesses (to support their allegations)—flog them with eighty stripes and reject their evidence ever after; for such men are wicked transgressors—unless they repent thereafter and mend (their conduct); for God is oft-forgiving, most merciful. (*Qur'an* 24:4-5)

Having presented the foregoing, it must be admitted that in Islam there is one way that a husband can bring a charge of sexual infidelity against his wife without having four eyewitnesses to the alleged event. In lieu of the four eyewitnesses, he can make four separate oaths declaring that his wife is guilty of sexual infidelity, provided that he then makes a fifth oath in which he invokes "the curse of God on" himself if he is lying. However, in total contrast to the Deuteronomic Law of the *Old Testament*, the wife may counterbalance her husband's oaths by her own oaths.

> And for those who launch a charge against their spouses and have (in support) no evidence but their own—their solitary evidence (can be received) if they bear witness four times (with an oath) by God that they are solemnly telling the truth; and the fifth (oath should be) that they solemnly invoke the curse of God on themselves if they tell a lie. But it would avert the punishment from the wife, if she bears witness four times (with an oath) by God that (her husband) is telling a lie; and the fifth (oath) should be that she solemnly invokes the wrath of God on herself if (her accuser) is telling the truth. (*Qur'an* 24:6-9)

As can be seen by the above situation, the oath of the wife is countenanced just as fully as the oath of the husband. In marked contrast to the *Old Testament* prescription that a husband can countermand and overrule his wife's oaths (see page 199: 'Women and Vows' in this chapter), Islam gives full credence to the woman's oaths and vows.

In further contrast to the *Old Testament*'s prescription that a wife who was able to prove her innocence had to remain married to the husband who falsely accused her of infidelity (see page 193: 'Women and Virginity' in this chapter), numerous sayings of Prophet Muhammad emphasize that if the husband undergoes the five oaths prescribed in *Qur'an* 24:6-9 and his wife does likewise, a divorce is then granted in the case.

> Said ibn Jubair narrated: "I said to Ibn 'Umar, 'If a man accuses his wife of illegal sexual intercourse (what is the judgment)?' He said, 'God's Prophet separated the couple of Bani 'Ajlan (when the husband accused his wife of having had illegal sexual intercourse).

The Prophet said, 'God knows that one of you two is a liar; so will one of you repent?' But they refused, whereupon he separated them by divorce.'" Aiyub (a sub-narrator) said: "'Amr ibn Dinar said to me, 'In the narration there is something which I do not see you mentioning, i.e., the husband said, 'What about my money (*Mahr* or the dowry initially paid to the wife)?' The Prophet said, 'You are not entitled to take back money, for if you told the truth you have already entered upon her (and consummated your marriage with her), and if you are a liar then you are less entitled to take it back.'" (*Al-Bukhari, Hadith* #7:226; see also *Al-Bukhari, Ahadith* #6:269, 272 & 7:185, 226, 228-229, 231-232, 261; as well as *Abu Dawud, Hadith* #2247).

Not only does the accused wife have her oaths honored on a par with that of her husband, she is freed from being married to him and still keeps the dowry (see page 230:'Women and the Marriage Dowry' in this chapter) given to her at the time of marriage.

Equality of the Sexes in Religion

Not only does Islam prescribe equality of the sexes in creation and in society but also in religion. Good works, deeds of righteousness, humbleness, charity, fasting, the guarding of chastity, and giving praise to God are prescribed for both men and women. Furthermore, with regard to such behavior, God has promised that, "Never will I suffer to be lost the work of any of you, be he male or female…"

> And their Lord hath accepted of them and answered them: "Never will I suffer to be lost the work of any of you, be he male or female: ye are members, one of another…" (*Qur'an* 3:195)

> If any do deeds of righteousness—be they male or female—and have faith, they will enter heaven, and not the least injustice will be done to them. (*Qur'an* 4:124)

> Whoever works righteousness, man or woman, and has faith, verily, to him will We give a new life, and life that is good and

pure, and We will bestow on such their reward according to the best of their actions. (*Qur'an* 16:97)

For Muslim men and women—for believing men and women, for devout men and women, for men and women who are patient and constant, for men and women who humble themselves, for men and women who give in charity, for men and women who fast (and deny themselves), for men and women who guard their chastity, and for men and women who engage much in God's praise—for them has God prepared forgiveness and great reward. (*Qur'an* 33:35)

Furthermore, men and women have the same religious obligations to observe prayer, practice charity, and obey God. God's mercy will pour forth on both men and women, and both sexes stand to inherit eternal bliss.

The believers, men and women, are protectors one of another: they enjoin what is just, and forbid what is evil: they observe regular prayers, practice regular charity, and obey God and His messenger. On them will God pour His mercy: for God is exalted in power, wise. God hath promised to believers—men and women—gardens under which rivers flow, to dwell therein, and beautiful mansions in gardens of everlasting bliss. But the greatest bliss is the good pleasure of God: that is the supreme felicity. (*Qur'an* 9:71-72)

Women and Modest Dress

As previously noted in 'Women and Veiling' on page 206 of this chapter, the *New Testament* prescribed modest dress for women, directed them to avoid ornamentation and expensive clothing that would draw needless attention to themselves, and maintained that they should veil or cover their heads at appropriate times. Similarly, the following passages from the *Qur'an* and sayings of Prophet Muhammad direct women to dress modestly and to refrain from displaying their beauty except to their husbands, their near relatives, eunuchs ("male servants free of physical needs"), small children, etc.

And say to the believing women that they should lower their gaze and guard their modesty; that they should not display their beauty and ornaments except what (must ordinarily) appear thereof; that they should draw their veils over their bosoms and not display their beauty except to their husbands, their fathers, their husbands' fathers, their sons, their husbands' sons, their brothers or their brothers' sons, or their women, or the slaves whom their right hands possess, or male servants free of physical needs, or small children who have no sense of shame of sex; and that they should not strike their feet in order to draw attention to their hidden ornaments. And, O ye believers! Turn ye all together towards God, that ye may attain bliss. (*Qur'an* 24:31)

O Prophet! Tell thy wives and daughters, and the believing women, that they should cast their outer garments over their persons (when abroad): that is most convenient, that they should be known (as such) and not molested. And God is oft-forgiving, most merciful. (*Qur'an* 33:59)

'Aisha narrated that Asma', the daughter of Abu Bakr, entered upon the Apostle of God wearing thin clothes. The Apostle of God turned his attention from her. He said: "O Asma', when a woman reaches the age of menstruation, it does not suit her that she displays her parts of body except this and this," and he pointed to her face and hands. (*Abu Dawud, Hadith* #4092)

However, the above prescriptions for women to dress modestly do not go to extremes, and the non-Muslim reader should note that there is some leeway in the above verses for personal interpretation as to what is meant by modest dress. Thus, devout Muslim women do not all dress exactly alike. Some choose to cover their entire body, including face and eyes, but most do not. Some choose to veil the lower portion of their face, especially if they are wearing makeup, but many do not. Many believe that a scarf over their hair and loose-fitting garments suffice to insure modesty in dress, and thus leave their face and hands exposed. Further, there are some commonsense exceptions to the rules governing dress, such as in the case of elderly women. However, even in the case of such exceptions, reasonable modesty is still expected.

> Such elderly women as are past the prospect of marriage—there is no blame on them if they lay aside their (outer) garments, provided they make not a wanton display of their beauty: but it is best for them to be modest: and God is One Who sees and knows all things. (*Qur'an* 24:60)

It should also be noted that the Qur'anic injunction to dress modestly is not exclusively aimed at women. Men are also prescribed modest dress and are told to lower their gaze respectfully in the company of women.

> Say to the believing men that they should lower their gaze and guard their modesty: that will make for greater purity for them: and God is well acquainted with all that they do. (*Qur'an* 24:30)

Thus, just as women should avoid transparent, tight fitting, or otherwise form-revealing clothing, so should men. Furthermore, men are always to be covered from just above the navel to just below the knee and are forbidden to wear gold and silk, which are materials that women may wear.

> Abu Musa Ash'ari narrated that the Prophet said: "Wearing silk and gold has been made unlawful for the males of my Ummah (community or nation) and lawful for their females." (*Al-Tirmidhi, Hadith* #808; see also *Al-Tirmidhi, Hadith* #4341)

Women's Property Rights

Throughout most of the world's recorded history prior to the 19th century, women have basically had no rights to own property or to earn an income in their own behalf. In fact, one of the very few avenues of employment that was open to them was prostitution. The marked exception to this sorry state of affairs has always been Islam, which guaranteed women the right to own property and assets, to work, to earn their own money in suitable employment, etc. As can be seen in the following Qur'anic verse, God specifically stated that women are allotted what they earn.

> And in nowise covet those things in which God hath bestowed His gifts more freely on some of you than on others: to men is allotted what they earn, and to women what they earn: but ask God of His bounty. For God hath full knowledge of all things. (*Qur'an* 4:32)

In considering the above verse, it should be noted that whatever remuneration a Muslim woman earns is strictly her own money. Thus, the money earned by a Muslim woman who is married and has a family is not family income, but it is strictly the income of the woman who earns it. It is her money, not the family's. She can do with her money whatever she wishes and is not in anyway obliged to help support the family with her income and assets. The financial support of the family lies with the husband and father. Furthermore, in the case of a Muslim woman who is not married, her basic sustenance and living requirements are the responsibility of her nearest male relative, and once again her income and assets belong to her alone. These general considerations are referenced in the following verse from the *Qur'an* and also apply to the property and assets that a woman inherits, an issue discussed in the subsequent section of this chapter.

> Men are the protectors and maintainers of women, because God has given the one more (strength) than the other, and because they support them from their means. (*Qur'an* 4:34a)

As an additional consideration regarding a woman's right to work and accumulate her own property and assets, one turns to an illustrious example from the life of Prophet Muhammad. His first wife, Khadijah, was a wealthy business woman who ran a successful caravan and international trade business. In fact, prior to their marriage, Prophet Muhammad actually worked for Khadijah. Sawdah, another of Prophet Muhammad's wives, worked as a skilled tanner of animal skins. Furthermore, several female Muslims at the time of Prophet Muhammad were engaged in various forms of work, including: (1) the wife of 'Abd Allah ibn Mas'ud, who was an artisan; (2) Khawlah bint Thalabah; (3) Qailah, who was involved in trade; and (4) Asma' bint Makhramah, who was involved in an international perfume business.[118]

Women and Inheritance

As noted previously in 'Women and Inheritance' on page 198 of this chapter, the *Old Testament* dictated that a woman could inherit only if there were no male heirs and then only if she married within her father's clan. In dramatic contrast, as the following verses from the *Qur'an* demonstrate, Islam mandates a woman's inheritance from her parents, her husband, her children, and her siblings.

> From what is left by parents and those nearest related there is a share for men and a share for women, whether the property be small or large—a determinate share. (*Qur'an* 4:7)

> God (thus) directs you as regards your children's (inheritance): to the male, a portion equal to that of two females: if only daughters, two or more, their share is two-thirds of the inheritance; if only one, her share is a half. For parents, a sixth share of the inheritance to each, if the deceased left children; if no children, and the parents are the (only) heirs, the mother has a third; if the deceased left brothers (or sisters) the mother has a sixth…If the man or woman whose inheritance is in question has left neither ascendants nor descendants, but has left a brother or a sister, each one of the two gets a sixth; but if more than two, they share in a third…Thus is it ordained by God, and God is all-knowing, most forbearing. (*Qur'an* 4:11-12)

> Those of you who die and leave widows should bequeath for their widows a year's maintenance and residence; but if they leave (the residence) there is no blame on you for what they do with themselves, provided it is reasonable. And God is exalted in power, wise. (*Qur'an* 2:240)

While some might object that a woman's inheritance is typically half that of a man's, it must be remembered that the man has all the financial responsibilities of maintaining a family, any unmarried women that are his next of kin, including the woman who may be inheriting alongside of him, etc. In contrast, the woman is free of all such responsibilities.

Men are the protectors and maintainers of women, because God has given the one more (physical strength, but also more from the inheritance) than the other, and because they support them from their means. (*Qur'an* 4:34a)

Thus, while the man's inheritance is really an inheritance by his family, the woman's inheritance is strictly her own. Seen from this perspective, it might even be argued that the woman's strictly personal inheritance is actually larger than that of the man's.

Women and the Marriage Dowry

As noted in 'Women and the Dowry' on page 202-203 of this chapter, the *Old Testament* prescriptions concerning the marriage dowry (*mohar*) were that this was an amount of money given by the bridegroom to the bride's father or male next of kin. In other words, the bride was being "sold" by her male relative to her husband, with the male relative pocketing the proceeds. In marked contrast, the *Qur'an* repeatedly stresses that the dowry (*Mahr*) must be paid to the bride herself. The *Mahr* becomes the bride's property and is under her control and direction. The following Qur'anic verses are illustrative of the concept of *Mahr* within Islam and stress that the *Mahr*   is to be paid directly to the bride.

> And give the women (on marriage) their dower as a free gift; but if they, of their own good pleasure, remit any part of it to you, take it and enjoy it with right good cheer. (*Qur'an* 4:4)

> ...except for these (who are prohibited to you in marriage), all others are lawful, provided ye seek (them in marriage) with gifts from your property—desiring chastity, not lust. Seeing that ye derive benefit from them, give them their dowers (at least) as prescribed: but if, after a dower is prescribed, ye agree mutually (to vary it), there is no blame on you, and God is all-knowing, all-wise. (*Qur'an* 4:24)

> (Lawful unto you in marriage) are (not only) chaste women who are believers, but chaste women among the People of the Book, revealed before your time—when ye give them their due dowers, and desire

chastity, not lewdness. (*Qur'an* 5:5b)

...there will be no blame on you if ye marry them on payment of their dower to them... (*Qur'an* 60:10b)

Within Islam, there are no exceptions to the need for the groom to pay a mutually agreed upon Mahr to the bride. Even Prophet Muhammad was directly enjoined to pay the *Mahr.*

O Prophet! We have made lawful to thee they wives to whom thou hast paid their dowers... (*Qur'an* 33:50)

Within Islam, the *Mahr* or dowry became the exclusive property of the bride. Furthermore, even in the case of subsequent divorce, no matter how large a dowry had been paid, the dowry remained the woman's property.

But if ye decide to take one wife in place of another, even if ye had given the latter a whole treasure for dower, take not the least bit of it back; would ye take it by slander and a manifest wrong? And how could ye take it when ye have gone in unto each other, and they have taken from you a solemn covenant? (*Qur'an* 4:20-21)

Women and Marriage

As previously documented earlier in this chapter, the Biblical tradition not only does not prohibit the involuntary marriage of women, it actually mandates involuntary marriage in certain situations, such as in cases of the rape of a woman who is not married or engaged, of women who stand to inherit because there is no male heir, of Levirate Marriage, etc. Against this historical background, it is indeed ironic that one of the false charges so often leveled against Islam is that it forces women into involuntary marriages. In fact, Islam prohibits the involuntary marriage of a woman, insists that the consent of a woman is needed before any marriage can transpire, regardless of whether that woman is a virgin or has been previously married, and specifically prohibits Levirate Marriage and other forms of marriage in which a man "inherits" a wife from a male relative.

O ye who believe! Ye are forbidden to inherit women against their will. (*Qur'an* 4:19a)

'Aisha narrated: "God's Apostle said: 'It is essential to have the consent of a virgin (for the marriage).' I said, 'A virgin feels shy.' The
Prophet said, 'Her silence means her consent.'" (*Al-Bukhari, Hadith*
#9:101)

Abu Huraira reported God's Messenger as having said: "A woman
without a husband must not be married until she is consulted, and
a virgin must not be married until her permission is sought."
They asked the Prophet of God how her (a virgin's) consent can
be solicited? He said: "That she keeps silence." (*Muslim, Hadith*
#3303; see also *Muslim, Hadith #3304*)

'Aisha reported: "I asked God's Messenger about a virgin whose
marriage is solemnized by her guardian, whether it was necessary
or not to consult her. God's Messenger said: 'Yes, she must be
consulted.'" 'Aisha reported: "I told him that she feels shy, where-
upon God's Messenger said: 'Her silence implies her consent.'"
(*Muslim, Hadith #3305*)

Ibn 'Abbas reported God's Messenger as saying: "A woman who has
been previously married has more right to her person than her
guardian. And a virgin should also be consulted, and her silence
implies her consent." (*Muslim, Hadith #3307*; see also *Muslim,
Ahadith #3306 & 3308*)

As noted in several of the above sayings of Prophet Muhammad, a
virgin's consent is required before she can be married to someone. However,
in order to preserve her modesty and to minimize any appearance that she
is overly eager to marry, the convention is that when a marriage proposal
is given to her through her guardian, she either assents to the proposal by
keeping her silence or she rejects the proposal verbally. While this convention may be subject to misinterpretation by some who are not familiar with
it, marital choice remains the prerogative of the virgin, as it does of every
woman.

Having established that there is no involuntary marriage in Islam, it
is instructive to turn to the teachings of the *Qur'an* on the nature of the
marital relationship. In a fitting metaphor, the *Qur'an* teaches that spouses

are like garments to each other, offering each other protection and warmth. Further, in daily life, nothing comes closer to a person than his or her own clothing. Thus, nothing is closer to a person than his or her spouse. The *Qur'an* also instructs that within the marital state one should "dwell in tranquility" with one's spouse and that there should be "love and mercy" between the two spouses. Husbands are specifically enjoined that they should not treat their wives "with harshness," should not infringe upon their wives' control of their dowry, and should "live with them on a footing of kindness and equity."

> They (your wives) are your garments and ye are their garments. (*Qur'an* 2:187b)

> And among His signs is this, that He created for you mates from among yourselves, that ye may dwell in tranquility with them, and He has put love and mercy between your (hearts): verily in that are signs for those who reflect. (*Qur'an* 30:21)

> O ye who believe! Ye are forbidden to inherit women against their will. Nor should ye treat them with harshness, that ye may take away part of the dower ye have given them—except where they have been guilty of open lewdness; on the contrary live with them on a footing of kindness and equity. If ye take a dislike to them, it may be that ye dislike a thing, and God brings about through it a great deal of good. (*Qur'an* 4:19)

Supplementing the Qur'anic instructions regarding the marital state, the following saying of Prophet Muhammad offers additional assurance as to the status of the wife in a Muslim marriage by noting that the best among Muslim men "are those who behave best towards their wives."

> Abu Huraira narrated that the Prophet said: "The most perfect Muslim in the matter of faith is one who has excellent behavior, and the best among you are those who behave best towards their wives." (*Al-Tirmidhi, Hadith* #278; see also *Al-Tirmidhi, Ahadith* #628 and 3264)

Despite the above instructions and despite the best of intentions, many marriages do encounter rough sailing at times. In an era preceding the advent of marital counseling professionals by over 1,300 years, the *Qur'an* even offers a guideline for resolution of marital strains and for the reconciliation of estranged spouses.

> If ye fear a breach between them twain, appoint (two) arbiters, one from his family and the other from hers; if they wish for peace, God will cause their reconciliation: for God hath full knowledge, and is acquainted with all things. (*Qur'an* 4:35)

Despite the above information regarding the status of the wife in a Muslim marriage, some Western commentators on Islam have seized on part of one verse of the *Qur'an* to insist that Islam permits husbands to beat their wives. The relevant verse is as follows.

> As to those women on whose part ye fear disloyalty and ill-conduct, admonish them (first), (next), refuse to share their beds, (and lastly) beat them (lightly); but if they return to obedience, seek not against them means (of annoyance): for God is most high, great (above you all). (*Qur'an* 4:34b)

The Arabic word that is translated as "beat" in the above verse is "*Udhdhribuu*," which literally means to strike. The English word "beat" is an unfortunate translation, as it conveys the erroneous impression of a beating being administered. In contrast, "strike" covers the whole range of possibilities from a slight tap to a forceful punch, and it is only upon turning to the sayings of Prophet Muhammad that a proper understanding of the above Qur'anic verse can be achieved.

There are numerous sayings of Prophet Muhammad that are relevant to a correct understanding of the above Qur'anic verse. Summing across these narrations, which are quoted below, one quickly discovers that husbands are not allowed to "strike" their wives except in the case "of flagrant misbehavior," and even then they may not "inflict upon them any severe punishment." Furthermore, a husband is enjoined that he may "not strike her on the face" etc.

> 'Amr ibn Al-Ahwas Al-Jushami narrated that he heard the Prophet say in his farewell address on the eve of his Last Pilgrimage, after he had glorified and praised God, he cautioned his followers: "Listen!

Treat women kindly...Should they be guilty of flagrant misbehavior, you may remove them from your beds and beat them, but do not inflict upon them any severe punishment..." (*Al-Tirmidhi, Hadith* #276)

Hakim ibn Mu'awiyah Al-Qushairi quoted his father as saying that he asked the Apostle of God, "What is the right of the wife of one of us over him?" He replied: "That you should give her food when you eat, clothe her when you clothe yourself, do not strike her on the face, do not revile her or separate yourself from her except in the house." (*Abu Dawud, Hadith* #2137)

Mu'awiyah Al-Qushairi said: "I went to the Apostle of God and asked him: 'What do you say about our wives?' He replied: 'Give them food what you have for yourself, and clothe them by which you clothe yourself, and do not beat them, and do not revile them.'" (*Abu Dawud, Hadith* #2139; see also *Abu Dawud, Hadith* #2138)

'Abd Allah ibn Zama narrated that the Prophet forbade laughing at a person who passes wind and said, "How does anyone of you beat his wife as he beats the stallion camel, and then he may embrace (sleep with) her?" (*Al-Bukhari, Hadith* #8:68)

...The Messenger of God...addressed the people, saying..."Fear God concerning women! Verily you have taken them on the security of God, and intercourse with them has been made lawful unto you by words of God. You too have right over them, and that they should not allow anyone to sit on your bed whom you do not like. But if they do that, you can chastise them, but not severely..." (*Muslim, Hadith* #2803)

The sum total of the above narrations illustrates that *Qur'an* 4:34b does not allow a husband to "beat" his wife in any way that causes injury or physical harm. In short, the "beating" referred to in *Qur'an* 4:34b is akin to a private psychodrama in which the husband symbolically expresses his displeasure, and it is similar to the American idiom of "being beaten with a wet noodle." Just as Shakespeare's Merchant of Venice could have his pound of flesh only if he did not spill a single drop of blood, so can the husband "beat" his wife only if he does not cause any physical pain, harm, or injury. So much for the erroneous and slanderous statements that Islam allows husbands to beat their wives.

Women and Divorce

Unfortunately, even within Islam, marriages are not always successful. Thus, while disapproving of divorce in principle, Islam recognizes that divorce is sometimes the only solution to a troubled marriage and thus authorizes divorce.

> 'Abd Allah ibn 'Umar narrated that the Prophet said: "Of all the lawful acts, the most detestable to God is divorce." (*Abu Dawud, Hadith* #2173)

> Muharib narrated that the Prophet said: "God did not make anything lawful more abominable to Him than divorce." (*Abu Dawud, Hadith* #2172)

> Mu'adh ibn Jabal narrated that God's Messenger said to him, "Mu'adh, God has created nothing on the face of the earth dearer to Him than emancipation, and God has created nothing on the face of the earth more hateful to Him than divorce." *(Al-Tirmidhi, Hadith* #3294)

Up until the last century or so, divorce within the Judaeo-Christian tradition was strictly the prerogative of the husband and remains so within Orthodox Judaism to this very date. In contrast, Islam acknowledges the right of both the husband and the wife to initiate divorce proceedings and did so well over a thousand years before the Christian West bestowed this right upon women.

> If a wife fears cruelty or desertion on her husband's part, there is no blame on them if they arrange an amicable settlement between themselves; and such settlement is best; even though men's souls are swayed by greed. But if ye do good and practice self-restraint, God is well-acquainted with all that ye do. (*Qur'an* 4:128)

Numerous *Ahadith* of Prophet Muhammad reiterate the above Qur'anic right of a wife to initiate a divorce, while disapproving of divorce in principle. Thus, a wife should have a "strong reason" for initiating a divorce, as should any husband who divorces his wife.

> Thawban narrated that the Prophet said: "If any woman asks her husband for divorce without some strong reason, the odor of paradise will be forbidden to her." (*Abu Dawud, Hadith* #2218)

> Ibn ʿAbbas narrated that the wife of Thabit ibn Qais ibn Shammas came to the Prophet and said, "O God's Apostle! I do not blame Thabit for any defects in his character or his religion, but I am afraid that I (being a Muslim) may become unthankful for God's blessings." On that, God's Apostle said (to her), "Will you return his garden to him?" She said, "Yes." So she returned his garden to him, and the Prophet told him to divorce her. (*Al-Bukhari, Hadith* #7:199; see also *Al-Bukhari, Ahadith* #7:197-198)

Further, once a divorce has been initiated, Islam guarantees a whole array of rights possessed by the divorced wife. She is guaranteed her reasonable maintenance, the dowry she received upon marriage, and any gifts her ex-husband gave to her.

> For divorced women maintenance (should be provided) on a reasonable (scale). This is a duty on the righteous. (*Qur'an* 2:241)

> There is no blame on you if ye divorce women before consummation or the fixation of their dower; but bestow on them (a suitable gift), the wealthy according to his means, and the poor according to his means—a gift of reasonable amount is due from those who wish to do the right thing. And if ye divorce them before consummation, but after the fixation of a dower for them, then the half of the dower (is due to them), unless they remit it or (the man's half) is remitted by him in whose hands is the marriage tie; and the remission (of the man's half) is the nearest to righteousness and do not forget liberality between yourselves. For God sees well all that ye do. (*Qur'an* 2:236-237)

> A divorce is only permissible twice: after that, the parties should either hold together on equitable terms, or separate with kindness.

It is not lawful for you (men) to take back any of your gifts (from your wives), except when both parties fear that they would be unable to keep the limits ordained by God. If ye (judges) do indeed fear that they would be unable to keep the limits ordained by God, there is not blame on either of them if she gives something for her freedom. These are the limits ordained by God; so do not transgress them. If any do transgress the limits ordained by God, such persons wrong (themselves as well as others). (*Qur'an* 2:229)

Within Islam, there is a waiting period (*'Iddah*) between the pronouncement of divorce and the time at which an irrevocable divorce takes place. This three-month period allows for reconsideration and for time to discover whether or not a pregnancy is in progress, the latter of which affects the husband's future obligations. During this waiting period, the husband must provide financial support to his wife and is forbidden to turn his wife out of the house, to annoy her, to restrict her, or to otherwise cause her discomfort or harassment. If a pregnancy is discovered and the divorce continues to its irrevocable stage, then the husband bears additional costs for the care of the child and must even recompense the mother for nursing the child.

When ye divorce women, and they fulfill the term of their (*'Iddah*), either take them back on equitable terms or set them free on equitable terms; but do not take them back to injure them (or) to take undue advantage; if any one does that, he wrongs his own soul. (*Qur'an* 2:231a)

O Prophet! When ye do divorce women...turn them not out of their houses, nor shall they (themselves) leave, except in case they are guilty of some open lewdness...Let the women live (in *'Iddah*) in the same style as ye live, according to your means: annoy them not, so as to restrict them. And if they carry (life in their wombs), then spend (your substance) on them until they deliver their burden: and if they suckle your (offspring), give them their recompense: and take mutual counsel together, according to what is just and reasonable... (*Qur'an* 65:1, 6)

The mothers shall give suck to their offspring for two whole years, if the father desires to complete the term. But he shall bear the cost of their food and clothing on equitable terms. No soul shall have a burden laid on it greater than it can bear. No mother shall be treated unfairly on account of her child. (*Qur'an* 2:233a)

Before leaving the topic of a woman's rights in divorce, it should be noted that the marriage contract typically specifies two *Mahr* or dowries. The first or initial *Mahr* has been previously discussed and becomes the wife's possession upon marriage. The second or delayed *Mahr* consists of a specified amount that the husband must pay to the wife in the event he divorces her.

Women, Free Speech and Education

As noted previously in 'Women in the Church' on pages 207-208 of this chapter, Paul of Tarsus forbade early Christian women from speaking in the church or congregation. In contrast, within Islam, women have been guaranteed their rights of free speech and free expression ever since the revelation of the *Qur'an* in the seventh century. Furthermore, women had the right to bring their concerns and complaints directly to the attention of Prophet Muhammad. One such notable example is directly referenced in the *Qur'an*.

God has indeed heard (and accepted) the statement of the woman who pleads with thee concerning her husband and carries her complaint (in prayer) to God: and God (always) hears the arguments between both sides among you: for God hears and sees (all things). (*Qur'an* 58:1)

Additional Qur'anic verses witness to women speaking openly, publicly, and in their own behalf, both to Prophet Muhammad and to the community of Muslim believers.

O Prophet! When believing women come to thee to take the oath of fealty to thee, that they will not associate in worship any other thing whatever with God, that they will not steal, that they will not commit adultery (or fornication), that they will not kill their children, that they will not utter slander, intentionally forging falsehood, and that they will not disobey thee in any just matter—then do thou receive their fealty and pray to God for the forgiveness (of their sins): for God is oft-forgiving, most merciful. (*Qur'an* 60:12)

O ye who believe! When there come to you believing women refugees, examine (and test) them: God knows best as to their faith: if ye ascertain that they are believers, then send them not back to the unbelievers. (*Qur'an* 60:10a)

As Prophet Muhammad was the Islamic government during his lifetime, the examples of women approaching him to voice their complaints or to ask for redress constitute the Islamic acknowledgement that women have equal rights with men to petition before the court of law. One such noticeable example concerns two slave girls, whose wicked owner had forced them into a life of prostitution. They protested their lot to Prophet Muhammad, and this resulted in additional revelation (*Qur'an* 24:33) that prohibited a master from prostituting his servants and slaves. This example is also significant in that it illustrates that even female slaves could petition before the court regarding their grievances and concerns. In contrast, slaves in Christian America never had any standing before the American justice system, a practice that continued until the abolition of slavery in the 1860s.

Jabir reported that 'Abd Allah ibn Ubayy ibn Salul had two slave girls, one was called Musaika and the other one was called Umaima, and he ('Abd Allah) compelled them to prostitution. They made a complaint about this to God's Messenger, and it was upon this that this verse was revealed: "But force not your maids to prostitution when they desire chastity, in order that ye may make a gain in the goods of this life. But if anyone compels them, yet, after such compulsion, is God oft-forgiving, most merciful (to those maids who are forced into prostitution) (*Qur'an* 24:33)." (*Muslim, Hadith* #7181)

Additional examples (*Al-Bukhari, Hadith* #7:197-199) of women petitioning directly to Prophet Muhammad were presented previously on pages 236-237 of this chapter.

In the wake of the publicity surrounding the decidedly non-Islamic practice of the former Taliban regime of Afghanistan in prohibiting women from receiving an education, it is helpful to note that Islam established the right of every woman to receive an education and did so over a thousand years before the Christian West finally did so.

> Anas reported that the Messenger of God said: "Search for knowledge is compulsory upon every Muslim male and Muslim female." (*Ibn Majah*[119])

Of special note, despite all his other duties and responsibilities, even Prophet Muhammad was directly involved in providing education for Muslim women. The following narratives illustrate this point, as well as reiterating that Muslim women were free to approach the Prophet directly and to petition him with their grievances and concerns.

> Abu Said narrated that a woman came to God's Apostle and said, "O God's Apostle! Men (only) benefit by your teachings, so please devote to us from (some of) your time a day on which we may come to you so that you may teach us of what God has taught you." God's Apostle said, "Gather on such-and-such a day at such-and-such a place." They gathered and God's Apostle came to them and taught them of what God had taught him. (*Al-Bukhari, Hadith* #9:413)

At a time and place in which slavery still existed, Prophet Muhammad strongly encouraged every slave owner to educate his female slaves and to manumit them. He stressed that the education of a female slave and her manumission would lead to additional divine reward for her owner, indicating that it was the pleasure of God that female slaves be educated and freed.

> Abu Musa Al-Ash'ari narrated that the Prophet said: "He who has a slave girl and teaches her good manners and improves her education and then manumits and marries her will get a double reward..." (*Al-Bukhari, Hadith* #3:723)

As a brief digression and as an additional reflection of Islam's encouragement of the abolition of slavery, it is fitting to reiterate the following *Hadith*, which was quoted earlier.

Mu'adh ibn Jabal narrated that God's Messenger said to him, "Mu'adh, God has created nothing on the face of the earth dearer to Him than emancipation, and God has created nothing on the face of the earth more hateful to Him than divorce." (*Al-Tirmidhi, Hadith* #3294)

Not only have Muslim women had the rights to free speech, free expression, and education ever since the early seventh century, they have also taught and produced some of Islam's greatest religious scholars. For example, numerous women were narrators of *Ahadith* and gave legal decisions, thus being teachers of both men and women. Other Muslim women memorized all or a good part of the *Qur'an* and were thus Qur'anic scholars in their own right. A very partial listing of such scholarly women among the early Muslim community would include: 'Aisha, Hafsah, Um Salamah, Um Waraqah, Hind bint Asad, Um Hisham bint Harithah, Ra'ita bint Hayyan, Um Sa'd bint Sa'd ibn Rabi', Um Asad, Safiyah, Um Habibah, Juwairiyah, Maimunah, Fatimah Zahra, Um Sharik, Um 'Atiyah, Asma' bint Abu Bakr, Haila bint Qanif, Khaulah bint Tuwait, Um Al-Darda', 'Atikah bint Zaid, Sahlah bint Suhail, Fatimah bint Qais, Zainab bint Abu Salamah, Um Aiman, and Um Yusuf. Other early Muslim women were renowned for their knowledge in such areas as speech, medicine and surgery, and poetry. A partial listing of these early Muslim women would include: Asma' bint Sakan, Rufadah Aslamiyah, Um Muta', Um Kabshah, Hamnah bint Jahsh, Mu'adhah, Laila, Umaimah, Um Ziyad, Rubayyi' bint Muawwidh, Um Sulaim, Khansa, Su'da, Umamah, Muridiyah, Hind bint Harith, Hind bint Uthathah, etc.[120]

However, 'Aisha, the wife of Prophet Muhammad, was probably the greatest of the female scholars within the early Muslim community, especially when it came to religious knowledge. She memorized the entirety of the *Qur'an* and narrated a total of 2,210 *Ahadith*, being surpassed in that regard only by Abu Huraira, 'Abd Allah ibn 'Umar, and Anas. In addition, she had few equals when it came to Islamic jurisprudence. With regard to her religious knowledge, the following narration of Abu Musa is relevant.

Abu Musa narrated: "We, the companions of God's Messenger,

never asked 'Aisha about a tradition regarding which we were in doubt without finding that she had some knowledge of it." (*Al-Tirmidhi, Hadith* #6185)

Women and Ritual Purity

Like the Judaeo-Christian tradition (see page 192: 'Women and Ritual Purity' in this chapter), Islam holds that a woman is ritually unclean during menses and for a short time following the birth of a child. During these times, she is excused from praying, fasting, and from reading the *Qur'an* and is prohibited from having sexual intercourse.

They ask thee concerning women's courses. Say: they are a hurt and a pollution: so keep away from women in their courses, and do not approach them until they are clean. But when they have purified themselves, ye may approach them in any manner, time, or place ordained for you by God. For God loves those who turn to Him constantly and He loves those who keep themselves pure and clean. (*Qur'an* 2:222)

While the Judaeo-Christian tradition prescribed that a woman's ritual impurity after delivering a female child was twice that as when she gave birth to a male, no such distinction exists within Islam. Following the birth of a child, the period of ritual impurity is 40 days, regardless of the gender of the child.

Women and Rape

As previously shown in this chapter, the Biblical response to rape was a far cry from any modern concept of justice. If an engaged or married woman were raped in a town or city, she was to be put to death along with her attacker, because she had not yelled loudly enough or fought strenuously enough to draw the attention of someone who could intervene and prevent the rape. If a woman who was not married or engaged were raped, she was to be forcibly married to her attacker, who got off with paying a small price to the victim's father as recompense for having assaulted the victim's father's honor.

Within Islam, a raped woman is always seen as the victim, not the criminal. She is never subjected to the Biblically mandated miscarriage of justice that sometimes necessitates that the raped woman be put to death or forcibly married to her attacker. Even in the case where the woman, no doubt secondary to the emotional trauma she has undergone, mistakenly identifies the wrong man as being her assailant, she is not penalized in any manner. In contrast, her assailant is always held to be guilty of having committed a capital crime, and his sentence is death. The following sayings of Prophet Muhammad illustrate these points.

> Wa'el ibn Hujr narrated that when a woman was forced against her will in the time of God's Messenger, he avoided punishing her, but inflicted it on the one who had molested her. (*Al-Tirmidhi, Hadith* #3571)

> 'Alqamah ibn Wa'el said on the authority of his father that a woman went out in the time of the Prophet for prayer, and a man attacked her and got his desire of her. She shouted and he went off, and when a man came by, she said: "That (man) did such and such to me." And when a company of the Emigrants came by, she said: "That man did such and such to me." They went and seized the man about whom they (mistakenly) thought that he had intercourse with her and brought him to her. She (erroneously) said: "Yes, this is he." Then, they brought him to the Apostle of God. When he (the Prophet) was about to award the sentence, the (another) man who had (actually) assaulted her stood up and said: "Apostle of God, I am the man who has done it with her." He (the Prophet) said to her: "Go away, for God has forgiven you." But he told the man (who was mistakenly seized) some good words, and of the man who had intercourse with her, he said: "Stone him to death." (*Abu Dawud, Hadith* #4366)

Summary

As can be seen from the above discussion, the status of women dictated by both the *Qur'an* and the sayings of Prophet Muhammad is infinitely better than that allowed to them by the *Bible*. In fact, as early as the seventh century, Islam mandated rights to women that they were not to receive within Western Christendom until the 19th and 20th centuries. In essence, Islam stressed the equality of men and women without obscuring those biological differences, e.g., in physical strength and reproduction, which do typically exist between the sexes.

ISLAM AND ORIGINAL SIN

As noted previously, Islam rejects the Western Christian concept of Original Sin as an inherited condition, as do Judaism and Eastern Christianity. However, along with Western Christianity, both Judaism and Eastern Christianity appear to blame Eve rather exclusively for initiating sin into the world.

> So when the woman saw that the tree was good for food, and that it was a delight to the eyes, and that the tree was to be desired to make one wise, she took of its fruit and ate; and she also gave some to her husband, who was with her, and he ate...And to the man he (God) said, "Because you have listened to the voice of your wife, and have eaten of the tree about which I commanded you, 'You shall not eat of it,' cursed is the ground because of you; in toil you shall eat of it all the days of your life..." (*Genesis* 3:6, 17)

> From a woman did sin originate, and because of her "we all must die." (*Ecclesiasticus* 25:24)

> For Adam was formed first, then Eve; and Adam was not deceived, but the woman was deceived and became a transgressor. (*I Timothy* 2:13-14)

As Eve is the prototype for all females, the Judaeo-Christian tradition tends to funnel this blame to all members of the female sex. In contrast, Islam views the initial sin of mankind as lying equally at the feet of both Adam and Eve, and thus women are held to be in no lower status than men.

> We said: "O Adam! Dwell thou and thy wife in the garden and eat of the bountiful things therein as (where and when) ye will; but approach not this tree, or ye run into harm and transgression." Then did Satan make them slip from the (garden), and get them

out of the state (of felicity) in which they had been. We said: "Get ye down, all (ye people), with enmity between yourselves. On earth will be your dwelling place and your means of livelihood for a time." (*Qur'an* 2:35-36)

Then began Satan to whisper suggestions to them, in order to reveal to them their shame that was hidden from them (before). He said: "Your Lord only forbade you this tree, lest ye should become angels or such beings as live forever." And he swore to them both that he was their sincere adviser. So by deceit he brought about their fall. When they tasted of the tree, their shame became manifest to them, and they began to sew together the leaves of the garden over their bodies. And their Lord called unto them: "Did I not forbid you that tree, and tell you that Satan was an avowed enemy unto you?" They said: "Our Lord! We have wronged our own souls: if Thou forgive us not and bestow not upon us Thy mercy, we shall certainly be lost." (God) said: "Get ye down, with enmity between yourselves. On earth will be your dwelling place and your means of livelihood—for a time." He said: "Therein shall ye live, and therein shall ye die; but from it shall ye be taken out (at last)." (*Qur'an* 7:20-25)

But Satan whispered evil to him: he said, "O Adam! Shall I lead thee to the tree of eternity and to a kingdom that never decays?" In the result, they both ate of the tree, and so their nakedness appeared to them: they began to sew together, for their covering, leaves from the garden: thus did Adam disobey his Lord, and allow himself to be seduced. (*Qur'an* 20:120-121)

The reader will note that in the above Qur'anic passages there is no portrayal of Eve as being the sinful temptress who leads Adam astray. In marked contrast to the *New Testament* statement that "Adam was not deceived, but the woman was deceived and became a transgressor," the *Qur'an* directly states that Adam was deceived by Satan every bit as much as was Eve.

ISLAM AND POLYGAMY

As demonstrated in 'Polygamy in the *Bible*' on page 215 of this chapter, the *Bible* licenses unlimited and unconditional polygamy, with the modest exception that a man cannot be married to multiple wives who are too closely related to each other, e.g., sisters. Further, the *Bible* actually mandates polygamy in certain cases of Levirate Marriage and in the case of a married man who rapes a woman who is neither married nor engaged. It was only with the issuance of the *Talmud* that post Biblical Judaism began to put restrictions on polygamy by limiting the number of wives of a commoner to four and the number of wives of a king to 18. Likewise, it was only several centuries after Jesus Christ that Christianity began to place limits and conditions on polygamy. However, as argued by such Christian stalwarts as Martin Luther, such limitations and conditions were not Biblically based.

In contrast to the Biblical license to unlimited and basically unconditional polygamy, the *Qur'an* acknowledges polygamy as a conditional right of men. As noted in the following Qur'anic verse, only if certain conditions are met is polygamy authorized. Further, even if those conditions are met, there is a limit of four placed on the number of wives that a man may have simultaneously.

> If ye fear that ye shall not be able to deal justly with the orphans, marry women of your choice, two, or three, or four; but if ye fear that ye shall not be able to deal justly (with them), then only one, or (a captive) that your right hands possess. That will be more suitable to prevent you from doing injustice. (*Qur'an* 4:3)

How likely is it that a man can actually meet the second condition specified above, i.e., that he "be able to deal justly" with multiple wives? The following verse from the *Qur'an* appears to answer that question and helps to explain why polygamy is actually a relatively rare phenomenon among Muslims.

> Ye are never able to be fair and just as between women, even if it is your ardent desire: but turn not away (from a woman) altogether, so as to leave her (as it were) hanging (in the air). If ye come to a friendly understanding, and practice self-restraint, God is oft-for-

giving, most merciful. (*Qur'an* 4:129)

SUMMARY AND CONCLUSIONS

In closing this chapter, there are two points that need to be emphasized. Firstly, it must be acknowledged that most contemporary Christians and Jews are probably horrified at the way that women are portrayed in the *Bible*. They undoubtedly reject the second-class status afforded to women in the *Bible*, as well as the blatant double standards involving women's rights or their lack thereof. Likewise, most Christians are probably appalled at the views on women expressed by many of the so-called Apostolic Fathers of Christianity. Nonetheless, the sorry facts remain that the *Bible* does teach a remarkably sexist and misogynist view of women and that this same *Bible* is the scriptural basis for both Christianity and Judaism. This leaves contemporary Jews and Christians in the unenviable position of having to reconcile the Biblical portrayal of women with their belief that the *Bible* is the revealed word of God. Appeals to historical circumstances and metaphorical interpretations, as well as attempts to decipher the divine inspiration lying behind the words of patriarchal authors who were the victims of their time and culture, provide reconciliation only by further undermining the claimed status of the *Bible* as revealed scripture. In such scenarios, contemporary human reason, not divine revelation, becomes the basis of religion.

Secondly, it must be admitted that not every Muslim practices Islam as it was revealed in the *Qur'an* and as it was clarified in the *Ahadith*. Too often, various cultural factors tend to taint the religious practice of many Muslims. This is especially prevalent when it comes to the role and status of women. However, a sharp distinction needs to be made between the cultural practices of certain Muslims when it comes to women and the teachings of Islam about women. While culturally determined conduct and behavior may undermine the role and status of women among some Muslims, Islam emphatically and consistently elevates the role and status of women and places women as the equals of men, while still acknowledging certain undeniable biological differences that generally hold between the sexes, such as issues pertaining to physical strength and reproductive functioning.

Chapter

8

Reconciliation and the Children of Abraham

Each of us, whether Jew, Christian, or Muslim, believes that his or her own religion is the one, true religion. After all, any other belief would be to make a mockery of one's religious affiliation. Why would any Jew adhere to Judaism if he or she actually thought that Christianity or Islam represented an equally viable religious alternative? Why would any Christian remain a Christian or any Muslim remain a Muslim if he or she actually believed that one or both of the other Abrahamic faiths were equally viable and correct? To hold that one's own religion is the best religion or only true revelation is not an expression of religious bigotry and intolerance, but an expression of spiritual faith and belief. It is only when a person cannot respect the religious traditions and beliefs of the other that one crosses the line between faith and bigotry. It is not lack of agreement that signifies religious bigotry, but lack of respect and tolerance.

However, sincere respect and tolerance cannot occur in a vacuum. To respect the religion of one's neighbor, one must first of all have at least some rudimentary and unbiased understanding of that religion. To a certain extent, at least within contemporary America, most Jews and Christians have managed to overcome the religious barriers separating them in the past and have come to have some understanding and respect for the religious beliefs of the other. With over seven million Muslims now living in America, with Islam being the fastest growing religion in America today, and with Islam now being the second largest religion in America, it is past time that the religious children of Abraham seek reconciliation among themselves as Jews, Christians, and Muslims.

As a first step in that direction, the adherents of the three Abrahamic faiths need to overcome the misconceptions of the past and blot out the distortions of the present. Jews and Christians need to recognize and understand that Islam is not represented by Osama bin Laden, suicide bombers, and third-world cultural examples of the suppression of women's rights. Jews and Muslims must appreciate that David Koresh and James Jones do not speak for Christianity and that the atrocities of the Crusades do not represent the higher ideals of contemporary Christianity. Muslims and Christians must acknowledge the fact that Judaism is not represented by Baruch Goldstein gunning down Muslims as they prayed in a Hebron mosque in 1994, by right wing Israeli settlers, or by the continuing violence against Palestinian civilians by the Israeli military. All of us, whether Jew, Christian, or Muslim, need to tone down our rhetoric when it comes to discussing the other Abrahamic faiths. We need to focus on the higher ideals that we share and not on the baser religious deviations in our midst.

To accomplish the above, we must begin to understand and acknowledge the tremendous common ground that binds these three Abrahamic faiths together within a common prophetic tradition. Additionally, we must begin to realize that the religious teachings and ethical instructions of these three religions also have much in common. Most importantly, we must acknowledge the common commitment to worship the One God and the common commitment to better the welfare of our neighbor and fellow man.

With regard to the above points, one cannot help but applaud certain statements that have been emanating from the Roman Catholic Church ever since 1964. These statements are worthy of reproduction and emphasis.

> Then (we refer) to the adorers of God according to the conception of monotheism, the Muslim religion especially, deserving of our admiration for all that is true and good in their worship of God. (Pope Paul VI, *Ecclesiam Suam 107*, August 6, 1965)
>
> But the plan of salvation also includes those who acknowledge the Creator, in the first place among whom are the Muslims: these profess to hold the faith of Abraham, and together with us they adore the one, merciful God, mankind's judge on the last day. (Second Vatican Council, Lumen Gentium 16, November 21, 1964)
>
> My brothers, when I think of this spiritual heritage (Islam) and the value it has for man and for society, its capacity of offering, particularly in the young, guidance for life, filling the gap left by materialism, and giving a reliable foundation to social and juridical organization, I wonder if it is not urgent, precisely today when Christians and Muslims have entered a new period of history, to recognize and develop the spiritual bonds that unite us, in order to preserve and promote together for the benefit of all men, "peace, liberty, social justice and moral values" as the Council (in *Nostra Aetate 3*) calls upon us to do. (Pope John Paul II, address to the Catholic community of Ankara, Turkey, November 29, 1979)

All of the above is not to say that there are no differences among the three Abrahamic faiths. The differences among Judaism, Christianity, and Islam are very real. Further, these differences are important and fundamental and should not be swept under the proverbial rug, simply in order to rush forward to an ecumenical embrace among the three Abrahamic faiths. We need to acknowledge honestly and discuss openly those differences. In doing so, our goal must be to seek mutual understanding, if not theological agreement. Moreover, our religious differences should not obscure our equally real and equally important similarities in religious history, heritage, and core beliefs. Nor should those differences blind us to the fact that we, as Jews, Christians, and Muslims, share a common core of ethical values, a common embrace of spiritual idealism, and a common religious belief in our social obligations and duties to our fellow man.

A common core of ethical values... A common embrace of spiritual idealism... A common religious belief in our social obligations and duties to our fellow man... At this point, we are no longer talking about a shared religious history and heritage. At this point, we are talking about our religious present and our religious future. To what extent is our religious present being defined by cooperative efforts among the three Abrahamic faiths, especially when it comes to our shared values, idealism, and social obligations? To what extent will our religious future be characterized by cooperative ventures and mutual assistance in seeking to realize those goals? Here is my challenge to the Jewish community, the Christian community, and the Muslim community. When and how are we going to learn to work together in cooperative and ecumenical fellowship, in order to actualize our shared ethical values, to promote our shared spiritual idealism, and to advance our shared religious commitment to our social obligations and duties to our fellow man?

For the last few years, the nightly news has been filled with headlines decrying the economic scandals of such major, American corporations as Enron and WorldCom. However, we have far more to worry about than mere corporate bankruptcy. I would submit to you that we are also facing a moral bankruptcy of our American culture and society. With regard to that claim, consider a few facts, figures, and examples.

Currently, we are witnessing the collapse of the traditional family structure in American society. About two out of every three marriages in America end in divorce, with all the pain, sorrow, and familial disruption that entails. Further, every major study of marriages within the last 40 years, of which I am aware, has consistently found that a majority of American husbands have had at least one affair over the course of married life. Likewise, those same studies indicate that large minorities of American wives have had at least one affair while being married. Still further, the frequency of spousal abuse within our society has been steadily rising decade after decade. Finally, study after study consistently finds that a majority of American teens engage in pre-marital sexual behavior. Are we so jaded that those numbers no longer shock us? Don't we all, whether Jew, Christian, or Muslim, view marriage as a sacred institution in one form or another? If so, why are we not working together to find constructive solutions to the breakdown of the institution of marriage within our society? Do not we adherents of the three Abrahamic faiths share a common goal with regard to the sanctity of marriage, especially given that one recent study found that the only demographic factor mitigating against divorce was a firm religious commitment on the part of the spouses? Why are we not actively working together to advance that goal?

According to another recent demographic study, about 14 percent of Americans classify themselves as non-believers—up from 8 percent a decade ago. One out of every seven Americans maintains that he or she is not a believer in a deity. This is a particularly striking statistic when one realizes that this 14% figure does not include those who only nominally consider themselves to belong to one religion or another, e.g., the so-called Christmas and Easter Christians. How do we expect to live in a moral society when at least 14% of our fellow Americans have no religious foundation upon which to erect a system of morality and ethics? Whatever our differences in how we conceptualize God, do not the three monotheistic religions have some common purpose in addressing this issue?

Another example of the moral bankruptcy of contemporary American society is the pervasive grip of organized gambling on so many Americans. In the absence of finding spiritual and moral bedrock in their traditional religious institutions, too many Americans are gambling away their money while dreaming of a better materialistic life—one that is filled with all the things that Madison Avenue has successfully convinced most Americans that they will need to find true happiness and contentment. In support of this hypothesis, allow me to present a few facts from a recent study.

According to the study results, Americans wagered two billion dollars in 1962 in various forms of organized gambling. Let me emphasize that we are talking about organized gambling, not about the office betting pool on Sunday afternoon's football game and not about the Thursday evening, boys-night-out poker game. Instead, the number given is reflective of such institutionalized forms of gambling as those provided by casinos, organized lotteries, and racetracks. Two billion dollars were wagered by Americans in various forms of organized gambling in 1962. In marked contrast, in just the one year of 2000, Americans wagered 866 billion dollars in various forms of organized gambling.[121]

Assuming that the population of the United States is about 300 million and assuming that only half of the American populace is of an age and inclination to gamble, that works out to 150 million people wagering 866 billion dollars a year or the equivalence of almost $5,800 per year per American who wagers! If one assumes that only 100 million Americans are wagering their money in organized gambling, the figure climbs to almost $8,700 dollars per person per year! Those are truly appalling figures, especially when one considers that compulsive gambling has been recognized as a mental illness for many years. They are even more appalling when one realizes that the American gambling addict is aided and abetted by government-sponsored lotteries and sweepstakes that reach out to and confront the compulsive gambler at almost every supermarket, gas station, and convenience store. How many poor and middleclass Americans sit each week with ticket in hand, avidly watching the live broadcast of power-ball and sweepstakes number results, which are being passed off as TV news on nightly programs? How many families are suffering the pain of an addict's gambling—gambling that has hollowed out personal and family finances until the pantry is empty and that has done irreparable damage to the moral fabric of our American society and local communities?

In Islam, gambling is simply and flatly prohibited. But whether one sees all gambling as religiously unlawful or not, aren't we all appalled at the thought of Americans wagering almost 9/10s of a trillion dollars in just one, single year? What else could be done with that kind of money? How many social problems could be addressed with an extra 866 billion dollars a year? Couldn't we, as adherents to the three Abrahamic faiths find some way to work together to alleviate this problem?

In 1999, I was living in the greater Denver area and, like most of you, was rocked back on my heels by the tragedy and senseless violence that transpired at Columbine High School. Yet, the Columbine massacre was not an isolated incident on the American landscape. Schoolhouse shootings had been taking place for years in American schools and have continued to occur since then. Do not Judaism, Christianity, and Islam have a joint and common mission in addressing such violence in our school systems and in correcting the social events and situations that precipitate such actions?

At the present time, thousands upon thousands of Americans are living a homeless or economically disadvantaged life. Every year, many thousands of Americans are afflicted by various natural disasters and calamities. Chronic illness and lack of educational opportunity plague many others. Would not the three Abrahamic faiths be more effective in addressing these ills if they worked together?

Consider one final example. For the last few years, Americans have been inundated with a tidal-wave of so-called reality game shows emanating from their nightly television screens. Contestants are put in difficult environments without significant supplies and resources and are asked to "survive" a series of tasks by climbing over the hopes and dreams of their fellow contestants. In another venue, male and female contestants live together in the intimacy of a single house, with individual contestants being voted out by their peers. In yet a third setting, the contestants are mixed couples who are placed together in an exotic and sexually tempting locale for what appears to be the express purpose of seeing whether the various couples can withstand the sexual temptation to be unfaithful to their significant other. What are such shows teaching our youth? They certainly appear to be glorifying interpersonal manipulation as the means to the ultimate end of "winning" and appear to be suggesting that sexual exploitation and gratification are the way to advance in the "game of life." Do not the three Abrahamic faiths have a common goal and concern regarding such nightly TV fare?

Are we finally ready, as members of the three Abrahamic faiths, to work together actively to confront the ills of our society? We have common concerns, common purpose, and common goals. Shouldn't we be working together to create a better society?

In closing, I would again point out that I am not suggesting that there are no differences among us. Nor am I suggesting that those differences be obscured or compromised. There may be times when we, each in good faith, disagree. There may be some issues where we cannot, in good faith, work together. At such times, perhaps all of us, whether Jew, Christian, or Muslim,

Notes

Chapter 2
The Quest for Abraham: Commonalities and Contrasts among Judaism, Christianity, and Islam

1. Smith WC (1957). Pages 25-26.
2. Hoffman MW (2002). Page 5.

Chapter 3
The *Qur'an*, *Ahadith*, and Judaeo-Christian Scriptures: Finding Common Ground

3. The Jewish examples used in this paragraph, as well as their citations, are taken from Hughes TP (1994). Pages 238-242.
4. Jeffrey Lang makes a cogent argument for Adam's earthly sojourn, and by extension the earthly sojourn of humanity, being an opportunity and a necessity for spiritual development and growth. See Lang J (1997). Chapter 2.
5. For an analysis of whether it was Prophet Ismail or Prophet Isaac who was the intended sacrificial victim, see Dirks JF (2002).
6. This concept of the gradual unfolding of divine revelation at a pace consistent with man's evolving spiritual development fits quite comfortably within the

framework developed by Jeffrey Lang regarding the earthly sojourn of mankind. See footnote #4. Both concepts have some intriguing parallels with the traditional thought within the field of developmental psychology about how individuals progress through developmental stages via resolution of conflict between their internal mental representations and the external reality of the world around them. In short, for growth to occur, the external world must present information that is just beyond the mental grasp and comprehension of the individual. This situation results in mental conflict, which spurs the individual to alter, modify, and eventually replace his prior mental representation(s). However, if external reality presents information that is too far advanced beyond the individual's mental representation of how the world works, the end result is incomprehensibility, which is not the sort of conflict that leads to growth and development.

7. Some scholars have suggested an alternative explanation of the phrase "woman of 'Imran." The Arabic word that is translated as "woman" in *Qur'an* 3:35 is "*Umur'at,*" which can mean either "woman" or "wife." Using the latter meaning, these scholars have interpreted *Qur'an* 3:35 to indicate that Mary's father was 'Imran, rather than that Mary was a member of the clan of 'Imran of the tribe of Levi.   As in all things, God knows best. However, *Qur'an* 19:34 states that Mary was a "sister of Aaron," which tends to suggest the interpretation that the 'Imran being referenced was the father of Prophets Moses and Aaron, and not the biological father of Mary.

8. It has been suggested that the statement by Mary's mother that "and no wise is the male like the female" refers back to the earlier dedication of the unborn babe to God, as gender had a direct bearing on what type of temple service could be performed by a person. See 'Ali 'AY (1992). Commentary note #378.

9. Despite its name, the Nicene Creed was not promulgated by the Council of Nicaea in 325 CE, but by the Council of Constantinople in 381 CE.   -
-- (T) (1998).

10. --- (U) (1998).

11. As quoted in Bin Bayyah 'A (2003). Page 8.

12. Wilson I (1985). Pages 54-55.

13. Al-Qathi Y (1996).

14. Richardson HN (1971).

Chapter 4
From Jesus to Muhammad: Early Christianity and Islam

15. Contrary presentations do exist in the canonical gospels of the *New Testament*. For a discussion and refutation of those presentations, see Dirks JF (2001). Ch. 6.

16. Armstrong K (1994). Page 79.

17. (A) --- (K) (1998). (B) --- (L) (1998). (C) Koester H (1982). Pages 198-207.

18. For a fuller discussion of these issues, as well as for the text of the cited passages from the various books of the *New Testament* apocrypha, see Dirks JF (2001). Ch. 5.

19, The Hebrew word from which the Anglicized "Messiah" is derived means "anointed one." The anointed ones of Israel were the kings of Israel, the high priests of Israel, and some of the prophets of Israel. It can thus be cogently argued that the condemned prisoner was a Jesus who was a revolutionary and who was claiming to be the king of Israel, while the Jesus who was released was the "son of the Father."

20. (A) Armstrong K (1994). Page 100. (B) Chadwick H (2003).

21. --- (T) (1998).

22. Qualben LP (1942). Page 122.

23. Pelikan JJ (1998).

24. (A) --- (K) (1998). (B) Koester H (1982). Pages 202-203. (C) Koch GA (1997). Pages 224-225.

25. Danielou J, Marrou H (1964). Pages 57-58.

26. Danielou J, Marrou H (1964). Pages 59-60.

27. --- (M) (1998).

28. (A) --- (N) (1998). (B) --- (E) (1998).

29. (A) Chadwick H (2003). (B) Kelly JND (2003).

30. Danielou J, Marrou H (1964). Pages 208-216.

31. (A) Armstrong K (1994). Page 99. (B) Danielou J, Marrou H (1964). Pages 212-218. (C) --- (J) (1998).

32. (A) Kelly JND (2003). (B) --- (F) (2003).

33. (A) Armstrong K (1994). Ch. 4. (B) Danielou J, Marrou H (1964). Ch. 28. (C) --- (H) (1998). (D) --- (I) (1998).

34. Armstrong K (1994). Page 107.

35. (A) Armstrong K (1994). Ch. 4. (B) Danielou J, Marrou H (1964). Ch. 28. (C) --- (H) (1998). (D) --- (I) (1998).

36. (A) Danielou J, Marrou H (1964). Pages 251 and 257. (B) Armstrong K (1994).

Chapter 4 and page 118.

37. (A) Danielou J, Marrou H (1964). Page 252. (B) --- (G) (1998).

38. --- (D) (2003).

39. (A) --- (A) (2003). (B) --- (B) (2003). (C) Danielou J, Marrou H (1964). Pages 259 and 261. (D) --- (H) (1998).

40. Danielou J, Marrou H (1964). Pages 259 and 261. (B) --- (H) (1998).

41. (A) Danielou J, Marrou H (1964). Pages 259 and 261. (B) --- (H) (1998). (C) --- (A) (2003). (D) --- (B) (2003). (E) --- (C) (2003).

42. (A) Godbey JC (1998). (B) --- (H) (1998). (C) --- (S) (1998). (D) ---(E) (2003).

43. (A) Kelly JND, et al. (1998). (B) Danielou J, Marrou H (1964). Pages 340 and 345. (C) --- (F) (1998).

44. (A) Danielou J, Marrou H (1964). Pages 369-372. (B) Kelly JND, et al. (1998). (C) --- (F) (1998).

45. (A) Kelly JND, et al. (1998). (B) --- (F) (1998).

46. --- (U) (1998).

47. Godbey JC (1998).

48. Qualben LP (1942). Page 107.

49. Qualben LP (1942). Page 122.

50. (A) --- (R) (1998). (B) --- (F) (2003).

51. (A) --- (R) (1998). (B) --- (Q) (1998).

52. (A) --- (R) (1998). (B) --- (P) (1998).

53. (A) Armstrong K (1994). (B) --- (O) (1998).

54. (A) Chadwick H (1998). (B) Qualben LP (1942). Pages 159-163.

Chapter 5
Islam, the "People of the Book," and Religious Pluralism

55. The second person pronoun is built into the form of the Arabic verb (translated as "cease") being used. As found in *Qur'an* 5:13, "*Tazaalu*" means "you (single person) cease."

56. Ibn Kathir (2000). Volume 3, page 129.

57. In both examples of "thou," the second person pronoun is built into the form of the Arabic verb (translated as "find") being used. As found in *Qur'an* 5:82, "*Latajidanna*" means "you (single person) find."

58. The reference to the Sabians in this and the following quotation have received different interpretations by different commentators on the *Qur'an.*

59. Safi LM (2002). Pages iii-iv.

60. McEvedy C, Jones R (1978).

61. Yahya H (2002). Pages 41-42.

62. (A) Yahya H (2002). Page 40. (B) Aprim F (---). Page 11.

63. (A) Arnold T (2001). Pages 88-89. (B) Yahya H (2002).

64. Ed-Din B (1988). Page 379.

65. Ed-Din B (1988). Page 239.

66. (A) Yahya H (2002). (B) Ed-Din B (1988).

67. (A) Yahya H (2002). (B) Armstrong K (2001). (C) Ed-Din B (1988).

68. Maalouf A (1984).

69. Hathout H (2002). Page 25.

70. Armstrong K (2001). Pages 461 & 469.

71. (A) Armstrong K (2001). Pages 458-459. (B) Koenigsberger HG (2003).

72. Hathout H (2002). Page 25.

73. Yahya H (2002). Pages 43-44.

74. Al-Sadlaan SG (1999). Page 78.

Chapter 6
Islamophobia in the Christian West

75. (A) Armstrong K (2001). Page 3. (B) --- (D) (1998). (C) Becker A (1998). (D) Baldwin MW (1998). (E) Hoffman M (1999). Pages xvi and 141.

76. John Paul II (1991).

77. Maalouf A (1984).

78. (A) Yahya H (2002). (B) Maalouf A (1984). (C) Gabrieli F (1984). (D) Armstrong K (2001).

79. (A) Yahya H (2002). (B) Maalouf A (1984). (C) Gabrieli F (1984). (D) Hathout M (2002). (E) Armstrong K (2001).

80. Krey AC (1921). Page 261.

81. Maalouf A (1984).

82. Maalouf A (1984).

83. (A) Armstrong K (2001). Pages 64-65. (B) ---(A) (1998). (C) --- (B) (1998). (D) --- (C) (1998).

84. (A) Armstrong K (2001). Pages 64-65. (B) --- (C) (1998).

85. Andrae T (1960). Page 173.

86. (A) Andrae T (1960). Page 173. (B) Hoffman M (1999). Page 151. (C) Quinones RJ (1998).

87. Meyer-Hoffman GI (2002). Pages 129-132.

88. Francois-Marie Arouet (1694-1778), who took the pseudonym of Voltaire, was a Deist of the French Age of Enlightenment, who dismissed divine revelation in favor of reliance on human reason. Despite his obvious slandering of Islam, he is often portrayed as a firm proponent of religious tolerance. See Pomeau RH (1998).

89. As quoted in Andrae T (1960). Page 174.

90. (A) Andrae T (1960). Page 174-175. (B) Hoffman M (1999). Page 151. (C) Pomeau RH (1998).

91. Hoffman M (1999). Page xiii.

92. Siddiqi 'AH (1971?). Volume III, page 941.

93. Hardon JA (1968). Page 69.

94. Watt WM et al. (1998).

95. Guillaume A (1968). Page 43.

96. Watt WM (1988). Page xvii.

97. Guillaume A (1968). Pages 61-62 and 71.

98. Qualben LP (1942). Pages 145-146.

99. Malcolm NR (2003).

100. Allcock JB (2003).

101. Beruni KR (2003).

102. (A) Goldenson RM (1970). Pages 247-249 & 929-931. (B) Ullmann LP, Krasner L (1975). Pages 144, 316, & 318. (C) Kimble GA (1967).

103. *The Wichita Eagle*, November 26, 2002. Page 4A.

Chapter 7
**Original Sin and the Role of Women:
Comparing the Abrahamic Faiths**

104. De Vaux (1965). Page 34.

105. Gordon GB (1971). Page 1285.

106. Gottwald NK (1971). Page 114.

107. Gordon GB (1971). Page 1285.

108. Armstrong K (1994). Pages 123-125.

109. Born circa 160 CE in Carthage, Quintus Septimus Florens Tertullianus was educated in Carthage and Rome, entered the priesthood, and became an important and highly opinionated Christian theologian and moralist. Prior to 210 CE, Tertullian converted from Christianity to Montanism and then later broke from the Montanists to form his own religious group. Wilken RL (2003).

110. Aurelius Augustinus was born on November 13, 354, in Tagaste, Numidia (Algeria), died on August 28, 430, in Hippo (Algeria), and is known to most Christians as St. Augustine. He was ordained a presbyter or priest in 391, and became the bishop of Hippo circa 395, serving in the latter capacity the rest of his life. A prolific writer, Augustine is best remembered today for his *Confessiones* (Confessions), *De Civitate Dei Contra Paganos* (City of God), *Retractationes* (Reconsiderations), *De Doctrina Christiana* (On Christian Doctrines), *De Trinitate* (On the Trinity), and *De Genesi ad Litteram* (Literal Commentary on *Genesis*). He was canonized a saint by the Roman Catholic Church, and his feast day is celebrated on August 28. O'Donnell J (2003).

111. Dentan RC (1971). Pages 521-522.

112. Beavin EL (1971). Page 550.

113. White SA (1993). Page 814.

114. De Vaux R (1965). Page 25.

115. Gershom bar Judah was born circa 960 CE in Metz, Lorraine (France), and died on October 28, 1040, in Mainz, Franconia (Germany). As head of the rabbinic academy at Mainz, he is generally credited with bringing the learning of the Talmudic academies of the Middle East to Western Europe.

116. Cyrus, bishop of Phasis, in the Caucasus, was appointed patriarch and governor of Alexandria by Heraclius. Given that he came from the Caucasus, he was known in Arab circles as Muqawqas. Kennedy H (1988). Page 6.

117. (A) Westermarck E (1968). Page 236. (B) Westermarck E (1969). Pages 335-336. (C) Cairncross J (1974). Pages 31-53, 80, & 121-125. (D) Bax (1966). Pages 203-206 & 254. (E) Hillman E (1975). Pages 22-24 & 217ff. (F) Tjernagel

N (1965). Page 89.

118. Chaudhry MS (1991). Page 133.

119. As cited in Chaudhry MS (1991). Page 117.

120. Chaudhry MS (1991). Page 124.

Chapter 8
Reconciliation and the Children of Abraham
121. Lambert C (2002).

Bibliography

The following represents a complete listing of all sources consulted, whether or not directly referenced within the text.

Qur'an and Commentaries

'Ali 'AY: *The Meaning of the Holy Qur'an.* Beltsville, Amana Publications, 1992.

Hilali MT, Khan MM: *Interpretation of the Meanings of The Noble Qur'an: A Summarized Version of Al-Tabari, Al-Qurtubi, and Ibn Kathir with Comments from Sahih Al-Bukhari in English Language:* Volumes 1-9. Lahore, Kazi Publications, 1989.

Ibn Kathir IA: *Tafsir ibn Kathir.* In Al-Mubarakpuri S et al. (trans.): *Tafsir Ibn Kathir:* Volumes 1-10. Riyadh, Darussalam, 2000.

Saheeh International: *The Qur'an: Arabic Text with Corresponding English Meanings.* Jeddah, Abul-Qasim Publishing House, 1997.

Syed AU: *Index of Qur'anic Topics.* Washington, DC, IFTA Office, Royal Embassy of Saudi Arabia, 1998.

Usmani MSA: *Tafseer-'E-Usmani.* In Ahmad MA (trans.): *The Noble Qur'an: Tafseer-'E-Usmani:* Volumes 1-3. New Delhi, Idara Isha'at-E-Diniyat (P) Ltd., 1992.

---: *Study the Noble Qur'an Word-for-Word:* Volumes 1-3. Riyadh, Darussalam, 1999.

Ahadith and Commentaries

Al-Asbahi MA (*Malik*): *Al-Muwatta.* In Rahimuddin M (trans.): *Muwatta Imam Malik.* Lahore, Sh. Muhammad Ashraf, 1985.

Al-Azdi SA (*Abu Dawud*): *Kitab Al-Sunan.* In Hasan A (trans.): *Sunan Abu Dawud.* New Delhi, Kitab Bhavan, 1990.

Al-Bukhari MI: *Kitab Al-Jami' Al-Sahih.* In Khan MM (trans.): *The Translation of the Meanings of Sahih Al-Bukhari.* Madinah, ---, undated.

Al-Bukhari MI: *Sahih Al-Bukhari.* In --- (trans.): *Alim Multimedia CD Rom.* ---, ISL Software Corporation, ---.

Al-Qushayri MH (*Muslim*): *Al-Jami' Al-Sahih.* In Siddiqi 'AH (trans.): *Sahih Muslim.* ---, ---, 1971(?).

Al-Tibrizi WMA: *Mishkat Al-Masabih.* In Robinson J (trans.): *Mishkat Al-Masabih: English Translation with Explanatory Notes.* Lahore, Sh. Muhammad Ashraf, 1963.

Al-Tirmidhi MI: *Sahih Al-Tirmidhi.* In --- (trans.): *Alim Multimedia CD Rom.* ---, ISL Software Corporation, ---.

Ibn 'Abd Al-Wahhab M: *Kitab Al-Tawhid.* In Al-Faruqi IR (trans.): *Kitab Al-Tawhid.* Malaysia, Polygraphic Press Sdn. Bhd., 1981.

Siddiqi 'AH (trans.): *Sahih Muslim.* ---, ---, 1971(?).

The *Bible*, Commentaries, and Aides

Beavin EL: *Ecclesiasticus* or the *Wisdom of Jesus the Son of Sirach.* In Laymon CM (ed.): *The Interpreter's One-Volume Commentary on the Bible.* Nashville, Abingdon Press, 1971.

Denton RC: The second book of Esdras. In Laymon CM (ed.): *The Interpreter's One-Volume Commentary on the Bible.* Nashville, Abingdon Press, 1971.

Eiselen FC, Lewis E, Downey DG (eds.): *The Abingdon Bible Commentary.* New York, Abingdon-Cokesbury Press, 1929.

Gordon GB: Measures and money. In Laymon CM (ed.): *The Interpreter's One-Volume Commentary on the Bible.* Nashville, Abingdon Press, 1971.

Gottwald NK: The book of *Deuteronomy.* In Laymon CM (ed.): *The Interpreter's One-Volume Commentary on the Bible.* Nashville, Abingdon Press, 1971.

Joines KR: Potiphar. In Miles WE et al. (eds.): *Mercer Dictionary of the Bible.* Macon, Mercer University Press, 1997a.

Joines KR: Eunuch. In Miles WE et al. (eds.): *Mercer Dictionary of the Bible.* Macon, Mercer University Press, 1997b.

Kohlenberger III JR: *The NRSV Concordance Unabridged: Including the Apocryphal/Deuterocanonical Books.* Grand Rapids, Zondervan Publishing House, 1991.

Koch GA: Ebionites, Gospel of. In Mills WE et al. (eds.): *Mercer Dictionary of the Bible.* Macon, Mercer University Press, 1997.

Laughlin JCH: Pharaoh. In Mills WE et al. (eds.): *Mercer Dictionary of the Bible.* Macon, Mercer University Press, 1997.

Laymon CM (ed.): *The Interpreter's One-Volume Commentary on the Bible.* Nashville, Abingdon Press, 1971.

Leon-Dufour X: *Dictionnaire du Nouveau Testament.* In Prendergast T (trans.): *Dictionary of the New Testament.* San Francisco, Harper & Row, 1983.

Marshall-Green M: Women in the *New Testament.* In Mills WE et al. (eds.): *Mercer Dictionary of the Bible.* Macon, Mercer University Press, 1997.

Metzger BM, Coogan MD (eds.): *The Oxford Companion to the Bible.* Oxford, Oxford University Press, 1993.

Mills WE et al. (eds.): *Mercer Dictionary of the Bible.* Macon, Mercer

University Press, 1997.

Morris WW: Women in the *Old Testament.* In Mills WE et al. (eds.): *Mercer Dictionary of the Bible.* Macon, Mercer University Press, 1997.

Platt RH, Brett JA (eds.): *The Lost Books of the Bible and the Forgotten Books of Eden.* New York, World Publishing Co., ---.

Richardson HN: The book of *Tobit.* In Laymon CM (ed.): *The Interpreter's One-Volume Commentary on the Bible.* Nashville, Abingdon Press, 1971.

White SA: Women. In Metzer BM, Coogan MD (eds.): *The Oxford Companion to the Bible.* Oxford, Oxford University Press, 1993.

---: *The Holy Bible: New Revised Standard Version.* Nashville, Thomas Nelson, Inc., 1989.

---: *Jubilees.* In Charles RH (ed.): *The Apocrypha and Pseudepigrapha of the Old Testament in English: Volume II. Pseudepigrapha.* Oxford, Oxford University Press, 1969.

---: *IV Ezra.* In Charles RH (ed.): *The Apocrypha and Pseudepigrapha of the Old Testament in English: Volume II. Pseudepigrapha.* Oxford, Oxford University Press, 1969.

---: *Ellis Maxima Bible Library.* Oklahoma City, Ellis Enterprises, 2001.

---: *Sirach.* In Charles RH (ed.): *The Apocrypha and Pseudepigrapha of the Old Testament in English: Volume I. Apocrypha.* Oxford, Oxford University Press, 1971.

Other References

'Abd Al-'Ati H: *Islam in Focus.* Beltsville, Amana Publications, 1998.

Allcock JB: Kosovo. In *Encyclopaedia Britannica 2003.* ---, ---, 2003.

Al-Faruqi L: *Women, Muslim Society, and Islam.* Indianapolis, American Trust Publications, 1991.

Al-Sadlaan SG: *Taysir Al-Fiqh.* In Zarabozo J (trans.): *Fiqh Made Easy: A Basic Textbook of Fiqh.* Boulder, Al-Basheer Company for

Publications and Translations, 1999.

Al-Qathi Y: *Riyaa: Hidden Shirk.* Sharjah, Dar Al-Fatah, 1996.

Al-Tabari MJ: *Ta'rikh Al-Rusul Wa'l-Mulak.* In Brinner WM (trans.):
The History of al-Tabari: Volume II. Prophets and Patriarchs.
Albany, State University of New York Press, 1987.

Andrae T: *Mohammed: The Man and His Faith.* New York, Harper
Torchbooks, 1960.

Aprim F: The A to Z of the ancient Chaldeans and their relation to
modern Chaldeans. http://assyria.nineveh.com/
education/20001021a.html.

Armstrong K: *A History of God: The 4,000-Year Quest of Judaism,
Christianity and Islam.* New York, Ballantine Books, 1994.

Armstrong K: *Holy War: The Crusades and their Impact on Today's World.*
New York, Anchor Books, 2001.

Arnold T: *The Spread of Islam in the World: A History of Peaceful Preaching.*
---, Gopodword Books, 2001.

Baker B: *More in Common than You Think: The Bridge between Islam
and Christianity.* ---, Defenders Publications, 1998.

Baldwin MW: The Crusades. In *Encyclopaedia Britannica CD 98.* ---,
---, 1998.

Bax EB: *Rise and Fall of the Anabaptists.* New York, American Scholar
Publications, 1966.

Becker A: Urban II. In *Encyclopaedia Britannica CD 98.* ---, ---, 1998.

Beruni KR: Give me that old time religion: Searching for God. In Dirks
DL, Parlove S (2003).

Bewley A: *Glossary of Islamic Terms.* London, Ta-Ha Publishers, 1998.

Bin Bayyah 'A: Despair not of God's grace. *Seasons: Bi-annual Journal of
Zaytuna Institute* 1: (1) 5-8, 2003.

Cairncross J: *After Polygamy was Made a Sin: The Social History of*

Christian Polygamy. London, Routledge and Kegan Paul, 1974.

Chadwick H: Christianity: The church and its history: The history of Christianity: The primitive church. In *Encyclopaedia Britannica CD 98.* ---, ---, 1998a.

Chadwick H: Christianity: The church and its history: The history of Christianity: Theological controversies of the 4th and 5th centuries. In *Encyclopaedia Britannica CD 98.* ---, ---, 1998b.

Chadwick H: Origen. In *Encyclopaedia Britannica CD 2003.* ---, ---, 2003.

Chaudhry MS: *Women's Rights in Islam.* Lahore, Sh. Muhammad Ashraf, 1991.

Danielou J, Marrou H: *The Christian Centuries: Volume 1. The First Six Hundred Years.* New York, McGraw-Hill, 1964.

Davies JG: Christianity: the early church. In Zaehner RC (ed.): *The Concise Encyclopedia of Living Faiths.* Boston, Beacon Press, 1959.

Davis HF: Christianity: St. Thomas and medieval theology. In Zaehner RC (ed.): *The Concise Encyclopedia of Living Faiths.* Boston, Beacon Press, 1959.

De Vaux R: *Ancient Israel: I. Social Institutions.* New York, McGraw-Hill, 1965.

Dirks DL, Parlove S: *Islam Our Choice: Portraits of Modern American Muslim Women.* Beltsville, Amana Publications, 2003.

Dirks JF: *The Cross and the Crescent.* Beltsville, Amana Publications, 2001.

Dirks JF: *Abraham: The Friend of God.* Beltsville, Amana Publications, 2002.

Ed-Din Beha: *The Life of Saladin.* Lahore, Islamic Book Service, 1988.

Gabrieli F: *Storici Arabi delle Crociate.* In Costello EJ (trans.): *Arab Historians of the Crusades.* Berkeley, University of California Press, 1984.

Godbey JC: Protestantism: The major Protestant denominations: Unitarians and Universalists: History: American Unitarianism. In *Encyclopaedia Britannica CD 98.* ---, ---, 1998.

Goldenson RM: *The Encyclopedia of Human Behavior: Psychology, Psychiatry, and Mental Health.* Garden City, Doubleday & Company, 1970.

Green J: *Jesus and Muhammad: The Parallel Sayings.* Berkeley, Seastone, 2003.

Guillaume A: *Islam.* Baltimore, Penguin Books, 1968.

Hardon JA: *Religions of the World: Volume Two.* Garden City, Image Books, 1968.

Hathout H: *Reading the Muslim Mind.* Burr Ridge, American Trust Publications, 2002.

Hathout M: *Jihad vs. Terrorism.* Los Angeles, Multimedia Vera International, 2002.

Hillman E: *Polygamy Reconsidered: African Plural Marriage and the Christian Churches.* Maryknoll, Orbis Books, 1975.

Hoffman M: *Islam: The Alternative.*Beltsville, Amana Publications, 1999.

Hoffman MW: Has Islam missed its enlightenment. *American Journal of Islamic Social Sciences* 19:(5) 1-11, 2002.

Hughes TP: *Dictionary of Islam.* Chicago, Kazi publications, 1994.

John Paul II: Message to the faithful of Islam at the end of the month of Ramadan, April 3, 1991. As cited in Vatican Council and Papal Statements on Islam, http://www.nccbuscc.org/comm/national tragedy/textsislam.htm.

Josephus F: *Jewish Antiquities.* In Whiston W (trans.): *The New Complete Works of Josephus.* Grand Rapids, Kregel Publications, 1999.

Kelly JND, et al.: Nestorius. In *Encyclopaedia Britannica CD 98.* ---, ---, 1998.

Kelly JND: Patristic literature. In *Encyclopaedia Britannica CO 2003.* ---, ---, 2003.

Kennedy H: *The Prophet and the Age of the Caliphates: The Islamic Near East from the Sixth to the Eleventh Century.* London, Longman, 1988.

Kent J: Christianity: Protestantism. In Zaehner RC (ed.): *The Concise Encyclopedia of Living Faiths.* Boston, Beacon Press, 1959.

Kimble GA: Pavlov and the experimental study of conditioned reflexes. In Kimble GA (ed.): *Foundations of Conditioning and Learning.* New York, Appleton-Century-Crofts, 1967.

Koenigsberger HG: Spain: History: United Spain under the Catholic monarchs. In *Encyclopaedia Britannica 2003.* ---, ---, 2003.

Koester H: *Introduction to the New Testament: Volume 2. History and Literature of Early Christianity.* Berlin, Walter De Gruyter, 1982.

Krey AC: *The First Crusade: The Accounts of Eye-Witnesses and Participants.* Princeton & London, 1921.

Lambert C: Trafficking in chance. *Harvard Magazine* 104:(6), 32-41, 2002.

Lang J: *Even Angels Ask: A Journey to Islam in America.* Beltsville, Amana Publications, 1997.

Maalouf A: *The Crusades through Arab Eyes.* New York, Schocken Books, 1984.

Malcolm NR: Bosnia and Herzegovina. In *Encyclopaedia Britannica 2003.* ---, ---, 2003.

McEvedy C, Jones R: *Atlas of World Population History.* New York, Facts on File, 1978.

Meyer-Hoffman GI: Pagans, Tartars, Moslems, and Jews in Chaucer's "Canterbury Tales." *American Journal of Islamic Social Sciences* 19:(5) 129-132, 2002.

O'Donnell J: Saint Augustine. In *Encyclopaedia Britannica 2003.* ---, ---, 2003.

Pelican JJ: Jesus: The Christ and Christology: The dogma of Christ in the ancient councils. In *Encyclopaedia Britannica CD 98.* ---, ---, 1998.

Pomeau RH: Voltaire: In *Encyclopaedia Britannica CD 98.* ---, ---, 1998.

Qualben LP: *A History of the Christian Church.* New York, Thomas Nelson and Sons, 1942.

Quinones RJ: Dante. In *Encyclopaedia Britannica CD 98*. ---, ---, 1998.

Ragg L, Ragg L. *The Gospel of Barnabas*. Karachi (?), The *Qur'an* Council of Pakistan (?), (1974).

Rohl DM: *Pharaohs and Kings: A Biblical Quest*. New York, Crown Publishers, Inc., 1995.

Safi LM: Overcoming the polemics of intolerance. *American Journal of Islamic Social Sciences* 19:(3), i-vii, 2002.

Smith WC: *Islam in Modern History*. New York, Mentor Books, 1957.

Tjernagel N: *Henry VIII and the Lutherans*. St. Louis, Concordia Publishing House, 1965.

Ullmann LP, Krasner L: *A Psychological Approach to Abnormal Behavior: Second Edition*. Englewood Cliffs, Prentice-Hall, 1975.

Watt WM: Translator's forward. In Al-Tabari MJ: *The History of Al-Tabari: Volume VI. Muhammad at Mecca*. Albany, State University of New York Press, 1988.

Watt WM et al.: Muhammad and the religion of Islam: The foundations of Islam: Muhammad: the prophet and his message: Character and achievements. In *Encyclopaedia Britannica CD 98*. ---, ---, 1998.

Werblowsky RJZ: Judaism, or the religion of Israel. In Zaehner RC (ed.): *The Concise Encyclopedia of Living Faiths*. Boston, Beacon Press, 1959.

Westermarck E: *A Short History of Marriage*. New York, Humanities Press, 1968.

Westermarck E: *Christianity and Morals*. Freeport, Books for Libraries Press, 1969.

Wilkin RL: Tertullian. In *Encyclopaedia Britannica 2003*. ---, ---, 2003.

Wilson I: *Jesus: The Evidence*. London, Pan Books, 1985.

Yahya H: *Islam Denounces Terrorism*. In Rossini C, Evans R (trans.): *Islam Denounces Terrorism*. Bristol, Amal Press, 2002.

Zernov N: Christianity: the Eastern Schism and the Eastern Orthodox Church. In Zaehner RC (ed.): *The Concise Encyclopedia of Living Faiths.* Boston, Beacon Press, 1959.

---: *The Catholic Encyclopedia.* http://www.newadvent.org/cathen/

Articles with unattributed authorship from the
Encyclopaedia Britannica CD 98

--- (A): La Chanson de Roland.

--- (B): Chanson.

--- (C): Chanson de geste.

--- (D): Council of Clermont.

--- (E): Monarchianism.

--- (F): Nestorian.

--- (G): Eusebius of Nicomedia.

--- (H): Arianism.

--- (I): Arius.

--- (J): Paul of Samosata.

--- (K): Ebionite.

--- (L): Nazarene.

--- (M): Theodotus the Gnostic.

--- (N): Theodotus the Tanner.

--- (O): Trinity.

--- (P): Jesus Only.

--- (Q): Priscillian.

--- (R): Sabellianism.

--- (S): Unitarian Universalist Association.

--- (T): Nicene Creed.

--- (U): Apostles' Creed.

Index of Names

Aaron 28, 41, 47-49, 55, 258

'Abd Allah ibn Mas'ud 155, 228

Abdon 216

Abel 39, 43

Abijah 216

Abraham 25-28, 30, 38, 40, 43-45, 55, 88, 130, 143, 216, 218, 270

Adam 37-39, 43-44, 65, 67, 101, 117, 210-211, 213-214, 220, 244-246, 257

Aetius 115-116, 274

Agabus 126

Ahab 216

'Aisha 132-134, 174, 226, 231-232, 242

Albert of Aix 170

Al-Nabhani, Khalid 12-14

Al-Nasir 168

Arius 112-116, 274

Artemon of Rome 111

Ashhur 216

Asma' bint Abu Bakr 242

Asma' bint Sakan 242

Asma' bint Makhramah 228

Athanasius 114

Athenagoras I 125

'Atikah bint Zaid 242

Augustine 124, 210, 212-214, 217, 262-263, 272

'Awad, 'Awad 20

'Awad, Wa'el 12-14

Babai 117

Barabbas 99

Barnabas 91, 98, 126, 135

Barsumas 117

Benjamin 200-202, 216

Bilqis (Queen of Sheba) 43

Cain 39, 43, 216

Cerinthus 111

Cerularius, Michael 125

Channing, William Ellery 122

Chaucer 172-173, 272

Clothilda 118

Clovis I 118

Dante 172, 274

David (Prophet) 28, 38, 42, 50, 93, 143, 216, 218

De Diogilo, Odo 159

Demetrius 112

Dionysius of Alexandria 112

Index of Subjects